# THE ANATOMY OF *LEVIATHAN*

# The Anatomy of
# Leviathan

## F. S. McNeilly

MACMILLAN
London · Melbourne · Toronto
ST MARTIN'S PRESS
New York
1968

*Published by*
MACMILLAN & CO LTD
*Little Essex Street London* WC2
*and also at Bombay Calcutta and Madras*
*Macmillan South Africa* (*Publishers*) *Pty Ltd Johannesburg*
*The Macmillan Company of Australia Pty Ltd Melbourne*
*The Macmillan Company of Canada Ltd Toronto*
*St Martin's Press Inc New York*

*Library of Congress Catalog Card No.* 68–12304

*Printed in Great Britain by*
*W & J Mackay & Co Ltd, Chatham*

# Contents

## INTRODUCTION

1 THE SCOPE OF THE DISCUSSION     3

2 THE APPROACH TO "LEVIATHAN"     7
    1 *Biographical*     7
    2 *Hobbes's reputation*     10
    3 *The situation*     16
    4 *The analysis of language*     18
    5 *The rejection of authority*     20
    6 *Conceptual revision*     25

## PART I: METHOD

3 LANGUAGE AND LOGIC     29
    1 *Sense and imagination*     30
    2 *Naming and signifying*     31
    3 *Universals*     35
    4 *Accidents*     39
    5 *Truth*     47
    6 *Definitions*     51
    7 *Verification*     54

4 SCIENTIFIC METHOD     59
    1 *A self-evidence theory of mathematics (in* De Corpore*)*     60
    2 *A conventionalist account of science (in* The Elements of Law*)*     66
    3 *A hypothetico-deductive theory of physics (in* De Corpore*)*     71
    4 *A mathematical paradigm*     76
    5 *A demonstrative science of politics (in* Leviathan*)*     83
    6 *Summary of Part I*     88

# PART II: MAN

5 HUMAN NATURE 95
   1 Egoism and hedonism 96
   2 Mechanistic materialism and the passions 100
   3 An hypothesis about pleasure (in De Corpore) 106
   4 A muddle about pleasure (in The Elements of Law) 110
   5 A neutral analysis (in Leviathan) 115
   6 The particular passions 117
   7 "Good" and "evil" 119
   8 Deliberation and the will 121
   9 Apparent good 125
   10 Two concepts of felicity 129

6 POWER AND GLORY 137
   1 Life as a race 138
   2 "All the pleasure and jollity of the mind" 141
   3 Power and glory in Leviathan 144
   4 "This inference, made from the passions" 147

# PART III: SOCIETY

7 THE STATE OF NATURE 159
   1 The primary sources of quarrel 159
   2 Anticipatory violence 164
   3 Liberty 168
   4 The right of every man to every thing 175
   5 "The terrible enemy of nature, death" 178

8 NATURAL LAW 183
   1 The fundamental law of nature 184
   2 The renunciation of rights 191
   3 Covenants 194
   4 Obligation, compulsion and necessitation 199
   5 The precepts of reason 204
   6 "The true and only moral philosophy" 209

9  POLITICAL SCIENCE                                    213
    *1 Authorisation*                                  214
    *2 The institution of a commonwealth*              218
    *3 An unconditional majority formula*             222
    *4 The absolute sovereign*                        231
    *5 God's prophet*                                 240
    *6 Equity*                                        245
    *7 Conclusion*                                    248

SHORT ENGLISH BIBLIOGRAPHY                              255

INDEX                                                   262

# Introduction

# CHAPTER ONE

# The Scope of the Discussion

To attempt to discuss the whole of Hobbes's philosophy in all his works would be a very big task, since Hobbes wrote at great length and in two languages on many and diverse topics. What this book is concerned with primarily is the fundamental elements of his political theory and his views on the nature and methods of "civil philosophy". I am specially—though not always exclusively—concerned with *Leviathan*. *The Elements of Law* and *De Cive* are in some respects more elegant; but *Leviathan*, although untidy and often confused, embodies not only great muddles but also, I think, deeper insights than the other works. Further, in my discussion of *Leviathan* I am attempting not so much to evaluate the conclusions which Hobbes reaches in his political theory as to examine the structure of the arguments which he employs in arriving at them. These two activities, of course, are not altogether independent, because one would expect that an analysis of the arguments would shed some light on the nature and value of the conclusions.

When students are introduced to Hobbes it is usually *Leviathan*, and only *Leviathan*, that they read. There have been periods, indeed, when it has been the only work of Hobbes's that has been readily available, except in libraries. That is a pity, because among his many interests two were dominant. One of these was politics. He lived through a period of civil disturbance and political instability, and he thought that these were great evils, which could be avoided only if men came to a rational understanding of political matters; and he was convinced that he possessed that understanding and could impart it to others. The other dominant interest was in geometry and scientific method. For although Hobbes has come to be thought of primarily as a political philosopher, and although his chief distinction as a mathematician is his abortive and even (for all I know) incompetent attempts to square the circle, his discussions of philosophical and scientific method are interesting and important, both in themselves and in their bearing on his political philosophy. In *Leviathan*, however, that aspect of his philosophy is not very prominent: that is to say, science and method are discussed, but sometimes rather fragmentarily, so that their importance for the political philosophy of *Leviathan* is concealed. Commentators on Hobbes, of course, have been aware of all of this. Yet I think that some aspects of his political theory, and the relations between it and other parts of his philosophy, have often been seriously misunderstood. Therefore, although I am concerned primarily with *Leviathan*, I shall at times have quite a lot to say about Hobbes's other works as well. For what I propose to show is that there were not only confusions but also a certain degree of development in Hobbes's views on method; that these are related to a systematic development of his views on the foundations of political theory; and that perhaps the most important clue to the understanding of *Leviathan* is the differences between it and *The Elements* and *De Cive*.

Thus after a very brief survey, in Chapter Two, of a few relevant aspects of Hobbes's life and times, Part I (Chapters Three and Four) examines his views on logic and methodology and tries to show, in the first place, that Hobbes did not adopt a single and consistent doctrine either of truth or of scientific method, but in different works —and sometimes in different parts of the same work—expressed a number of quite different and mutually incompatible views; and, secondly, that there is a certain pattern of development in these changes of standpoint. It becomes clear that in *Leviathan*, although not in *The Elements* or *De Cive*, political doctrine is presented as a deductive system which has logical affinities with mathematics and not with science as the term is understood nowadays. Part II (Chapters Five and Six) tries to show that Hobbes's doctrine of human nature, which is the foundation of his political theory, shows a similar pattern of confusion, inconsistency, and development, and in *Leviathan* has been largely formalised as part of the deductive system. What Hobbes does in *Leviathan* is to construct a system of concepts—the notions of *endeavour*, *good*, *hope*, and so forth—which are required for the analysis of rational deliberation, both at an individual and at a social level; and Part III (Chapters Seven, Eight and Nine) examines the way in which Hobbes uses these concepts to construct a formal account of political relationships, from which he goes on to draw conclusions. The difference between *Leviathan* and Hobbes's other works is that in *The Elements* and *De Cive* Hobbes attempts to derive political conclusions from certain (very doubtful) propositions about the specific nature of individual human beings, whereas in *Leviathan* the argument depends on an analysis of the *formal* structure of the *relations* between individuals. This is of some importance, because while the political theory of the earlier works rests on a confused and distorted view of human nature, the political theory of *Leviathan*, although confined by the limitations of the demonstrative method, has some considerable value within these limitations, and is not based upon defective foundations.

Although this is an exercise in philosophical analysis and not a piece of political science I cannot help hoping that political theorists with an interest in Hobbes may regard these issues as relevant to their interest. They might, however, wish to be spared some of the details of the examination of Hobbes's views on logic and method. Consequently I have concluded Part I with a summary of the conclusions which it reaches and I suggest that any reader whose interest in Hobbes is exclusively in his political theory should confine himself to the summary, which gives the gist of the argument and a sufficient foundation for the discussion which follows.

Now there exists already an extensive literature on Hobbes, offering a variety of interpretations and evaluations, and in recent years there have been a number of distinguished additions to it. I owe a heavy debt of gratitude to this literature, for I know of no part of it which has failed to contribute to the understanding of his philosophy, although none which I have been able to agree with completely. There have been, I think, some very widespread misunderstandings of some aspects of Hobbes's philosophy, and especially of *Leviathan*. But that presents a problem to anyone who proposes to contribute to the discussion. One has to decide whether one is writing a book about Hobbes or a book about books about Hobbes. If I acknowledged all my debts, or if I attempted to deal carefully and explicitly with every element of every interpretation contrary to my own, the book would extend to twice its present length. From time to time, when it is convenient to my own purposes, I mention and develop specific points of agreement or disagreement with other commentators. But in the main I confine myself to expounding my own interpretation, with evidence from Hobbes's works. In the bibliography at the end, however, I attempt both to acknowledge debts and to indicate areas of disagreement.

The references to Hobbes's works are as in the following examples:

*Leviathan*, XVII 111 = chapter XVII and p. 111 of Oakeshott's edition.

*De Corpore*, IV xxv 9 = part IV, chapter xxv, paragraph 9 of Molesworth's *English Works*, vol. I; or chapter 25, paragraph 9 of the passages of *De Corpore* reprinted in Peters, *Body, Man and Citizen*.

*The Elements [of Law]*, I vii 2 = part I, chapter vii, paragraph 2 of the Tönnies edition; or chapter 7, paragraph 2 of the passages reprinted in *Body, Man and Citizen*.

*De Cive*, I xiv = chapter I, paragraph xiv.

CHAPTER TWO

# The *Approach* to Leviathan

BEFORE discussing the details of Hobbes's views there are some features of his life and times, and of his general approach to philosophy, which ought at least briefly to be mentioned. His philosophy is pervaded by hostility towards scholastic modes of thought, as he conceived them. Many of the views which he developed on particular topics (his nominalism, for example) were developed as weapons with which to attack what he regarded as a completely bankrupt approach to philosophy. He was a philosophical radical who, in common with many of his contemporaries in different fields, thought that great advances could be made in human knowledge provided that philosophers turned away from the confusions of the past, made a fresh start on new foundations, and strove, above all, to think with clarity and method.

## 1 BIOGRAPHICAL

Hobbes was born in 1588, and in due course went to Oxford. Then he went into service, in a gentlemanly sort of way, with the Cavendish family, tutoring the sons of the Earl of Devonshire. His own interests for a long period were chiefly classical, and included a translation of Thucydides. But in 1629, at the ripe age of forty-one, yet with fifty years of active life still ahead of him, one of the great events of his life occurred—he came across Euclid. During the time that he had been working on Thucydides he had been developing views on the causes of political degeneration—views which were relevant to the troubles of the times, since Charles I and Parliament were becoming involved in the struggles which ultimately erupted in the Civil War. What impressed Hobbes in Euclid was the demonstrative method, which deduced conclusions with logical rigour from premisses regarded as self-evident. He found in Euclid a paradigm of clarity and method. These were virtues, he thought, which had been specially lacking in moral and political philosophy. Sometimes he contrasted the good method of mathematicians with the bad method of other thinkers. Thus in *The Elements of Law* Hobbes described the success of those who had pursued mathematical studies, and he explained it thus: "The *reason* whereof is apparent to every man that looketh into their writings; for they proceed from most *low* and *humble* principles, evident even to the meanest capacity; going on *slowly*, and with most *scrupulous ratiocination. . . .*" He called them *mathematici*, and contrasted them favourably with the *dogmatici* who in two thousand years had failed to achieve any advances in moral and political philosophy. Their failure was due to the fact that they "*take up* maxims from their *education*, and from the *authority* of men, or of custom, and *take the habitual discourse of the tongue for ratiocination*" (*Elements of Law*, I xiii 3, 4). And in *Leviathan* he talked contemptuously about "those men that take their instruction from the authority of books, and not from their own meditation", and concluded the paragraph with one of his most famous and typical aphorisms: "For words are wise men's counters, they do but reckon by them; but they are the money of fools, that value them by the authority of an Aristotle, a Cicero, or a Thomas, or any other doctor whatsoever, if but a man" (IV 22).

This gave Hobbes the clue to the solution of the political problems of his troubled times. The country, he thought, was full of people each of whom was convinced that he knew how the State should be constructed and run, and was prepared to bicker endlessly with everyone else. The consequence of this was civil disorder and increasing violence. It was obvious that the salvation of society depended on the emergence of a political Euclid, who would demonstrate political truth beyond all possible doubt. In the years following, his travels took him to Italy, to visit Galileo, who was presiding over the renovation of natural philosophy. Thus he had been provided with a political motive, a methodological inspiration, and the stimulus of contact with the radical new thinking of the times. Hobbes conceived the ambition to reconstruct the whole of philosophy on a methodologically sound basis, ultimately deducing from incontestable premisses the political truths which would save the nation.

But in order to establish truth it is necessary to remove error, and here Hobbes had no difficulty in identifying the enemy. Lack of method, he thought, produced confusion and absurdity. Conceited men, each seized by his own particular brand of nonsense, contended with each other and with lawful authority. The most pernicious purveyors of nonsense were certain unbridled theologians (for Hobbes approved of theologians, but only when saddled and harnessed), their minds fogged, often with Aristotelian absurdity, who set up an authority against the civil power and thereby provoked disorder and sedition.

The religious whom he criticised for their pretensions refused to turn the other cheek: he was their enemy, but they could not bring themselves to love him. David Hume was later to complain that his first great work of philosophy fell still-born from the press, but Hobbes never had reason to feel so neglected. He did not always succeed in winning friends and influencing people, but he had no difficulty in winning a reputation. His philosophical progeny came into the world screaming; and the noise of them echoed through the land, to the scandal of all and the discredit of their parent in the eyes of respectable people. In *The Elements of Law* Hobbes for the first time systematically worked out and presented his views on human nature and politics, and in 1640 the work was circulating in manuscript form, although it was not yet printed. Then he fled to France, for fear of the Parliamentarians, and spent eleven happy years in the company of courtiers and philosophers. He had conceived the project of a systematic work covering the whole field of philosophy. It was to be composed of three parts, the first on body, the second on man, and the third on society. In view of the political situation at the time, and his saving message for the world, it is not surprising that it was the third part of the project that was the first to appear—*De Cive*, in 1642. He was then able to start work on the first part, *De Corpore*. He was making progress with this until 1647, when it seemed that he should try to make his political views more widely known, for *De Cive* was in Latin. Instead of simply translating *De Cive* (a translation was to appear a few years later), Hobbes began to write a new work in English, the famous *Leviathan*, which was published in 1651. Thereupon he thought that it was safe to return to England—at all events, safer than to remain in France. He returned to England and resumed work on *De Corpore*, which was published in 1655. Three years later what should have been the second part of the trilogy—*De Homine*—

appeared at last, rather cursorily done. He had in any case already discussed human nature at some length, and pungently, both in *The Elements* and in *Leviathan*.

He lived on, disputing vigorously about religion, politics and the squaring of the circle, among other topics. In 1679, after an astonishingly long life of ninety-one years, he died—in peace, if not in the odour of sanctity. He never actually was persecuted. But what might be described as some of the best minds in the country thought that he ought to have been. He was Hobbes the Atheist, the Monster of Malmesbury. Sometimes his books were burned, and there were bishops who thought that he should have been burned with them. In the considered and plausible opinion of some members of Parliament the scandal of his doctrines was the probable cause of the Great Fire of 1666. Poor Daniel Scargill was expelled from Cambridge for being *an Hobbist*. He was allowed back after publicly recanting his views. He confessed that he had asserted

divers wicked, blasphemous, and atheistical positions . . . professing that I gloried to be an Hobbist and an Atheist; . . . agreeably unto which principles and positions, I have lived in great licentiousness, swearing rashly, drinking intemperately, boasting myself insolently, corrupting others by my pernicious principles and examples, to the dishonour of God, the Reproach of the University, the Scandal of Christianity, and the just offence of mankind. (From Mintz, *The Hunting of Leviathan*, pp. 50–51.)

## 2 HOBBES'S REPUTATION

Scargill's recantation expressed what was a fairly general view of Hobbes and Hobbism. Times have changed, and he is no longer so fiercely criticised. We do not object to his wicked, blasphemous and atheistical views, because now we share them. Easily swallowing these much diminished camels, however, we still find ourselves straining at a certain unsavoury gnat, which is Hobbes's view of human nature. For the pattern of Hobbes's argument was to begin with a certain account of the passions of man, and to use this as the foundation of his political theory.

The Hobbesian argument goes something like this. All voluntary human actions are necessarily self-regarding. Pleasure is a certain bodily condition—a quickening of the vital motion, which is the circulating of the blood. We are disposed by our nature to seek pleasure and avoid pain, and that is the pattern of all human striving. When I say that something is good I mean nothing more than merely that it pleases me. People do sometimes act charitably, it is true, but the motive of it is merely that nothing can give a man a greater sense of his own power than to be able to help his friends. If we benefit strangers it is either from a desire to buy their friendship and its advantages, or out of fear, to placate them. Life is a race, with every man competing against every other. It has no aim nor prize, except merely to be first. Misery is to be falling behind, and felicity is to be out in front. All pleasures are either sensual, or else are *glory*, which is to have a good opinion of oneself; and when we seek society it is either for profit or for glory—that is, not so much for the love of others as for the love of ourselves. Above all, we are dominated from birth to death by an insatiable desire for power. And power itself is a relative notion, because to be powerful is essentially to be *more* powerful than other people. Human nature being what it is, if there were no laws and coercive forces to keep us at peace, we should be at each others' throats in a savage and remorseless war of all against all. Our condition would then be inexpressibly wretched and insecure. It is worth our while to pay a high price for deliverance from such misery, and the price is submission to political absolutism.

This summary statement of the Hobbesian view of human nature is easily recognisable, and something very like it is commonly accepted as perhaps a brief and incomplete, but not an inaccurate or seriously misleading, representation of Hobbes's opinions. Certainly every one of the propositions which are strung together to make it up has in fact been asserted by Hobbes, except perhaps the last.

Most philosophers are at least a little critical of this Hobbesian view. People may very often be selfish, it is argued, but they are not invariably, and certainly not necessarily, so brutally and exclusively selfish as Hobbes makes them out to be. Since Hobbes explicitly based his political conclusions on his account of human nature, any serious weakness in the latter is liable to have damaging consequences for the argument. Some regard Hobbes's whole view of man and politics as a nightmare of fantasy and exaggeration. Others criticise the theory of the passions but still find some merits in the political theory, where this does not presuppose the egoistic psychology. We are fairly generally agreed, however, that one of the most conspicuous and interesting, and important if debatable, features of his philosophy is his insistence that all human behaviour is essentially self-seeking. This is the point from which much discussion of Hobbes *begins*. Thus in his illuminating chapter on Hobbes in *Man and Society*, Plamenatz begins by pointing out very briefly (because "Hobbes's account of human nature is simple") that Hobbes held a theory of psychological egoism. According to Hobbes, we can take an interest in the good of another person only in so far as we ourselves get pleasure or pain from the thought of being in the other person's position. "Hobbes therefore implies that man is by nature self-regarding and can never be otherwise." Psychological egoism is regarded nowadays as an exploded doctrine, a compound of fallacies and confusions. Plamenatz does not discuss this, but makes an interesting suggestion about the political relevance of the doctrine. Psychological egoism, he argues, is not necessary to Hobbes's political theory. For Hobbes's purpose was to explain the existence of stable society. Then even if pity and benevolence are genuinely altruistic, contrary to the egoistic analysis, this is not relevant to political theory, because they "are not emotions strong enough to explain the existence of political society". Benevolence, indeed, can thrive only in an orderly social context, and is therefore an effect of social stability and cannot be postulated as its cause. "The less orderly and secure men's lives, and the less they are bound by rules, the more ruthless, narrow and selfish they are." (*Man and Society*, I, pp. 118–19.)

Of course there are disagreements among commentators. Peters argues that Hobbes was not really a *hedonist* (*Hobbes*, pp. 158–9), but he argues—as most if not quite all commentators have agreed—that in Hobbes's view human nature was entirely or predominantly selfish.

Yet there is room for doubt. The summary statement of Hobbes's view of human nature which I produced above was composed of genuine Hobbesian bricks. But who was the architect? Not Hobbes! He made the bricks, but he never put them together quite like that. What I did was a piece of reconstruction, taking a brick from here and a brick from there, building them into a structure which Hobbes, perhaps, might have refused to acknowledge as his own. That, indeed, has become almost a standard method of Hobbes-scholarship. Thus Warrender, for example, says:

I have chosen for exposition those parts of Hobbes's text which appeared to state his position most clearly and concisely, without regard to their source. There is some variation to be found in the different versions of his political doctrine, but it is of secondary importance, and I could find no special evidence of a development or change in his thought, of which special note had to be taken for the purpose in hand. (*The Political Philosophy of Hobbes*, pp. 7–8.)

It was not part of Warrender's purpose, certainly, to discuss Hobbes's views on human nature. But too many commentators adopt this approach throughout their discussion of Hobbes. The assumption is that Hobbes has *a view* on, say, pleasure and desire. It is found that in one place he has said one thing about them and in another place something else. It is assumed then that there is still really one view; but that it has come to pieces, and it is the commentator's job to put the pieces together again. Thus Peters gives an account of Hobbes's view of pleasure and desire which is made up of little bits and pieces from *De Corpore*, *The Elements* and *Leviathan* chiefly. He brings in the notion of felicity (found in *The Elements* and *Leviathan*) to pad out the empty spaces in the brief and vague reference to fruition in *De Corpore*. Laird's *Hobbes* is the classic example of the view-mending approach.

Of course it would be mere pedantry to object to such an approach. Far from objecting to it, I propose to adopt it myself. That is just to treat Hobbes's works as live philosophy. But it is important to recognise and admit that one is taking liberties with the texts. And before taking the liberties it is desirable to approach each one whole and with respect. There may be a philosophy of Hobbes which is variously expressed in a number of works. But there may be no such thing. It may be rather that Hobbes produced a number of arguments which have no more than a certain family resemblance to each other. For Hobbes's works certainly differ in their date of composition and in their subject-matter, and it is possible—I shall argue that it is the case—that in some important respects they differ substantially in their views.

### 1. *The dates of composition*

It may not be possible to date all of them very precisely. But *The Elements* was circulating in manuscript in 1640, though not printed until 1650. Hobbes seems to have begun work on *Leviathan* some time after 1647, and it was published in 1651. *De Corpore* was not published until 1655, but there is evidence that at least parts of it had existed in draft in 1644 or earlier. *De Cive* was published in 1642 and a new preface added to the edition of 1647. *De Homine* was not published till 1658. *The Elements* and *De Cive*, then, are early works compared with *Leviathan*. The new preface to *De Cive* falls between them, and the remarks on politics and on the passions in *De Corpore* might derive from an earlier period than *Leviathan*. Obviously we have to look out for possible changes and developments in Hobbes's views, and I am convinced that in some cases it is possible to detect a certain pattern of development.

## 2. *The subject-matter*

*The Elements of Law* is in two parts: the first part, called "Human Nature", has the subject its title implies; and the second, arguing political conclusions and based on the first part, is called "De Corpore Politico". *De Cive* is concerned almost exclusively with political questions. *De Corpore* says almost nothing about politics, and little about the passions, but a great deal about philosophical method, among other things. The discussions of method in *De Corpore* are Hobbes's most systematic treatment of the topic. *Leviathan* is primarily political, but with a fairly extensive treatment of the passions. Both *The Elements* and *Leviathan* have something to say about philosophical method, but not much, and sometimes very vaguely. Difference of subject-matter may be important. Peters suggests, for example, that:

it is possible to defend the view that when he is speaking in a predominantly political context he stresses always the importance of definitions and usually puts forward a conventionist theory of truth; whereas when he is thinking about the natural sciences this theory is less conventionist and more like a self-evidence theory such as Descartes' (*Hobbes*, p. 57).

I shall be discussing this suggestion in a later chapter, because I am not altogether convinced that it is correct in this particular case. But certainly it is the sort of possibility which one ought to have always in mind.

### 3. *The views expressed*

When one work of Hobbes's is compared with another, one certainly finds a lot of similarities. Sometimes, however, it is no more than that. An argument appears in one place and then seems to reappear in another. But sometimes it is expressed differently and put in a different context, and is in fact a new argument. I shall be arguing that there are quite a number of substantial and important differences; and especially, that reference to the views of *The Elements, De Cive,* and *De Corpore* can be very misleading when used in interpreting the account of human nature in *Leviathan.* Sometimes the differences are more important than the similarities.

Of these three points, however, the first is the least important to my arguments. My own information about Hobbes's life and the provenance of his writings is both scanty and second-hand. This would be a disgraceful admission if my declared purpose were to achieve a complete insight into Hobbes's thought. I am not attempting to survey the whole of Hobbes's thought, however, but only certain aspects of the political philosophy of *Leviathan;* and I am concerned rather with what Hobbes actually wrote in *Leviathan* than with what he may have been thinking when he wrote it. Now I am not suggesting that what a person thinks and what he says or writes are two quite different things which *may happen* to be related to each other and which can be investigated quite independently. That would be a most un-Hobbesian approach to take to Hobbes, and would lead to a lot of nonsense. When we read some of the reverential remarks which Hobbes makes about God, for example, we ought to question whether sincerity and conviction lie behind them. I do not think that one could read *Leviathan,* or any other important work, without raising that kind of question. I shall myself make a few (always tentative) suggestions about some patterns of development in Hobbes's thought. But there is an important matter of emphasis here. The purpose of these speculations will be not so much to contribute to an understanding of Hobbes's inner thoughts, though if there is any ground for them they must make some small contribution, as to bring out and emphasise some features of the arguments which he actually presented. Of course the most interesting and illuminating thing that could be done with Hobbes would be to trample all over and through him and his works in a thoroughgoing philosophical-cum-historical sort of way—the kind of job Laird and Peters set out to do. That is a big and worth-while sort of job, but it is not my job, and I have not got the tools to do it.

Nevertheless, my own more limited ambition has something to be said in favour of it. For in the first place, we cannot make a great deal of progress in penetrating into his thought until we have looked very carefully at his writings. If we are careless in this, our notions about his philosophy, and about his thought and intentions in general, will not be worth very much. What I am mainly concerned to argue is that there are some important parts of his arguments which have not always been looked at carefully or closely enough. And secondly, it is quite an apt approach to adopt towards Hobbes. After all, when we examine the Theorem of Pythagoras we are not concerned to *get behind* the theorem to penetrate the mind and personality of Euclid. We examine the proof, agree that it is valid, and then *use* the theorem. Hobbes's arguments can be treated like that too. We can examine them to see how good they are; and if we like them we can use them. There are some arguments of his which I like and which I think can be used. In some cases I suspect that they are not exactly as Hobbes intended them to be, but from one important point of view that just does not matter at all. If we like them we can still have them, and enjoy them, and use them. Hobbes would have approved of the analogy.

## 3 THE SITUATION

Hobbes's views on philosophy generally and on method in particular did not just spring into existence quite spontaneously, but arose partly in reaction to the views which he thought were current in the universities, and which had been developed through the Middle Ages under the influence of Plato and Aristotle. There are notorious examples of the sort of attempts which some medieval thinkers made to explain phenomena; and the stock example, which everyone who is not well-disposed to medieval thought must (and does) learn off by heart, is the statement that opium puts people to sleep because of its soporific faculty. This is the sort of pseudo-explanation which Hobbes had much in mind, and throughout *Leviathan* he is scathing in his denunciations. It is temptingly easy to go along with Hobbes here, and to regard the Middle Ages as a period of scientific darkness, suddenly transformed by revolutionary illuminations, generated out of nothing by a group of radical innovators such as Copernicus and Galileo; and Hobbes's remarks on scholastic thinkers would lead us to picture them as, at best, contemptible pedants who thought they could construct knowledge of the world out of their own imaginings, supplemented by rummaging around in the musty books of ancient authors no less credulous than themselves. Fairness to the enemy, however, was never one of Hobbes's more conspicuous weaknesses; and it must be admitted that there is a small element of injustice in his strictures. For in the Middle Ages a fair amount of progress was made in a number of scientific fields. Advances were made in the diagnosis, and to a lesser extent in the treatment, of disease; and the methods of medieval scientists were sometimes impeccably systematic and experimental, as in the study of reflection and refraction of light. Although experimental method was not unknown to the Middle Ages, however, the use of it was a matter of sporadic outbursts, rather than the steady development and general acceptance of a systematic approach. In order that the sciences should be well-based and capable of progress there were a number of conditions that had to be met: it had to be recognised that while language, carefully used, was an indispensable tool in thinking and communicating, it could also be a source of confusion, obscurity and error; a certain dead weight of authority had to be challenged; and whole ways of thinking had to be laid aside to make room for new concepts. However conservative he was in some of his political conclusions, in his doctrine of method Hobbes was an extreme radical. He was not alone in that, of course: in respect of his hostility to scholasticism, his conviction that attention to method was of supreme importance, his concern with clarity, and his choice of mathematics as a model for the sciences, there is a very strong similarity between his views and those of his contemporary, Descartes. Philosophical radicalism was not an isolated phenomenon, but something called forth by and meeting the real needs of the times.

## 4 THE ANALYSIS OF LANGUAGE

One very important element of Hobbes's radicalism was his conviction that philosophers were in danger of talking nonsense unless they paid close and critical attention to the use of language. Thus *Leviathan* abounds in references to the need for definitions, and in scathing denunciations of those whose misuse of language allows them to present mere nonsense as philosophical profundity. He objected to the use of "names that signify nothing; but are taken up, and learned by rote from the schools, as *hypostatical, transubstantiate, consubstantiate, eternal-now*, and the like canting of schoolmen" (*Leviathan*, v 28). This was not merely a commonsense insistence on the need to use language carefully, but was developed into a general theory of language and signification. Some of the elements of Hobbes's account of language are discussed in more detail in Chapter Three, but there are some features of it which it is appropriate to discuss here.

1. Hobbes thought that all "conceptions" in the mind were determinate images, and were derived from particular perceptual experiences; and he went on to claim that language was used significantly only if there were conceptions in the mind of the speaker corresponding to the names which were used. Sometimes (but not always) Hobbes put this in a very extreme form, and claimed that there must be a one–one correspondence between names and conceptions, with a different conception corresponding to each different name. This was an overstatement of what prima facie is a reasonable demand—namely, that abstract terms should be used only when their meaning can be related systematically to observable facts. Thus Berkeley was later to argue that although "force" was not the name of something observable, it was a legitimate term because it had a use within theories and calculations whose conclusions could be checked against observed facts. Hobbes, certainly, was making too rigid a demand, and over-simplifying, and Berkeley's account of the matter was an improvement. But Hobbes's insistence on relating language to observation, even if over-simplified and overstated, presented the philosopher with a challenge: he must be prepared to examine, and to expound the utility and legitimacy of, every element of the language which he used in his arguments. Hobbes, perhaps more clearly than any other philosopher until recent times, saw that reasoning

essentially involved the use of language, so that logical misadventures could be avoided only by a thorough understanding and scrupulous maintenance of linguistic machinery.

2. He did not limit himself to general pronouncements, but attempted to construct a doctrine of categories which could be used in the diagnosis of absurdity. What he did, in both *De Corpore* and *Leviathan*, was to divide names into a number of distinct categories. One of these was *names of bodies*, such as "living", "rational", "cold", "moved", etc. These are all words whose proper use, in Hobbes's view, was to describe bodies. Another category is *names of names*, such as "general", "universal", "equivocal", etc.: for it is words, Hobbes argues, that are universal, and not things or ideas, and hence "universal" is a word which describes a certain kind of word—is the name of a name. Hence someone who says that "there be things universal" is not stating an opinion that might be true or false, but simply uttering nonsense, because he is coupling together two names which belong to different categories—he is coupling a name-word, "universal", with a body-word, "thing" (*Leviathan*, IV 22–23 and V 28). Now this distinction of categories, of course, by itself proves nothing. The philosophers whom Hobbes is criticising might simply reply, "But 'universal' is *not* the name of a name: it is the name of a thing." What is of value in the list of categories is that it is a summary, in systematic form, of an extended analysis of the nature and uses of language in general, and of universal terms, and the word "universal" itself, in particular. What Hobbes has done, in respect of a wide range of philosophical issues, such as the theory of universals, is to compel philosophers to re-examine their arguments and to abstain from conclusions unless and until they can work within the framework of an adequate theoretical analysis of the uses of language. Anyone who ignores this challenge does so at his peril.

3. Hobbes shows an unusual awareness of how philosophical problems may be generated by special features of particular languages. He thought that Scholastics were great exploiters of nonsense, and one of his favourite examples of their "insignificant speech" was their theorisings about "essence". In *Leviathan* he suggests that talk about essences is sheer confusion, which arises from misconstruing the verb "to be". Those who believed in a doctrine of essence were assuming that just as there are objects in the world corresponding to the name "stone", so there must be objects corresponding to the word "is". But

this is a mistake, Hobbes argues, because the verb "to be" does not have any sort of referring function, but does a quite different kind of job. In the proposition "man is a body", the word "is" signifies a connexion between the terms "man" and "body". The word "is", in fact, is quite dispensable, because its job could be done simply by placing the names in a determinate order in the proposition, so that the order in which they occurred signified the connexion between them (*Leviathan*, XLVI 441). Now not even Hobbes's most devoted admirers can pretend that this is a very adequate account of the use, or uses, of the verb "to be". For in the first place, it mentions only the copulative use and ignores the very different use which occurs in a proposition such as "There is a time-bomb in my briefcase". This existential use is relevant, one imagines, to a discussion of the notion of real essences. Again, it is not at all clear why he thinks that the fact that the copulative function of "is" could be performed simply by the word-order of a sentence should imply anything about the function of the word. Hobbes, indeed, has done nothing more than to make merely a small beginning of an analysis of the uses of the word "is". Nevertheless it is some virtue, to have seen the necessity of making the attempt.

## 5 THE REJECTION OF AUTHORITY

Not only sophisticated scientific knowledge of the world, but even the most elementary commonsense knowledge of things, is a social and not merely an individual product, and every individual contribution depends on and presupposes some acceptance of the testimony and theories of others. Nevertheless, this has to be balanced by a critical approach to the authority of others, and in the Middle Ages, although this was not altogether lacking, and was even conspicuous in some individuals, it had hardly become a settled and generally accepted habit of mind. The philosopher was prone to seek the truth in the pages of some musty text, whose nonsense he would copy down and embellish with fantasies of his own. The natural history of the period was an extraordinary ragbag of acute observation and old-wives' tales. A. C. Crombie records that even as late as the seventeenth century one of the founders of the Royal Society (admittedly, a bishop) could mention being carried through the air by birds and by witches as "recognised methods of human transport" (*Augustine to Galileo*, vol. i, p. 53).

One particular authority which badly needed attacking was the Church. Although justice compels one to admit that all the scientific eggs of medieval Christendom were laid and incubated by ecclesiastical hens, the rate of production was not very impressive. For this the Church itself was partly to blame, because in the first place it was committed to a belief in the divine authority of the Bible, and in the second place, partly by its own efforts and partly with the help of Aristotle, it had built up a theological-cum-philosophical world-view, which it did not regard as a product of supernatural revelation but still tended to identify with divine truth. The wretched scientist thus had to cope not only with common or garden old-wives' tales but with a special brand of divine nonsense which he challenged at his peril. For the Church, in the very early stages of its development, had acquired an influential and even dominant position in political affairs, and used its powers effectively to suppress criticism of beliefs which it regarded as fundamental. Sometimes and in some respects this hardly seemed to matter. A scientist may believe, or pretend to believe, in the existence of God and the divinity of Jesus Christ; and this may do no harm, because in the laboratory he can put this belief aside and get on with the job in hand. But sometimes it mattered very much. The most famous instance of this, perhaps, is the issue between heliocentric and geocentric astronomy. For the religious the earth was the stable centre of the universe, with the sun and the planets revolving around it. But there were a few who thought differently because they found that the apparent motions of the sun and planets could be explained, on the geocentric hypothesis, only in terms of the most fantastically complicated formulae. What is important is not to decide in favour of either hypothesis, but to notice the way in which the issue developed. The religious authorities saw it as a challenge to divinely inspired truth, and as such it was to be resisted, regardless of the merits of the rival hypotheses. Even this would not have mattered too much if the Church had had less power. But in those days the religious were not limited to pressurising the B.B.C. and lobbying M.P.s; and independent thinkers, whose bodies were less tough than their minds, grew timid at the thought of the rack and the thumbscrew.

It was not just that the stories in Genesis made it difficult to account for particular phenomena, like the motions of the stars and the existence of fossils. It was that religious beliefs encouraged and required the suspension of criticism generally. Where conformity with religious dogma is made a criterion, not merely of theological truth but of truth generally, honest men are involved in mental gymnastics which in the end produce a sort of intellectual depravity. Hobbes and his contemporaries and immediate predecessors did not react simply by rejecting religion. Most of them at least went through the motions of affirming belief in the tenets of whichever church had corporal power over them, and it seems likely that this was not merely a diplomatic pretence but the expression of genuine belief. But they were increasingly prepared to claim that religious truth could not be contrary to reason; to seek the truth about the world independently of religious dogma; and to insist that if well-based beliefs came in conflict with dogma, it was the latter which must yield (*Leviathan*, XLVI 450). Considerations such as these are things which we have to be able to *take for granted* if we are to make much progress in the pursuit of knowledge, but Hobbes and Descartes had to assert them *defiantly*.

God moves in a mysterious way, his wonders to perform. The Bible view, with which medievals tended to sympathise, was that God was always at it, performing wonders. He was the Prime Minister of the universe, governing busily from day to day. In Hobbes's philosophy, and in most of the philosophy of his time, God was kicked upstairs: not assassinated, but retired into constitutional monarchy. He was held to be the creator of the world; but rather like a clockmaker, who designs and constructs the machine but keeps his finger out of the works once he has set it going. A number of convenient assumptions were made. It was assumed that the world had been designed in an intelligible sort of way (according to Galileo the world was an open book, waiting to be read, and the language was mathematics). It was assumed that God was not constantly interfering with the works so as to render their operations unpredictable. And it was assumed that human beings had the capacity to understand how the machine worked. Finally, human ambition was limited to the attempt to understand *how* the machine worked and not to discover *why* it had been constructed as it was. This was expressed in the abandonment of the Aristotelian notion of *final causes*. The notion of final causes imported purposes into the world, and if the world was created by God, these purposes must be divine. Since God was an infinite and incomprehensible being, the investigation of final causes was always liable to become a blind alley. Philosophers ultimately got round to regarding them as dispensable, and showed a certain amount of low cunning in representing this as theological virtue. Thus Descartes, who never mentions the Almighty except in terms so cringing and servile that it is embarrassing and shameful to read him, writes that the notion of final causes cannot be usefully employed in the sciences, "for it does not appear to me that I can without temerity seek to investigate the [inscrutable] ends of God" (*Meditation* IV). Hobbes always insists that God is so incomprehensible that we cannot really say anything at all about him, but can only direct honorific noises towards him. The only causal notions which Hobbes is prepared to accept into his philosophy are the concepts of the material and of the efficient cause, and he sharply defines these together as the sum of the conditions which are jointly sufficient for the production of an effect, so that if these conditions are fulfilled the effect must follow. This is a commendable analysis, for it directs attention towards aspects that are susceptible of investigation and at the same time provides a framework for embodying and formulating the results of these investigations.

Hobbes never admitted to being an atheist. This was probably because he did actually believe in the existence of God, as a remote first cause. And in any case, even if he had been an atheist he would have been very foolish to admit it. It is not merely that he would have had to face persecution. But in addition, he thought that his political arguments were matters of the greatest public importance, and that people must attend to them if there was to be any prospect of peace and security. It was not likely that people would have much attention to spare for his politics if they were obsessed with the scandalous possibility of atheism. Indeed Hobbes not only proclaims his belief in God, but also is prepared to confirm some of his conclusions by appeal to Scripture. This has led some commentators to suggest that Hobbes's political theories are, to a greater or lesser extent, actually based on explicitly theological premises. That is a matter which can only be fully discussed in connexion with some of the specific arguments themselves, and, in particular, in the context of his treatment of natural law. But generally it seems to me to be a most implausible supposition. For Hobbes was very adept at getting under the skins of theologians. The evidence for this is both the irritated screaming of his victims and the nature of the arguments which so offended them. For in the first place Hobbes asserted not only the existence but the total incomprehensibility of God: he allowed theologians to say *that* there was a God, but not to say anything at all about him. And in the second place, although he was prepared to appeal to Scripture as an authority, the way in which he did this was well designed to give offence. Thus in an epilogue to *Leviathan* he writes:

To conclude, there is nothing in this whole discourse, nor in that I writ before of the same subject in Latin, as far as I can perceive, contrary either to the word of God, or to good manners; or to the disturbance of the public tranquillity. Therefore I think it may be profitably printed. . . . (*Conclusion*, 467).

This is not the only occasion in *Leviathan* on which Hobbes insultingly combines appeal to divine authority with a reference to considerations of public order. Indeed, although he admits the legitimacy of appeal to Scripture, he insists that the sovereign, if a Christian, has indisputable authority in the *interpretation* of Scripture. Hobbes argues that even a *heathen* sovereign is the supreme pastor of his people, with the right to judge what should be taught and who should teach it; and that it would be absurd to suppose that conversion to Christianity should deprive a sovereign of this right (XLII 355). Hobbes later defines "heresy" as "nothing else but a private opinion obstinately maintained, contrary to the opinion which the public person, that is to say, the representant of the commonwealth, hath commanded to be taught" (XLII 381).

Hobbes, of course, like Galileo, Descartes and others, was compelled to pretend to orthodoxy in order that theological squabbling should not divert attention from the important things which needed discussing and could be rationally discussed. This is the excuse for Descartes' excesses of piety. But although Hobbes refused to offer himself up as a victim for persecution, his discussions of religion were infused with mockery and derision, and he preserved theology only by pickling it in political vinegar.

## 6 CONCEPTUAL REVISION

The conclusions people reach about the world depend not merely on what they discover in their investigations (if any), but on their ways of thinking about the world—the basic concepts in terms of which they formulate propositions about the world. This is because in the first place these concepts, taken together, may add up to some sort of world-view which to a greater or lesser extent encourages fruitful kinds of investigation; and because in the second place there are facts which cannot exist for us at all unless we have the appropriate concepts with which to express them.

One may regard the world as an irreducibly mysterious place in which many things happen quite inexplicably, sometimes merely by chance, and sometimes because they are the unpredictable whim of some human or supernatural agency. Such a view of the world does not encourage the growth of science, because the world in effect is seen as resistant to systematic investigation. Hobbes, however, had a materialistic metaphysics, which offered a very different view of the world. According to Hobbes the world is just bodies moving in space, acting and interacting with each other. Everything which happens is explicable in terms of motions of physical particles.

Hobbes and Descartes can be usefully compared here. Hobbes was a materialist and Descartes was not. Nevertheless Descartes, equally with Hobbes, saw the material world as a mechanism whose mode of operation was fully explicable with the help of mathematics. Over a wide range of phenomena their approach, and the methods appropriate to it, were going to be the same. Now in a sense this was something that just had to be produced out of a hat. There could be no scientific justification of this view of the world, because some such view must be presupposed in the systematic acceptance of canons of scientific justification. Hobbes and Descartes, however, would certainly have refused to regard it as a mere private fiction of their own. Hence Descartes—and sometimes Hobbes also—was driven back to appeals to self-evidence. This was not entirely satisfactory, yet it was defensible. It was not satisfactory, because the principles involved are not necessarily at all *evident*. It was defensible because they are still susceptible of a sort of justification that is not viciously circular. This justification is in part *a priori*, in the reflection that the principles constitute a framework of systematic investigation. And in part it is *a posteriori*, in the discovery that investigations inspired by them have in fact been fruitful.

It was not merely a general view of the world which needed re-thinking but some specific concepts as well. The concept of cause needed revising, and it is no accident that Hobbes and Descartes were agreed about this. And there were other concepts which equally needed overhauling. One of the most obvious, and perhaps the most important, of these was the concept of inertia. On the Aristotelian view the motion of a body was a process caused by the continual action on it of some moving force, and the motion would stop when the force was removed. This view was in no way contrary to common sense, and was consistent with, and even suggested by, elementary observations. Galileo, however, replaced it with the notion that a body would continue *either* in a state of rest *or* in a state of uniform recti-linear motion unless acted on by a force. This notion was not sug-gested by either common sense or observation, but scientifically it was in fact an advance on the commonsense Aristotelian concept.

The possibility of scientific knowledge of the world, then, depends in the first place on the adoption of some general scheme of concepts, some view of the world which will encourage, and within which it will be possible to frame, a system of theories and investigations; and in the second place, in specific fields of investigation, on the choice of certain concepts, in terms of which the construction of adequate theories will be possible.

What was needed, in fact, was a conceptual revolution, and Hobbes accepted and welcomed it, even although he did not invent it. But what is more important, the conceptual revolution posed logical problems about the nature of scientific method. A certain empiricist tradition of philosophy grew up after Hobbes, which regarded con-cepts as necessarily derivative from simple perceptual data, and claimed that the truth of propositions about the world was to be established by reference to these data. Hobbes never developed any single and consistent alternative to this account, but the rich muddles and con-fusions which developed in his views on scientific method originated partly in some genuine insights which prevented him from achieving clarity through over-simplification. In the next two chapters I shall be following out some of the different accounts which Hobbes gave of matters of logic and scientific method.

# Part One

# METHOD

# CHAPTER THREE
## *Language and Logic*

IN the first three chapters of *Leviathan* Hobbes gives an account, in physical, mechanistic terms, of what is involved in perception and thought. They are a *description* of what (Hobbes thinks) is going on within the human organism when it is exercising its cognitive capacities. In chapters IV and V he discusses reasoning and the use of language, and his discussion is no longer merely descriptive, but much more extended in scope. It is an analysis of the uses of language and the modes of reasoning, and it is concerned not so much to describe how people *do* think and talk, as to prescribe how they *ought* to think and talk if they are to avoid absurdity. This extends to a discussion of philosophical and scientific method generally. Matters of method—especially close attention to definitions—were regarded by Hobbes as supremely important, and it would be ludicrous to make any pretence of studying Hobbes seriously unless one were prepared to look closely at his views on method.

In chapter IX of *Leviathan* Hobbes distinguishes two kinds of knowledge. One is "knowledge of fact", and by this Hobbes means particular facts such as that King Charles I of England was beheaded in 1649. The "register" of such knowledge is called *history*, and may be either *natural history*, which is the history of such facts as have no dependence on human contrivance, or *civil history*, "which is the history of the voluntary actions of men in commonwealths" (IX 53). The other kind of knowledge is "knowledge of the consequence of one affirmation to another", and this is science. Its distinguishing feature is that it is *conditional*, as, for example, in the proposition that *"if the figure shown be a circle, then any straight line through the centre shall divide it into two equal parts*. And this is the knowledge required in a philosopher; that is to say, of him that pretends to reasoning" (IX 53). *Leviathan*, of course, is to be regarded as a contribution to science. And the first thing to notice here is that Hobbes does not distinguish, as modern philosophers do, between philosophy and science. The two words "science" and "philosophy" are used interchangeably by Hobbes, and cover a wide range of enquiries which not only share the same methods and procedures but even, to a large extent, form a single deductive system depending on the same fundamental premisses. Thus *geometry, architecture, optics, ethics, logic* and many other particular sciences are all branches from the single stem of *natural philosophy*. This is shown graphically in a chart given in chapter IX, which displays the connexions and ramifications of the sciences with great clarity. The only thing that is not so clear is why this simple picture of the systematic unity of the sciences is spoiled by a fundamental division, which the chart shows, between *natural philosophy* and *civil philosophy* or *politics*. Since natural philosophy includes physics, which in turn includes ethics and the science of just and unjust, it is obvious that there must be some points of interest in Hobbes's views on the sciences. Indeed there are, and I shall be discussing them in the next chapter. But in order to do that I have to begin with Hobbes's views on language and logic. For on the various occasions when he expounded his views on philosophical method, Hobbes began by describing the nature, use and rules of language; and his account of philosophical method in some respects is expressed as an element of his theory of language and in most respects presupposes it.

## 1 SENSE AND IMAGINATION

Hobbes begins *Leviathan* with an account of "sense" and "imagination", which terms he uses to cover, respectively, perception and thought generally. It is not unreasonable to make a beginning there, even in a book which is concerned with political knowledge, because in Hobbes's philosophy thinking is nothing more than a succession of images (or conceptions) which originate in sense experience. According to Hobbes, the world, and our experience of it, is all to be explained in terms of the actions and interactions of physical objects —motions of bodies. We see objects as coloured, feel them as hot and cold, and so forth. The colour and the heat, however, are not properties inhering in the objects, but are how the objects appear to us: they are *appearances* in us, caused by the action of the objects on our sense organs. (Hobbes uses a great number of synonyms for "appearance"—"representation", "fancy", "seeming", "image", "apparition" are some of them. In the *Elements of Law* he uses the word "conception" to cover all the contents of our experience, whether in perception or in imagination.) We ourselves are material objects, with physical sense organs which react to the stimulus of objects external to us. We have knowledge of these objects only through the images which they cause in us; and these images, strictly speaking, are merely our awareness, not of the objects causing them, but of the physical state of our own organism produced by the action of the objects upon it. Even when the object is absent its effect lingers on, so that the image may remain, though more obscurely; and this is imagination, which is just "decaying sense". All the activities of the mind—imagining, dreaming, remembering, all kinds of thinking—are simply successions of images or conceptions.

Such an account as this raises some obvious questions. Since images might be hallucinatory, how is it possible to infer from the occurrence of images to the existence of external physical objects? How can we know that there are *ever* any objects corresponding to but distinct from images? Descartes and subsequent philosophers were much concerned with such questions. They may or may not be answerable, and may or may not be bogus questions, but prima facie they do seem to arise naturally out of the sort of account which Hobbes gave. Hobbes, however, simply ignores them. Chapters I and II of *Leviathan* represent not so much the weakest part of Hobbes's philosophy as an area within which he had no philosophy at all. He has no philosophy of perception, but is content to make a number of dogmatic assumptions. Their only significance is that these provide the framework within which his theories of language and method are expounded.

## 2 NAMING AND SIGNIFYING

Hobbes distinguishes between thoughts which are *"unguided, without design, and inconstant"* from those which are *"regulated* by some desire, and design" (*Leviathan* III 14). The first is when "the thoughts are said to wander", without apparent connexion with each other, as in dreaming or day-dreaming. Even here, however, Hobbes thinks that at least sometimes we see the connexions between succeeding thoughts, by means of a sort of association of ideas. But what Hobbes is more interested in is the *regulated* train of thoughts, which is thought directed by desire. The train of regulated thoughts is either (i) seeking the means to produce something which we imagine and desire, or (ii) seeking all the possible *effects* of a thing.

This, of course, is a grossly over-simplified account of thought, but it is of no importance to Hobbes's argument anyway. It purports to be a *description* of how people think. As such it is a contribution to psychology, and a very unimpressive contribution. But in chapters IV and V he abandons merely describing, and produces a *critical analysis* of thought and language. What he is concerned with then is to discuss how language *can* be used and *ought* to be used and to show how misuses can result in absurdity.

"Regulated" thinking, Hobbes argues, is possible without the use of words, but is then limited to the exercise of prudence. For our memory is not merely of particular conceptions but also of the original *sequence* of these in our experience. Hence when we come across $X$ we may recall conceptions like $X$ followed by a conception, $Y$, or conceptions like $Y$. Then we expect to find $X$ soon followed by something like $Y$. "As he that foresees what will become of a criminal, re-cons what he has seen follow on the like crime before; having this order of thoughts, the crime, the officer, the prison, the judge, and the gallows" (III 15). The greater one's experience, the more reliable are one's conjectures, but at best they are still uncertain. "Experience concludeth nothing universally", Hobbes says in *The Elements of Law* (I iv 10), and he has not changed his mind in *Leviathan* (see III 16 and V 29–30 especially). Even with language to help us we are not justified in drawing universal conclusions from particular cases. But without language it is impossible to generalise at all. For the primary purpose of language is to serve as *marks* that will recall conceptions which otherwise are "apt to slip out of our memory" (IV 18). Hobbes tries to show the importance of this by means of an example. A man without the use of language might see a triangle, and beside it, two right angles. He might then compare them and find that the sum of the three angles of the triangle was equal to the two right angles. If another, differently-shaped triangle were to be shown to him, however, he would have to do his sums all over again. But if he had the use of words he could notice that the equality followed, not from particular features of either triangle, but merely from its having straight sides and three angles—that is, from those things "for which he named it a triangle"; and then he could conclude universally that *every* triangle has its three angles equal to two right angles (IV 20, also *De Corpore*, I vi 11). There is another example, with the same import, in *De Corpore*, where Hobbes argues that syllogistic argument involves not only having the appropriate conceptions but also using the relevant *names* (I iv 8). There is an interesting difference of emphasis, however, in *The Elements of Law*, where he provides no such examples, but is concerned rather to insist that speech which is not accompanied by corresponding conceptions is merely parrot-talk (I vi 3).

In addition to this private use of words in reasoning, when Hobbes calls them *marks*, there is also a public use in signifying one's conceptions to an audience, when Hobbes calls them *signs*. He has already defined a sign as "the evident antecedent of a consequent" (III 16). His discussion of signs in *De Corpore* is similar to that in *Leviathan*, but much fuller. He gives as an example of a *natural* sign, clouds, which are usually followed by rain, and as an example of an *artificial* sign, a stone to mark the bounds of a field (I ii 2). Words are artificial signs, and what they signify is conceptions in the mind of the speaker. Hobbes distinguishes between words and names, because one name may be composed of several words: "For all these words, *he that in his actions observeth the laws of his country*, make but one name, equivalent to this one word, *just*" (IV 20).

He also distinguishes—in effect, if not explicitly—between naming and signifying. Thus he talks of names as imposed on *things*, universal names as common to many *things* (IV 19) and names generally as names *of things*, whereas when he talks abut their signification it is conceptions which they signify. Thus he says: "For seeing all names are imposed to signify our conceptions, and all our affections are but conceptions, when we conceive the same things differently, we can hardly avoid different naming of them" (IV 24). There is a passage in *De Corpore* where he argues that a name cannot be a sign of a thing— "for that the sound of this word *stone* should be the sign of a stone, cannot be understood in any sense but this, that he that hears it collects that he that pronounces it thinks of a stone" (I ii 5). Presumably if it were the sign of the thing, the utterance of the word would indicate the presence or imminence of a stone. It has been argued in connexion with this by Watkins that Hobbes "identified a name with physical expressions of itself", because his "materialism did not allow him to regard a name as an abstract entity immanent in, but not identical with, its various physical expressions. He regarded each such expression as a name. . . ." (*Hobbes's System of Ideas*, p. 141.) But this reading of Hobbes is not very convincing.

1. Hobbes never actually says that he regards each expression of a name as a name.

2. He sometimes talks about one name "comprehending" another, and this is certainly not to identify the name with the physical expression of itself.

3. The distinction between word-tokens and word-types can usefully be applied here. If I send you a telegram with the message "Happy birthday, happy New Year", the postal official counts five words, and you, who have a linguistic interest in the poverty of my vocabulary, count four words, and you are both right, because the official is counting tokens while you are counting types. Hobbes, however, had not heard of the type–token distinction. He describes names as "sensible marks" and "sounds", but if he *had* thought of the type–token distinction I think that he might well have been prepared to identify the "physical expressions" with the tokens. For Watkins says that Hobbes could not regard a name as "an abstract entity immanent in, but not identical with, its various physical expressions"; but the fact is that Hobbes does come near to saying something very like that. The job of a name is to signify conceptions. That means not merely to be related in a certain way to the conceptions of the speaker but also to cause the appropriate conceptions to arise in the mind of the hearer. Unless it had the latter capacity it would be of no use as a name. Now Hobbes argues in *De Corpore* that both names and conceptions have the same cause, namely, a certain power in the thing conceived, otherwise called an *accident* of it (I iii 3). He also says that an accident is a part of the nature of a thing, though not a physically separable part of the thing itself (I vi 2); and he argues frequently and consistently that causes are not bodies as such (for then all causal agents would produce the same effects, being all equally bodies) but *accidents* of bodies (fire warms, not because it is a body, but because it is hot) (II ix 1–3; also I vi 2–10). I think that everything that Hobbes says about names is consistent with regard-

ing them as accidents of those physical marks which are name-tokens, and indeed it is only so regarded that they could be considered capable of doing the jobs which Hobbes ascribes to them.

Having defined the signification of a name in terms of the capacity to cause appropriate conceptions, Hobbes defines *understanding* as "conception caused by speech"—not *any* conceptions, but "those thoughts which the words of that speech and their connexion were ordained and constituted to signify" (IV 24). (This indeed would be a hard saying if Hobbes identified names with their physical expressions. For how then could we ordain and constitute? If I said "My name is to be Joe Soap", I should be deluded if I imagined that I had thereby named myself, for I should merely have "ordained" something (but what?) about that particular occurrence of the noise "Joe Soap". Someone who said "You are *not* Joe Soap" would be uttering another name and therefore not contradicting me. Even Hobbes cannot have intended such nonsense.) Now there are two aspects to this account of understanding. Hobbes always insists that speech must *signify* conceptions, and he uses this as a rather blunt instrument with which to attack the metaphysicians and theologians whom he dislikes, accusing them of using *mere* words which are meaningless—that is, to which there are no corresponding conceptions. But (i) this could be taken as the claim that all significant speech involved the actual occurrence of conceptions corresponding one–one to the names used. Or (ii) it could be taken as a demand that all names used should be *capable* of being given a cash value in terms of conceptions. Hobbes at various times expresses both of these views, and one of the differences between *The Elements of Law* and *Leviathan* is that the first view is conspicuously present in *The Elements* (I v 14), whereas in *Leviathan* there is very little trace of it, but a constant reiteration of the second. This is a point which will arise again in connexion with Hobbes's doctrine of accidents, and yet again in the discussion of definition.

## 3 UNIVERSALS

Having given an account of language and its uses in general terms, Hobbes goes on to distinguish two kinds of name. A name is either "*proper*, and singular to one only thing, as *Peter, John, this man, this tree*", whose standard use is to pick out some particular individual; or "*common* to many things, *man, horse, tree*", each of which names an indefinite number of human, equine or arboreal objects. Hobbes goes on to say that "in respect of" all the various things of which it is the name, a common name is called *universal*; and he insists immediately that it is the *name* which is *universal*, "there being nothing in the world universal but names" (IV 19). This is an expression of the *nominalism* for which Hobbes is famous, and there is no question that he was consistent in rejecting any variety of the view that a general word like "man" has corresponding to it some general idea or universal which can be identified neither with the word itself nor with any *particular* object. (Readers who are not familiar with philosophical problems and theories about universals will find an elementary and lucid account in A. D. Woozley's article on "Universals" in *The Encyclopedia of Philosophy*, Collier–Macmillan, 1967.)

Now Watkins has argued that the consistent adoption of a strictly nominalistic position can have far-reaching implications (see *Hobbes's System of Ideas*, chapter VIII). For we have to be able to answer the question how we are to tell which objects should have any given common name applied to them. Suppose we consider three objects whose proper names are "Fido", "Mount Everest" and "The Archbishop of Canterbury". Suppose also that Fido has been given the common name "dog", and since "not-dog" is, in Hobbes's view, also a name, suppose that Mount Everest has been given the common name "not-dog". The question is, whether the third object, the Archbishop, is to be called a dog or a not-dog. How are we to answer such a question? Can we call the Archbishop a dog, or not, just as the whim takes us? Or must we ask whether he is sufficiently *like* Fido to share the same common name with him? But such a consideration, by itself, will not take us very far, Watkins argues, since any object can be represented as being like any other object in an indefinite number of respects. Thus the Archbishop and Fido are like each other in having two eyes, in having at least one good meal every day, in not being encrusted with a layer of snow and ice, and so forth. Mount Everest and the Archbishop are alike in being mentioned sometimes in British newspapers, in being objects of religious veneration to some, in not having waggly tails, and so forth. How then are we to decide whether the Archbishop is a dog or a not-dog? On an extreme nominalistic view this would have to rest simply on a decision: it is we who use words who give them their meaning, and have to *decide* whether the Archbishop goes in the dog or not-dog category.

But this is a conclusion which cannot very easily be accepted. For it seems to make the truth of propositions a matter simply of verbal convention. Of course, it is obvious that you cannot determine whether a proposition is true or false if you are uncertain about the meanings of the terms involved, but it does not seem very plausible to suggest that the question whether the Archbishop is a dog or a not-dog can be settled *just* by attending to the meanings of the words "dog" and "not-dog". Most of us have no hesitation in conceding that the Archbishop is a not-dog. But this is not just because we know the language, but also because we have no reason at all for suspecting the occurrence of a stupendous deception or a sensational mutation. Nevertheless, however implausible this view may seem, there are times when Hobbes appears to insist on it. "Truth consisteth in the right ordering of names in our affirmations", he says in *Leviathan* (IV 21); and in *De Cive*, even more explicitly, "And to *know truth*, is the same thing as to *remember* that it was made by ourselves by the very usurpation of the words" (xviii 4). And in *De Corpore* he says, "And it is for brevity's sake that I suppose the original of names to be arbitrary, judging it a thing that may be assumed as unquestionable" (I ii 4). Yet there is difficulty in knowing exactly how to take these assertions. For to say that names are imposed arbitrarily may be to say any one of three different things.

1. It may be to say that there is no reason why this rather than that word in any given language has come to have the meaning it has. This thesis is obviously false in some cases—onomatopoeic words, for example—and if Hobbes believed it, he could easily have abandoned it without damage to his other views on language.

2. It may be to say that there is no good reason why we should not choose words arbitrarily, if we please. This is not to say that we *do* choose words arbitrarily, but that there is no harm in it if we do. If we all agreed that "kong" was to mean what "king" now means, then "kong" would *have* that meaning, just because we had agreed that it was to. There are some obvious limitations here. The word "kong" could not possibly do *all* the jobs that "king" does: it rhymes differently, for example, and it might not acquire precisely the same emotive overtones as "king". This, however, would not worry Hobbes very much. At the end of chapter IV of *Leviathan* he

distinguishes between names of *constant* and names of *inconstant* signification. Because different things please or displease different people, and the same person at different times, the names for the things that please and displease us have "*inconstant* signification"—that is, their meaning varies from occasion to occasion. Hence these can never, Hobbes argues, be used for *reasoning* (IV 24–25). Part of what Hobbes is saying, then, when he says that words are "arbitrary", is that so long as the signification is settled and constant it does not matter, *for purposes of reasoning*, whether the word is "king" or "kong".

3. But Hobbes might be saying that the signification of words is also arbitrary. He might be saying, to revert to our previous example, that when the name "dog" has been given to Fido, the question whether to give this name also to the Archbishop of Canterbury can be answered only by making an arbitrary decision. And what is involved here might be either a lesser or a more extreme claim. For (i) there is some room for manoeuvre in the procedure of classifying. We do not classify whales as fish, for example. If the distinction between mammals and non-mammals was not important to us, however, we could use the word "fish" to cover, say, all non-crustacean creatures which live in the sea and swim by moving fins and tail. Then, in terms of that classification, whales would be fish. How things are classified depends to some extent on *why* they are classified. This, however, only applies to the adoption of classificatory *schemes*. Once we have decided in favour of one scheme rather than another the question of whether any given object is a fish or not a fish, or whatever the question may be, is no longer a matter for arbitrary decision but depends on the nature of the object. But (ii) one might make the very extreme claim that *every* step involved in classifying objects is a matter of arbitrary decision. Then we should not merely have to *decide* whether to call whales "fish" or not, but each time we came across a whale we had not met before we should have to decide whether to call *it* a "fish". It is hard to imagine why anyone should make a claim so extreme, which is so patently untrue to actual classification procedure, and which would make a shambles of all conceivable verbal processes of communication. But it has sometimes been thought that Hobbes is asserting it when he insists on the "arbitrary" nature of language.

Which of these views *does* Hobbes have in mind? I think that no firm answer can be given to this question. For what I have done is to distinguish a number of different views. I think the distinctions which I have made are useful and necessary. Unfortunately they simply did not occur to Hobbes. In the main his remarks on the arbitrary nature of language are rather vague, and when he does become specific it is not always in the same way. Thus in *De Corpore* Hobbes explicitly propounds first View 1: "how can any man imagine that the names of things were imposed from their natures?"; then View 2: "moreover, whatsoever the common use of words be, yet philosophers . . . had always the liberty, and sometimes they both had and will have a necessity, of taking to themselves such names as they please for the signifying of their meaning, if they would have it understood" (I ii 4). In *De Cive*, when he says that truth is "made by ourselves", and in *Leviathan*, when he says that "truth consisteth in the right ordering of names", I think that it is universal propositions which he has in mind. There is no evidence that he would have applied these views to *singular* propositions, of the form "This object is a fish". In other words, Hobbes never explicitly commits himself to View 3 (ii), which is the extreme claim about the arbitrary nature of classification of individuals. His position seems to be nearer to View 3 (i), which is a modest claim about arbitrary features of classificatory schemes. This cannot be explored further, however, until we examine Hobbes's pronouncements about truth, in a later section.

Whatever may be the correct interpretation of those passages which we have been considering, when Hobbes himself discusses how universal names are applied to individual things he produces a doctrine of accidents which is a straightforward and downright denial of the extreme conventionalist position.


## 4 ACCIDENTS

Having distinguished between proper and common (or universal) names, Hobbes goes on immediately in *Leviathan* to explain the very simple principle on which universals are applied: "One universal name is imposed on many things, for their similitude in some quality, or other accident" (IV 19). A few pages later he gives "life", "heat", "length", "motion" as examples of "names of the accidents and properties by which one matter and body is distinguished from another", and these are called *abstract* names. Hobbes goes on immediately to insist that the abstraction is in the *names*: it is not that accidents can be separated from bodies, but merely that names of accidents are a special way of referring to bodies (IV 23).

The discussion in *Leviathan* is little more than a brief mention of the topic, and such discussion as there is is by no means as clear as it might be. But in *De Corpore* he goes into it much more fully, although perhaps not very much more clearly. He distinguishes between concrete and abstract names. The former are names of things which we suppose to exist, such as "body", "moved", "hot", etc. Abstract names are names which "denote only the causes of *concrete names*, and not the things themselves", for example, "corporeity", "motion", "heat", etc. "So when we see a thing appear sometimes here, sometimes there, and call it *moved* or *removed*, the cause of that name is that it *is moved* or the *motion* of the same." The names of things and our conceptions of things, Hobbes goes on, have the same causes, "namely, some power of action, or affection of the thing conceived, which some call the manner by which anything works upon our senses, but by most men they are called *accidents*. . . ." And these accidents, "being neither the things themselves, nor parts thereof, do nevertheless accompany the things in such manner, that (saving extension) they may all perish, and be destroyed, but can never be abstracted" (I iii 3). Later Hobbes says that an accident is a part of the *nature* of a thing, though not a physically separable part of the thing itself (I vi 2).

Now one thing at least emerges very clearly from this, and that is that Hobbes is asserting the very contrary of an extreme conventionalist view. We are not free arbitrarily to decide to call the Archbishop a dog. Whether we call the Archbishop a dog or not depends not on our decision but on "some quality, or other accident", of the Archbishop.

Hobbes's doctrine is very complicated, because he thinks that the analysis of language has to expound the relations not just between words and things but between words *and conceptions* and things. Thus Berkeley held that all imagery must be determinate, although particular images could have a general, representative *function*: a particular, determinate image of a man could be general in its function because it *stood for* all images of men. But Hobbes thought that it was only the name, and not the image, which had even so much as a general use.

It has been commonly recognised that the interposition of conceptions between names and things complicates matters for Hobbes,
but I do not think that it has always been realised just what difficulties
this makes for him. The two elements of his account which, in combination, make difficulties for him are his account of *universals* and his
account of *understanding*.

### 1. *Universals*

We have already discussed his insistence that only names are universal,
not things or images of things.

### 2. *Understanding*

In *Leviathan* Hobbes defines "understanding" as "conception caused
by speech" (IV 24). If a man, hearing some words, has the conceptions
which the words and their connexions are "ordained and constituted
to signify", then he understands them. One important source of
absurdity is using words that have no signification, and to signify is
to be the sign of a conception. This is a matter about which Hobbes has
very little to say in *Leviathan*, but a great deal more in *The Elements*
and *De Corpore*. What he actually says in *Leviathan* amounts to very
little more than a rather vague and innocuous claim that thoughtless
chatter is not a significant use of language. Thus he says that "the
general use of speech, is to transfer our mental discourse, into verbal
. . ." (IV 18), and his account of the use of *marks* and *signs* suggests
that what corresponds to them in the mind is thoughts *that something
or other is the case*. He does not claim explicitly that each name in any
speech must have some thought, in the sense of a particular mental
image, corresponding to it. But in *The Elements* it is this second, more
extreme, claim that he makes. "A NAME or APPELLATION therefore
is the voice of a man, arbitrarily imposed, for a mark to bring to his
mind some conception concerning the thing on which it is imposed"
(I v 2). Later he refers slightingly to the beggars' habit of muttering
the words of the *paternoster*, "having no images or conceptions in their
minds answering to the words they speak" (I v 14). And he argues
that knowledge requires not only truth but also something which he
calls "evidence", by which he means, not "evidence" in the sense of
"facts supporting a certain belief, allegation or conclusion", but

simply "the concomitance of a man's conception with the words that signify such conception in the act of ratiocination". If a man reasons in words only, without having in his mind a succession of conceptions corresponding to his words, then he is speaking only parrot-like (I vi 3). One might almost say that Hobbes is constantly harping on this theme in *The Elements*, and this is in contrast with the vague and cursory way in which he touches on it in *Leviathan*. There are many passages in *De Corpore* also, when Hobbes's account is given in similar terms to that of *The Elements*. Thus in his discussion of universals he argues for a one–one correspondence between names and conceptions in the mind (I ii 9–11). He defines "absurd and insignificant" speech as that in which "there is a succession of words, to which there can be no succession of thoughts in mind to answer them" (I iii 1). Again, he analyses the argument of a syllogism in order to show that the argument could not be conducted without the use of names; and yet alleges—working this out in great detail—that the thought involved is a succession of "conceptions" (or "phantasms") with the occurrence of one of these corresponding to the occurrence of each of the names in the syllogism (I iv 8).

There seems to be a distinct difference, then, between the doctrine of *The Elements* and *De Corpore* on the one hand and that of *Leviathan* on the other; and I suspect that this is reflected in a difference in Hobbes's choice of *words*. I have remarked already that Hobbes uses a wide range of expressions, more or less interchangeably, for the "contents" of the mind: "thought", "appearance", "representation", "fancy", "seeming", "image", "apparition", "conception", "idea". Now when he is talking in *Leviathan* about the relation between speech and thought, the term he uses is "conception", and this is perhaps significant, because the word is vague. In Hobbes's own usage "conceive" is used in two different ways: (i) "conceive (that is, form) an image", and (ii) "conceive (that is, think) that something is the case". Thus Hobbes describes how "the mind conceives first an image of a man . . .", and talks of conceiving a "phantasm" (*De Corpore*, I iii 3), and these are examples of the first usage. But his account of a proposition is that it signifies that the speaker conceives "that the former name is comprehended by the latter" (*De Corpore*, I iii 2). This is an example of the second usage. Now whereas in the first sense a conception is a particular, determinate mental image, a sort of *picture*, in the second, propositional sense, the existence of such an image is not entailed by the use of the word "conception" itself. Hobbes may well think that all "acts of the mind" are reducible to the occurrence of images. He does think so, as we have seen, and says so on many occasions. Indeed, right at the beginning of chapter 1 of *Leviathan* he says that our "thoughts" are "every one a *representation* or *appearance*, of some quality, or other accident of a body without us" (1 7). But the significance of this pronouncement is less than it might seem, because it is implicitly restricted to the subject in hand, which is the *source* of our conceptions of *things*: the subject of the chapter is *sense*, and not thought in general. He is not concerned to affirm that all thinking is reducible to a succession of particular images, but to deny that there can be any ideas of things which do not originate in sense perception. The fact is that, whereas in *The Elements* and *De Corpore* Hobbes goes to great lengths to state, unambiguously and in detail, that significant speech involves the occurrence of images corresponding to each name employed, in *Leviathan* he avoids committing himself to this; and whereas in the other works he uses words like "image" and "phantasm", which leave no room for doubt, in *Leviathan* he avoids these words and uses the vague and ambiguous word "conception".

The fact that this difference of language exists can be determined simply by looking at the relevant parts of the texts involved. But when I say that Hobbes "avoids" certain words in *Leviathan* I am implying that he has changed his mind, and denying that the difference is merely fortuitous. But why should we not simply suppose that Hobbes, carelessly or whimsically, or merely accidentally, has used one sort of language on one occasion, and another sort on another occasion, without intending any difference of view? There are, I think, some reasons, though not conclusive ones, for rejecting this supposition. The dates of publication of Hobbes's works are sometimes misleading. *The Elements* was circulated in manuscript form in 1640. Hobbes had been at work on *De Corpore* as early as 1642, and substantial parts of it already existed in draft form in 1644, and by 1647 Hobbes himself was reporting that it was nearly complete. But he only *began* work on *Leviathan* in 1647. *The Elements*, then, is unquestionably a relatively early work compared with *Leviathan*. And it seems possible, perhaps even probable, that in respect of some of its doctrines *De Corpore* should be placed between *The Elements* and *Leviathan*. This, combined with the fact that the relation between language and conception is treated similarly in *The Elements* and *De Corpore* and differently in *Leviathan*, suggests that the doctrine of *Leviathan* (or rather, the absence of a doctrine) may be regarded as a later development.

What tends in some small measure to confirm this is the fact that the doctrine of *De Corpore* involved Hobbes in a number of difficulties, especially in combination with his theory of accidents. Thus in his first account of a proposition, Hobbes describes it as containing two names, "both which names raise in our mind the thought of one and the same thing, but the copulation makes us think of the cause for which those names were imposed on that thing" (I iii 3). This postulates the occurrence of only one "thought". But when he describes the thoughts corresponding to the propositions in a syllogism Hobbes gives a more complex account. Thus if the minor premiss is the proposition "man is a living creature", what happens in the mind is that first one conceives a phantasm of the thing, with the accident on account of which it is named "man"—that is, an image of a man speaking; then an image of the same man with that accident on account of which it is called "living creature"—that is, an image of a man moving; and one remembers that a thing which appears thus is called "living creature" (I iv 8). According to this account *two* images are involved, an image of a man speaking, and an image of a man moving—two images, although of the same man. And this is simply bristling with difficulties. *What* does Hobbes mean by requiring that the two images should be of the same man? Not that they are both images of some actual man, since then it would be impossible for anyone to entertain a proposition about unicorns, or for me to entertain a proposition about dinosaurs. That I think of them as ("feign" them to be) the same man conceived twice over? This involves reference and identification, and what images do these involve? What *is* it to refer two images to the same (real or imaginary) individual? I do not think that Hobbes can give any satisfactory answers to these questions. And in any case he is not prepared to insist that two images *are* involved, because later he tells us that "proposition signifies only the order of those things one after another, which we observe in the same idea of man; so that this proposition, *man is a living creature* raises but one idea in us, though in that idea we consider that first, for which he is called man, and next that, for which he is called living creature" (I v 9). This may seem a more promising approach, but it only introduces us to a new batch of problems. What is it to "observe" one thing and then another in the same idea, or in the one idea "consider" one accident and then another? The things observed are not separable *parts*, like arms and legs, but "accidents" like motion. Suppose that the two accidents were length and motion. The idea involved would have to be the idea of a long, moving body. It seems simple enough to suppose that we might observe first the length and then the motion. But it is not so simple if we are assuming that all thinking is nothing more than a succession of images, and that all images are particular and determinate. For just what sort of imaging can possibly do all the jobs that Hobbes requires? First there must be a long-body-image, that much is clear. We observe only the length. What account are we to give of observing the length to distinguish this from observing the motion? Perhaps the distinction lies in the image itself, so that we observe first a long-stationary-body-image and then a short-moving-body-image. But that will not do, because then we have two ideas instead of one. Is it then that we have first a long-body-image which is indeterminate in respect of motion, neither moving nor stationary, so that there is no motion to observe? And then a moving-body-image which is indeterminate in respect of length, neither long nor short, so that there is no length to observe? But this contradicts the initial assumption that all imagery is of particular, determinate images. It seems that we are stuck with just one, complex, long-moving-body-image, and two different acts of observing it. Assuming that all acts of the mind are conceptions or images, then observing image $x$ must be the having of some image $y$ which is somehow related to $x$. Indeed, observing the length must be image $y$, and observing the motion, image $z$. One wonders what $y$ and $z$ can be *like*, and what the difference between them is.

What causes all the trouble, of course, is the assumption that all images must be determinate. We may regard this as a false assumption, and sometimes Hobbes seems to agree with that, for his description of our conception of space is that having a phantasm of something without considering any of its properties "but only that it had a being without the mind, we have presently a conception of that we call *space*" (II vii 2). This sounds like a very indeterminate conception. Yet it is also Hobbes who has insisted that only names are universal; that images are of individuals (I ii 9); that one of the jobs of a definition of "man" is to produce a conception (1 vi 15); and that this conception is like a painting, which may be *used* to represent men generally, but is still a painting of some actual or possible determinate individual (1 vi 15; and also *The Elements*, 1 v 6). The point of the analogy with a painting is that although it may not be a picture of any actual man, it must still have the determinate characteristics of some *possible* individual.

These are only some of the difficulties, and only a few examples, of the confusions and contradictions which Hobbes gets himself into as a consequence of combining together a doctrine of accidents along with the assumptions that thought is a succession of images, that these are all individual and determinate, and that the significance of verbal discourse depends on a simple, one–one correspondence between names and images. It is inevitable that in the course of his discussion he should abandon sometimes one and sometimes another of these assumptions.

Presumably Hobbes was satisfied with what he wrote, since he published it. *De Corpore* was a long time in the writing, and much of this time may well have been spent in the attempt to remove the obscurities, confusions and contradictions which we have been discussing. On the other hand, he may have been too much concerned with other matters to give much thought to these. For in 1651, the year in which *Leviathan* was published, Hobbes returned from France to England, and took up residence in London, where he could benefit from the intellectual stimulus of friends such as Harvey. And for some time preceding the publication of *De Corpore* what Hobbes devoted much effort to was the constant revision of his attempts to square the circle. It seems to me possible that most of the theory of language in *De Corpore* was already complete before the writing of *Leviathan*; that Hobbes was sufficiently aware of its deficiencies to play safe in *Leviathan* by modifying the extremity of his position; and that he was not *so* aware of these deficiencies, nor so interested in the issues themselves, as to go to the trouble of revising an already finished theory.

Yet that is only a speculation, not so much supported by positive grounds, as merely allowed by a general absence of relevant evidence. I am concerned more to analyse the actual arguments which Hobbes produced than to discover his intentions in producing them; and from that point of view what is important is the fact that the theory of language contained in *Leviathan* avoids some of the worst confusions of the doctrines of *The Elements* and *De Corpore*. And I think that it is important to insist on this, and that it has been worth while following out some of the details involved. For some commentators, from a laudable desire to inform and instruct, have presented what Hobbes says in *Leviathan* as merely a part of a whole doctrine which is expounded at length elsewhere. But I can find no warrant for this in the text, and I am convinced that the clue to understanding some parts of *Leviathan* is to notice as often the differences as the similarities between it and his other works.

## 5 TRUTH

Having distinguished proper names from common names or universals, Hobbes tells us that universal names can be of greater or lesser extent, those of greater comprehending those of lesser signification. Thus "body" comprehends "man", while "man" and "rational" are of equal extent, comprehending each other. And Hobbes goes on to discuss truth in terms of this logical relation of comprehension. In a proposition such as "man is a living creature", either the latter name "living creature" comprehends the former name "man", in which case the proposition is true, or it does not, in which case it is false. Hobbes goes on immediately to draw some conclusions: since "truth consisteth in the right ordering of names in our affirmations", it is necessary to pay great attention to definitions; and indeed geometry, the only science so far achieved by man, begins with definitions.

The first question that arises here is what Hobbes means by "comprehension". His account of it in *Leviathan* is very brief. He could mean either of two things.

I. He might mean nothing more than a relation of class-inclusion. That is, to say that the name "body" comprehends the name "man" might be to say that the class of all those things which it is correct to call "man" is in fact included in the class of all those things which it is correct to call "body".

2. He might mean that the meanings of "body" and "man" are so related that anything that is a man *must* be a body. If, for example, "man" is defined as "rational body", then anything that is a man is a body. In that case the class of bodies includes the class of men: not

merely as a matter of fact, but necessarily, by virtue of the definitions of the terms involved.

Now the first of the two meanings of "comprehension" is innocuous: it merely unfolds what is involved in saying that all $x$'s are $y$'s. It is only the second, when presented as a criterion of truth, that commits Hobbes to a philosophical thesis; the conventionalist thesis that the truth of a proposition is completely determined by the definitions of its terms, or that all true propositions are analytic.

This conventionalist thesis is often attributed to Hobbes, and there is much justification for this in *Leviathan*. For in the first place, he chooses for an example a proposition which might easily be represented as analytic: the example is "man is a living creature", and "living" and "creature" would not be out of place in a definition of "man". Secondly, he says that when a proposition is false, its terms, put together, signify nothing: for example, if it is false to say "a quadrangle is round", then the expression "round quadrangle" signifies nothing (IV 23–24). Now Hobbes here distinguishes two kinds of insignificant expression. One is a *new* expression which has not been defined. The other is a compound expression which combines inconsistent names, such as "round quadrangle". Thus Hobbes has here made falsity the same as self-contradiction, which is to apply the conventionalist criterion to falsity. Thirdly, he follows his brief account of truth by saying that "truth consisteth in the right ordering of names in our affirmations" (IV 21), and goes on immediately to emphasise the importance of definitions. This is a theme he returns to more than once: whenever he mentions truth and science in *Leviathan* he goes on to preach a sermon about the necessity of definitions. Finally, the one thing he conspicuously *fails* to mention in connexion with truth is the relevance of (non-linguistic) facts about *things*.

Yet this may lead us to give undue emphasis to the conventionalist element in Hobbes's discussion. For the fact is that on several occasions explicitly, and on others implicitly, his account of truth is restricted to *universal* propositions. Thus he says, indeed, that the terms of a false proposition, put together, signify nothing; but he follows this by saying that there can be no understanding of false propositions "in case they be universal" (IV 24), and a few pages later asserts that "when we make a general assertion, unless it be a true one, the possibility of it is inconceivable" (V 27). This restriction is not surprising, because what Hobbes is talking about all the time is the use of language in *science*, which is a search after universal (and hypothetical) truths, not a catalogue of particular facts—the latter Hobbes calls "history", either natural or civil. I do not think that there is any indication—either in *Leviathan* or elsewhere—that Hobbes ever regarded the truth of singular propositions as depending simply on the definitions of their terms.

Further, in restricting his conventionalist theory of truth to universal propositions Hobbes, I think, is to be regarded as giving a very narrow interpretation to "universal". *De Corpore* is the only work of Hobbes's in which he deals with distinctions of logic in any detail. There he distinguishes between *universal* propositions (e.g., "every man is a living creature"), *particular* propositions (e.g., "some man is learned"), *indefinite* propositions (a doubtful category, exemplified by "man is a living creature"), and *singular* propositions (e.g., "this man is black") (1 iii 5). And he also distinguishes between necessary (that is, necessarily true) and contingent (that is, contingently true) propositions. Thus a necessary proposition is one in which it is inconceivable that anything of which the subject is the name is not also named by the predicate. This is a simple matter of definition, for Hobbes goes on to explain that in every necessary proposition, either the subject and predicate names are equivalent, as in "man is a rational living creature", or else the predicate is part of a name which is equivalent to the subject, as in "man is a living creature", where "living creature" is part of "rational living creature", which is equivalent to "man". A contingent proposition, Hobbes explains, is one "which at one time may be true, at another time false; as *every crow is black*; which may perhaps be true now, but false hereafter". A contingent proposition *may* always be true: *every man is a liar* may always be true, but it is contingent because it *might* be false, since "liar" is not part of a name equivalent to "man".

He does not develop the distinction between "necessary" and "contingent" in *De Corpore*, and, so far as I know, he does not even mention it elsewhere. Hence we have to speculate about its significance. This does not seem to be a matter of great uncertainty, however. At the beginning of *De Corpore* he distinguishes between on the one hand, sense and memory, which are knowledge, and which are the source of *prudence*, which is the attempt to foresee the future, based on experience; and on the other hand, philosophy, which is something "gotten by ratiocination" (1 i 2). This contrast between science and knowledge of sense is a standard element of Hobbes's discussions of knowledge, and occurs also in *The Elements of Law* and *Leviathan*. In the former he distinguishes science from "knowledge original", which is knowledge of particular facts obtained through the senses. If a person has much knowledge of fact then he is said to have *prudence*. As we have seen, there is a similar distinction in *Leviathan*, although there, as in *De Corpore*, "prudence" means rather the judicious *use* of "knowledge original" to make predictions (which are always rather chancy). Now in *The Elements of Law* Hobbes does not talk about the *necessity* of propositions, but he does say something similar. For he discusses prudence in some detail, and argues that assurance in predicting can never be "full and evident", because "experience concludeth nothing universally" (*Elements*, 1 iv 10). In *De Corpore* he summed up his account of a necessarily true proposition as one that is "*eternally* true" (1 iii 11), and in *The Elements* he gives a similar rendering of "universal": experience does not yield universal conclusions, or fully reliable predictions, because although we have always seen day and night follow each other we cannot conclude that they will do so eternally. Thus "universal" in *The Elements* seems to have the same force as "universal and necessary" in *De Corpore*. "Every crow is black" is described in the language of *De Corpore* as universal and contingent. In the language of *The Elements*, which does not include the terminology of "necessary" and "contingent", this proposition might simply be denied the title "universal", since certainly nothing can be concluded universally about the blackness of crows.

I think that it is possible, therefore, to reconstruct a single account which is given most fully in *De Corpore* and very sketchily in *Leviathan*. There are propositions which express matters of fact, are singular in form, and belong within "history" or "knowledge original". Science is concerned with universal propositions. But propositions of the form "every *x* is a *y*" are of two radically different kinds. In one kind "*x*" and "*y*" are connected not merely universally, but necessarily, by virtue of their definitions. In the other kind they are not connected necessarily. Propositions of this second kind depend on experience of particular *x*'s, of this *x* which is a *y*, that *x* which is a *y*, and so forth. Hence they belong to "knowledge original" and not to science. The conventionalist theory of truth applies only to the universal propositions of science, because factual propositions, if singular, are verified by sensc, and if universal, cannot be fully verified and are therefore conjectural.

That is the position which Hobbes adopts in *De Corpore*. His discussion in *Leviathan* is fragmentary, but what there is of it does not suggest a different view. Nor, I think, are the gaps significant, because he has given sufficient and quite clear indication that his conventionalist criterion of truth applies only to universal propositions.

## 6 DEFINITIONS

In *Leviathan* Hobbes has much to say about the importance of definitions and the demonstrative nature of science. But he has little to say about what definitions are, and still less about how exactly they are used. In *De Corpore*, however, he analyses these matters in some detail.

Reasoning, he says, is always either resolutive (or analytical) or compositive (or synthetical). Demonstration is compositive, and consists in putting propositions together and drawing conclusions from them. Thus what composition produces is a deductive chain. An example would be Euclidean geometry which begins from a few axioms, puts these together as premises from which conclusions may be deduced, uses these conclusions (theorems) as premises from which to derive further theorems, and so on indefinitely. Composition, however, presupposes some principles from which a beginning can be made. Resolution is a procedure in the opposite direction which, if carried far enough, takes us back to the principles from which demonstrations are derived. Thus we begin with a compound notion (for example, of some particular thing, like a man) and analyse it. This analysis is an analysis of its *parts*, not in the sense of physically separable parts, like arms, legs, trunk, and so forth, but the parts of its "nature", which are universals like "rational", "sentient". Thus "man" might be resolved into "rational", "animal". These parts are universal, but they are not necessarily the most universal of their kind. "Animal" is more universal than "man", because if a thing is a man it is an animal, but if it is an animal it is not necessarily a man— that is, "animal" comprehends "man". And "body", in turn, is more universal than "animal". So further analysis is possible, as into "rational, animated, sentient body". This yields us the proposition, "man is a rational, animated, sentient body", which is a definition of "man". Such definitions are the principles from which all demonstration must begin.

Definitions, Hobbes explains, are of two sorts. If a name is not the most universal of its kind then it can be defined in terms of more universal names, by genus and difference. Thus "man" can be defined as "rational animal", where "animal" is the genus to which man belongs, and "rational" the difference between men and other animals. But if the name to be defined is the most universal of its kind, for example, "body" or "motion", then the definition cannot be by means of genus and difference. All that can be done in such a case is to produce "such circumlocution, as best explicateth the force of that name" (*De Corpore*, I vi 14)—some form of words which will give the hearer a clear idea of the thing named, as when "motion" is defined as "the leaving of one place, and the acquiring of another continually" (I vi 13).

Now the *aim* of science is to demonstrate the causes of things. But the pattern of scientific demonstration is the deduction of conclusions from basic principles which are just definitions—in *Leviathan* Hobbes says that science is "a knowledge of all the consequences of names appertaining to the subject in hand" (v 29). If a reference to causes is to appear in the conclusions then, Hobbes argues, it must be present in the premisses. Therefore a definition must, where possible, express the cause of the thing named by the term which is being defined. This complicates the distinction between definition of names which are the most universal of their kind and names which are not. For names can be divided into those which signify a thing which has some conceivable cause, and those which signify things of which we cannot conceive a cause. This is really just the same as the other distinction, because names which signify things of which we cannot conceive a cause are such as "body" and "motion", which are "common to all matter", and names of things of which we can conceive a cause are "whatsoever we can distinguish one body from another by" (*De Corpore*, I vi 13). The former kind of name can only be defined by using any words that will give the hearer a clear idea of the thing named. "But definitions of things, which may be understood to have some cause, must consist of such names as express the cause or manner of their generation, as when we define a circle to be a figure made by the circumduction of a straight line in a plane, etc."

This requirement, that definitions should mention causes, is one which is not so much added to, as in effect contained in, the notion of definition by genus and difference. For in defining "man", by genus and difference, as "rational, animated, sentient body" we are, as has been noted already, analysing the *nature* of man into its "parts". But the parts of the nature of a thing are just its accidents (*De Corpore*, I vi 2), and an accident of a body is the way in which the body is conceived by us, or a power of the body to produce in us a conception of it (II viii 2–3). All definitions, then, on this account necessarily refer to causes—that is, to causes of our conception of the thing named by the word which we are defining. The reference to a cause is not always explicit, but it is a fact that the definitions which Hobbes gives of the terms which are fundamental to his argument in *Leviathan* are definitions explicitly in terms of causes: thus "sense" is *defined* in terms of the effect on our organs of the motion of external objects ("sense is motion in the organs and interior parts of man's body, caused by the action of the things we see, hear, etc."; "voluntary motions" are those which "depend always upon a precedent thought"; "appetite" is endeavour towards something which causes the endeavour); and so forth (VI 31).

The most interesting and difficult feature of this account of definitions is what Hobbes says about the fundamental propositions which are the ultimate end of analysis and the beginning of demonstration. These are definitions, and Hobbes calls them "principles" and "primary propositions". All primary propositions are definitions, and those definitions are primary propositions which are either (i) the resolution of a name, at the most universal level, so that no further resolution is possible, or (ii) the explanation of a name by means of a circumlocution, without resolution. The distinction between definition and primary proposition, then, seems to be that not every definition is a primary proposition, and when it is, the same proposition, if used to convey the meaning of a term, is to be called a definition, and if used as the beginning of a demonstration, is to be called a primary proposition. Since these primary propositions are the beginnings of demonstration, they cannot themselves be demonstrated. What is both interesting and difficult about Hobbes's account of primary propositions is what account, if any, he can give of a criterion for determining whether any alleged primary proposition should be accepted or rejected. That raises some further problems.

## 7 VERIFICATION

When Hobbes first mentions primary propositions he says that they are "truths constituted arbitrarily by the inventors of speech, and therefore not to be demonstrated" (*De Corpore*, I iii 9). But this simple statement of a conventionalist view is contradicted in his later, extended account of primary propositions. There he says something very different, and says it several times over. ". . . the causes of universal things (of those, at least, that have any cause) are manifest of themselves", and although the proposition that all change consists in motion cannot be demonstrated, its contradictory is unintelligible (I vi 5); if one conceives motion "*aright*", one *must* know that "motion is the privation of one place, and the acquisition of another" (I vi 6); "primary or most universal propositions" need no demonstration but are "manifest of themselves" (I vi 12).

These seem like two very different and plainly incompatible accounts, for if they are manifest of themselves when conceived correctly it must be possible to be right or wrong about them—Hobbes says that people fail to see their truth if their minds are lazy, or corrupted by authority (I vi 5)—and then it can hardly be a matter of *arbitrary* decision by the inventors of speech. In view of the suggestion that a conventionalist theory predominates in political contexts and a self-evidence theory in works concerned with the natural sciences, it is interesting to notice that in *De Corpore*, which is in fact the only work in which self-evidence has a prominent place at all, the self-evidence theory does not have things all its own way. The fact is that both a conventionalist and a self-evidence theory are expressed. Nor is the situation any different in either *The Elements* or *Leviathan*. In *The Elements* Hobbes says in one place that universal propositions can be concluded only "from remembrance of the use of names imposed arbitrarily by men" (I iv 11), but in the very next chapter he talks about reasoning "from principles, that are found indubitable by experience" (I v 12). There is no sharp contrast to be drawn here, because while Hobbes at times connects the use of words with sense experience, he does not explain in any detail what he means, and the whole issue is left quite vague. Nevertheless he does seem to be saying two different things, rather as in *De Corpore*. In *Leviathan* the conventionalist view occurs frequently, and I have discussed this at some length in Section 4. Nevertheless Hobbes has no hesitation in putting a *self-evident* proposition at the beginning of chapter II: "That when a thing lies still, unless somewhat else stir it, it will lie still for ever, is a truth that no man doubts of." But he makes no attempt to present this either as a definition or as a consequence of a definition. On the contrary, he goes on to give an explanation of why so many people *do* doubt it, which is always the first thing a wise philosopher does after propounding an indubitable proposition.

It seems then, that throughout Hobbes's works there is a conflict between a conventionalist and a self-evidence account of truth, which is never settled decisively in favour of either view. It cannot be questioned that these are two different views. Yet I think that it is too readily assumed that these are completely incompatible, and I think that it is at least possible to understand why Hobbes went on so stubbornly adhering to both. That involves considering his account of definition in the context of the whole view of scientific method to which it belongs; which will be discussed in the next chapter. Certainly there are some problems that are going to need solving. Thus in *De Corpore* Hobbes says that political science can be established in either of two ways. We may argue deductively from first principles of philosophy, in a long chain of reasoning which brings us ultimately to a knowledge of the causes of human passions, and thence to a knowledge of political matters; or we may take a short cut, *beginning* with the knowledge of the passions and proceeding to the political conclusion. This short cut is possible because "the causes of the motions of the mind are known, not only by ratiocination, but also by the experience of every man that takes the pains to observe those motions within himself" (I vi 7). (This passage has parallels in *The Elements* and *Leviathan*, with differences which will be explored in the next chapter.) On this view there are some observations—introspective observations—which can be used (although they are not *needed*) in the construction of political science. And Hobbes claims in *Leviathan* that the propositions of political science, as deduced by him, are *confirmed* by common experience (*Leviathan*, XIII 82). Again, he sometimes argues in favour of a proposition by showing that its contradictory is not compatible with observed facts. Thus in chapter I of *Leviathan* he argues that colours cannot be properties of objects, and the form of his argument is to mention certain facts which, he claims, are incompatible with the proposition that colour is a property of the object—e.g., the fact that if I look in a mirror I see colours in one place although the object is in another. Thus Hobbes does allow that observations are relevant to determining the truth or falsity of propositions of science. Yet he also claims that science is derived deductively from self-evident axioms. And he also claims that truth is constituted *merely* by the (arbitrary) imposition of names.

Thus it is clear that Hobbes's views embody a certain amount of confusion, inconsistency and change.

1. According to Hobbes names *name things* but *signify conceptions*. This is the basis of his attack on philosophical absurdity. Thus in *The Elements* he claims that significant speech involves the actual occurrence of conceptions corresponding one–one to the names used, but in *Leviathan* he tends to make the more modest demand that names should be *capable* of being related to actual conceptions.

2. Hobbes rejects any view of universals as real existences. It is only names that are universal. This nominalism, however, does not of itself commit him to an extreme conventionalist account of the imposition of names.

3. In parts of *De Corpore* Hobbes departs very far from the extreme conventionalist position, by expounding a theory of accidents as parts of the nature of a thing. This, combined with the claims that thought is a succession of individual and determinate images, and that significant discourse depends on a one–one correspondence between names and images, leads him into difficulties in his account of syllogistic thought. In *Leviathan* a simpler view is presented; and this *may* be an indication that Hobbes had become aware of the problems involved.

4. There are elements of a conventionalist theory of truth in *Leviathan*. But we have to be careful about this. For when he is expressing his conventionalist account of truth, he limits this to *universal* propositions. Further, in *De Corpore* he also gives a narrow meaning to "universal"—only the necessary propositions of science are universal, and not contingent propositions such as "All crows are black". This latter distinction is not made in *Leviathan*, but it is not abandoned, either explicitly or by implication.

5. In *Leviathan* Hobbes insists that science is demonstrative and depends on definitions. But he says little about what definitions are and how, precisely, they are to be used. In *De Corpore* he discusses this in great detail. The "primary propositions" on which any deductions must rest are definitions; and this raises the question of how these can be validated.

6. Hobbes seems to combine conventionalist and self-evidence theories, and in addition he sometimes allows that observation is relevant to determining the truth of the propositions of science.

It is some very diverse elements, then, that are going to the making of Hobbes's account of science. This chapter can be ended appropriately by mentioning a passage in which almost in one and the same breath Hobbes appeals to different, and, perhaps, incompatible criteria of truth. This is a passage in *The Elements*, in which Hobbes gives an account of truth and falsity. In a proposition, "*S* is *P*", either *P* comprehends *S*, in which case the proposition is true, or it does not, in which case it is false. This is similar to the account given in *Leviathan*, which is discussed in Section 5. When Hobbes illustrates and discusses the criterion, however, a difference emerges. As an example of a true proposition he gives "Charity is a virtue". This is a tricky example, because I think that it is not terribly easy to decide whether this is an analytic proposition or not. Since Hobbes's account in *The Elements* of how the truth of universal propositions is established is always in terms of definitions, I think that it is safe to assume that Hobbes regards this proposition as true by virtue of the definitions of its terms and that he is here exemplifying the conventionalist theory of truth which is clearly present elsewhere in the book. His example of a false proposition, however, is "Every man is just", which is false, he says dryly, because "unjust is the name of the far greater part of men" (*Elements*, I v 10). But surely not even Hobbes would be tempted to say that the meaning of "unjust" is, or includes, "the far greater part of men"? Hobbes, one thinks, is calling here not merely on his understanding of language but on his unfortunate experience of the world; and what is wrong with the proposition "Every man is just" is that it does not correspond to the facts. This is the only case I know of where a philosopher has expounded in the same breath a conventionalist theory of truth and a correspondence theory of falsity. The lustre of this achievement would shine more brightly if Hobbes had shown more signs of knowing what he was up to. Nevertheless, it is an achievement, and its merits are discussed in a later chapter (see Chapter Four, Section 4).

What I have to do now is to examine Hobbes's account of the logical structure of science, to discover whether the diverse elements which I have been discussing in this chapter lead merely to confusion or are combined together into some sort of consistent whole.

# CHAPTER FOUR

# *Scientific Method*

ANY study of Hobbes's philosophy must pay some attention to his views on scientific method, because, in the first place, his arguments are in some respects interesting and illuminating in themselves; because, secondly, Hobbes's was a period much concerned with questions of method, and Hobbes himself, however confused he was about it, regarded the adoption of correct methods as a matter of overwhelming philosophical importance; and because, finally, one's understanding of the nature and significance of Hobbes's political conclusions depends on one's understanding of his views on the methods by which these conclusions were to be reached.

What we have discovered so far is that a number of disparate and incompatible elements must be included in Hobbes's account of science, and that no single and consistent account is likely to emerge. In fact there are several different views, which it is hard to number because although some are sharply opposed, some shade off imperceptibly into each other. Thus there is to be found in Hobbes a conventionalist theory of science which can be sharply opposed to an hypothetico-deductive account of physics. There is a self-evidence theory of mathematics which also can be sharply opposed to the conventionalist view of science in general. And there are some minor variations in his account of the foundations of political science—variations which it is difficult to describe accurately because of the fact that the references to the matter are scattered and vague.

Now up to this point I have used the word "science" in a very wide and Hobbesian sense. In this usage it does not mean the same as we understand nowadays by the term, which we restrict primarily to the experimental sciences, and extend, with some hesitation, to those disciplines, such as sociology, which are unable to experiment but have to rely on observation and statistical analysis. (One might still say, however, that sociology is an experimental science, even if it

does not experiment, because only practical considerations and humane motives *prevent* experiments, and it is so constructed that if these
obstacles were removed, experimental results would be immediately
relevant to its conclusions, and would be of use in confirming or
refuting them.) In Hobbes's use of the term, of course, it applies to
any study at all which can proceed by rational methods and which may
reasonably hope to reach well-founded conclusions. Therefore it
includes mathematics and other disciplines. Now, however, some
distinctions have to be made. It would be confusing to adopt a new
meaning for the word "science", and I shall continue to use it in a
very vague way. I shall use the term "philosophy" to denote only the
study of what we might regard as philosophical questions, and to
exclude *experimental* science. I need, however, to have a term to apply
to what we now call the experimental sciences. The term "experimental science", unhappily, will not serve the purpose, because
Hobbes sometimes adopted a view of these sciences which would make
the expression a ludicrous misnomer. The term "physics" is available,
however, and I shall use this term in a way which includes, I think,
the sort of science which we now call "physics", but so as to include
also some sciences such as chemistry, which we might distinguish
but which Hobbes did not. For Hobbes did have a theory about
physics which is to be distinguished from (and which in some cases
he himself explicitly distinguished from) his theories about science
in general and about mathematics.

## i A SELF-EVIDENCE THEORY OF MATHEMATICS (IN *DE CORPORE*)

For Hobbes, as for many other philosophers before and since, mathematics was the paradigm of knowledge. It is not surprising that
mathematics was regarded as pre-eminent among the sciences. The
Greeks knew little chemistry, and the medievals had not greatly
advanced it. Astronomy was in a better state, but still full of un-
certainties. (Theology, of course, was queen of the sciences. But this
was more a matter of great pretensions than of clear arguments and
agreed conclusions.) Geometry, Hobbes thought, was alone in having
been established for many centuries as a demonstrative science which
claimed and won the assent of all rational men.

Sometimes Hobbes asserted that all science (including mathematics) was demonstrative knowledge, a system of propositions derived from premises which were merely arbitrary definitions. This is a view which will be discussed in the next section. But in *De Corpore* he expounded a different and complex view, some important details of which seem to me to be stated less clearly than might be desired. There he constructed the elements of a demonstrative science in two parts. The first of these was called "The First Grounds of Philosophy" or "*Philosophia Prima*" and this consisted in definitions of some very fundamental terms, such as "space", "place", "body", "number", "motion", and some conclusions drawn from these definitions. The second he called "Proportions of Motions and Magnitudes", and he identified this with geometry, which includes projects such as squaring the circle. Since Hobbes treated both parts as logically continuous with each other, composed of deductions resting ultimately on the same premises laid out in *philosophia prima*, this discussion will not take any account of the distinction. (There is, indeed, a logical gap between the two chief divisions of science which Hobbes expounds in *De Corpore*, but it is not between *philosophia prima* and the geometry, but between *philosophia prima* and geometry taken together, on the one hand, and physics on the other hand. That is discussed in Section 3 of this chapter.) Hobbes regarded mathematics as deductive in form, and there is nothing unusual or distinctive in such a view. What is distinctive in the account of mathematics given in *De Corpore* is the logical status of the primary propositions on which all the deductions ultimately rest.

Mathematics (indeed, all demonstrative reasoning) is a matter, Hobbes says, of starting from first principles and deducing consequences from them. "Now, such principles are nothing but definitions" (*De Corpore*, I vi 13). But definitions are of two sorts. Firstly, there are definitions which "resolve" the term to be defined. Thus in "Man is a rational animal" the subject "man" is resolved into "rational and animal". The notions into which the subject is resolved are "more universal" than the subject (I vi 14)—that is, the class of animals (and also the class of rational beings) includes the class of men, but not vice versa; or being a man entails being animal (and rational), but not vice versa. But, secondly, such resolution comes to an end when we reach a term which is "the most universal in its kind". "Man" can be subsumed under "animal", and "animal" can be subsumed under "body", each term being more universal than the last. But we must come at last, Hobbes says, to some terms that are so universal that they cannot be subsumed under anything else. And then definition by resolution is impossible. Then all that can be done by way of definition is to produce some "circumlocution" which will raise in the mind of the speaker an adequate conception of the thing to be defined (1 vi 13, 14). Hobbes calls this an "explication" of a simple conception.

Now what is to be said about a proposition which contains such an explication? The conventionalist account would hardly fit here. For the view which we are discussing here belongs to Hobbes's theory of accidents, which was discussed in Chapter Three, Section 3. Primary propositions "explicate" simple conceptions, terms which are the most universal of their kind; and these are parts of the *nature of things*, not matters for arbitrary decision. Thus Hobbes says: "For example, he that has a true conception of *place*, cannot be ignorant of this definition, *place is that space which is possessed or filled adequately by some body*; and so, he that conceives *motion* aright, cannot but know that *motion is the privation of one place, and the acquisition of another*" (1 vi 6). Thus it is not just a matter of deciding how a word is to be used, but of conceiving something *correctly*. And there is something which someone who conceives correctly "cannot be ignorant of": but if he cannot be ignorant of it he must *know* it. Therefore those definitions which are primary propositions do not on this view express linguistic decisions but embody some fundamental knowledge about the nature of the world. Hobbes returns a few pages later to this matter of knowledge. He supposes that a master is instructing a scholar and considers whether the scholar may dispute the definitions. What he does not say is that the master is entitled to define terms as he chooses, and he ends the discussion by asserting that "principles are either known by themselves, or else they are not principles" (1 vi 15).

Hobbes is asserting, then, that mathematics is derived by a process of logical deduction from a set of first principles which are "known by themselves". This has considerable implications. *Why* is it that no one can doubt that motion is privation of one place, and the acquisition of another? It might be that the English word "motion" was (arbitrarily) defined to mean "privation of one place, and the acquisition of another". Then the proposition "motion is privation of one place, and the acquisition of another" might be regarded as being either a rendering of the definition, (*D*), "the word 'motion' is defined as 'privation of one place, and the acquisition of another' ", or else of the proposition, (*P*), "motion is privation of one place, and the acquisition of another" which is tautologically true because of definition *D*. If *D* is accepted, then the terms of *P* are logically equivalent to each other, and *P* is then necessarily true, but tautologous. One might say, perhaps, that *P* was self-evidently true because to understand its terms would be to accept *D*, by virtue of which *P* is a tautology. This, however, is certainly not what Hobbes has been saying. For (i) this view would make the truth of *P* depend on *D*, whereas Hobbes says that first principles are *known by themselves*. Since he has just been arguing that demonstration proceeds from definitions, a proposition that can be demonstrated *from* a definition is precisely *not* what he intends by "first principle", which is a definition which *cannot* be derived from a further definition. (ii) The definitions which are first principles embody, on Hobbes's account, not truths about language but truths about the simple features of the world—features which we can *correctly conceive*. Mathematics, then, is derived from a set of first principles which state certain elementary truths about the world which are "known by themselves". As to *how* they are known—there is perhaps not much to be said, and at all events Hobbes does not say it.

Hobbes, then, regarded Euclidean geometry as a system of demonstrated truths about the world, deduced from a set of first principles which were certain but non-tautologous. Nor was he alone in this, for many before and since Hobbes have shared this view. Indeed it is because geometry was so regarded that it was an object of such veneration. For there seemed to be something very remarkable about the achievement of constructing a true science about the world, without recourse to observation, and merely by deducing consequences from a small set of self-evident first principles. It is not that there was anything unusual about the notion of a demonstrative science. Theologians had been busy for centuries demonstrating theological propositions, and there was a big body of armchair physics as well. But theology and armchair physics, although attempting the *methods* of mathematics, had signally failed to achieve comparable *success*. Mathematics was the only science which both was demonstrative and stated true propositions about the nature of the world.

When Hobbes stopped theorising about how to do mathematics and got down to actually doing it, I am not convinced that his practice was always consistent with his theories. Thus in one passage in which he is discussing first principles he mentions the proposition that "motion is the privation of one place, and the acquisition of another" (I vi 6). But he does not later *treat* this as a first principle. On the contrary, in the development of "The First Grounds of Philosophy" he *redefines* motion as "a continual relinquishing of one place, and acquiring of another" (II viii 10), and supports this amended definition with arguments intended to convince, and not merely with "circumlocutions" intended to "explicate". But I do not propose to discuss Hobbes's actual practice in mathematics. For in the first place, happily it is not relevant, since what I am concerned with is only his *theories* of method, and not his practice, except in his political philosophy. And in the second place, I am not competent to analyse or criticise his contributions to mathematics. I have asked many mathematicians whether Hobbes's attempts to square the circle were successful, and they have all denied it. But obviously it is impossible for me to tell whether this is fair criticism, or mere professional jealousy.

Quite apart from the question of Hobbes's competence *in* mathematics, his self-evidence account of the nature of mathematics was acceptable to many of his contemporaries and some of his successors. Yet since his time, mathematics has developed, and so also have views about the nature of mathematics. In particular, there have been radical changes in the status of Euclidean geometry. Euclidean geometry can be defined as that geometry which depends on a particular set of postulates (the Euclidean postulates). But non-Euclidean geometries have been developed from non-Euclidean postulates. And if you asked a mathematician, he would probably refuse to express a preference for one rather than another of the possible geometries. On a certain view of mathematics, indeed, the demand that such a choice should be made would betray a misunderstanding. For on this view, the only mathematical criteria are consistency in the postulates and rigour in the deductions. There seems to be no reason for supposing that there may not be many possible different sets of consistent postulates, and therefore many possible geometries. But how can many *different* geometries all be true of the world? The obvious answer is that geometry does not consist at all of a set of propositions (true or false) about the nature of the world. A geometry is a formal system, and the mathematician is concerned only with its formal aspects. Mathematics, of course, can be *used* in investigating, describing and explaining the world. Scientists *do* use it, and physics, and other sciences, involve the use of applied mathematics. It is up to the scientist, and not to the mathematician, to decide which geometry to prefer. And this choice will be made on empirical grounds. Thus it may be found that in some contexts Euclidean geometry is adequate, while in other contexts a non-Euclidean geometry is required. The question of *which* geometry will be most fruitful can only be answered on empirical grounds.

On this view, then, questions about the nature and truth of mathematics involve making a distinction.

1. There are systems of pure mathematics—Euclidean geometry, for example. These are formal systems, and there is no need to wonder whether they are self-evidently true propositions about the world, because they are not propositions about the world at all: the space which they describe is not necessarily the same as any actual space which we may investigate by physical means.

2. There is mathematics *applied in* the sciences. There is no need to wonder whether its propositions are self-evidently true propositions about the world, because their truth can be decided empirically, and there is no need for any recourse to self-evidence. Empirical tests, of course, do not provide demonstrative certainty. But demonstrative certainty belongs to *pure* mathematics, to the formal system, which does not claim to describe the world.

Hobbes, then, has simply failed to distinguish between pure mathematics and applied mathematics. His problems have arisen because he has thought of mathematics as combining the descriptive content of applied mathematics with the demonstrative certainty of pure mathematics. This is certainly an excusable lapse, because it is a fault which he committed in company with almost all of his predecessors and contemporaries, and many also of his successors (such as Kant, for example).

But it is not a mere historical curiosity, that Hobbes failed to construct a certain theory which was to be developed subsequently by mathematicians. My reasons for sharply contrasting Hobbes's view of mathematics with a later was not merely to condemn Hobbes of a blunder, nor to plead that it was excusable. What is of interest, I think, is that although he never remedied the deficiencies of his philosophy of mathematics, one of his theories of philosophical method in general (including mathematical method) avoided the weaknesses of his self-evidence theory. In the next section I begin to discuss this other theory.

## 2 A CONVENTIONALIST ACCOUNT OF SCIENCE (IN *THE ELEMENTS OF LAW*)

The story which Hobbes tells in *The Elements of Law* is substantially different from the self-evidence account in *De Corpore*. Since *The Elements of Law* is concerned with human nature and politics, the discussions in it of language, logic and scientific method are relatively brief and cursory. Some important issues are only barely touched on, and then sometimes in terms which are vague and ambiguous. And whereas in *De Corpore* a distinction (which is discussed in the next section) is drawn between mathematics and physics, *The Elements of Law* simply gives an account of science in general.

Hobbes's basic distinction in *The Elements of Law* is between two kinds of knowledge. The first is "nothing else but sense, or knowledge original . . . and remembrance of the same". This is "the experience of the effects of things that work upon us from without". The "register" of it is history (*Elements*, I vi 1). Hobbes also calls this sort of knowledge "experience of fact", which, when it is "great", is called "prudence" (I vi 4). Apparently "knowledge original" is constituted primarily of knowledge of singular propositions about matters of fact, based on experience. *Generalisations* based on experience also belong to prudence, and Hobbes distinguishes these from the universal propositions of science: "for though a man have always seen the day and night to follow one another hitherto; yet can he not thence conclude they shall do so, or that they have done so eternally: *experience concludeth nothing universally*" (I iv 10).

The second kind of knowledge is "science or knowledge of the truth of propositions, and how things are called, and is derived from understanding". Whereas knowledge original is sense experience, science is "the experience men have of the proper use of names in language" (I vi 1). Understanding, from which science is derived, is a *linguistic* capacity: "It is therefore a great ability in a man, out of the words, contexture, and other circumstances of language, to deliver himself from *equivocation*, and to find out the true meaning of what is said: and this is it we call *understanding*" (I vi 8). Knowledge, Hobbes goes on, implies two things.

1. Knowledge implies truth (I vi 2). Truth is defined in terms of the comprehension of the subject by the predicate, and I have argued (in Chapter Three, Sections 5 and 7) that what Hobbes seems to mean by this is comprehension by virtue of the definitions of the terms involved; and I have argued also that this is restricted to the truth of *universal* propositions. So far as the universal propositions of science are concerned, then, Hobbes seems to be asserting that they are true by virtue just of the definitions of their terms.

2. Truth must be *"evident"* if it is to be knowledge. That is not quite what it sounds, because Hobbes attaches his own special meaning to "evidence". "Evidence", in Hobbes's usage, is "the concomitance of a man's conception with the words that signify such conception in the act of ratiocination", or, more briefly, "evidence, which is meaning with our words, is the life of truth" (I vi 3). The requirement that truth should be evident, then, does not mean that knowledge has to be supported by facts, but merely refuses to ascribe knowledge to one who utters true propositions without understanding them—a parrot may *say* "The world is round", but this does not mean that it *knows* that the world is round.

What this all adds up to is something very like a conventionalist account of science. The truth of scientific propositions is not established by appeal to observation, because "experience concludeth nothing universally", but depends on understanding—that is, on understanding the meanings of words. There is what seems like a very clear and unambiguous statement of such a view in a passage in which Hobbes is commending the procedures of mathematicians. Hobbes says that "they proceed from most *low* and *humble* principles, evident even to the meanest capacity". And that sounds like a self-evidence theory. But Hobbes continues: ". . . going on slowly, and with most *scrupulous ratiocination*; viz. from the imposition of names, they infer the truth of their *first* propositions. . . ." (I xiii 3). One obvious interpretation of this (though, I shall suggest, not the only possible one) is that the first principles of science are not definitions, as in the account given in *De Corpore*, but propositions immediately derived from definitions, and "evident to the meanest capacity" because their truth can be immediately established by appeal to the definitions of their terms. Since the criterion of truth and knowledge which Hobbes gives in *The Elements of Law* is a linguistic criterion, this account is substantially different from that of *De Corpore*. The two chief differences are (1) that in *The Elements of Law* no distinction is made between the sciences, but one single account represented as true of them all, whereas in *De Corpore*, as we shall see, the logical structure of physics is distinguished from that of mathematics; and (2) that in *De Corpore* Hobbes says several times over, not merely that primary propositions are manifest of themselves, but that they express a *true conception* of that to which they refer, whereas this notion is absent from *The Elements of Law*. The account which we have been considering, then, comes near to being a straightforward conventionalist account: it is stated that the universal propositions of science are true simply by virtue of the definitions of their terms, and there is at least no indication that the definitions are not arbitrary.

Nevertheless, there are some places where Hobbes goes beyond a merely linguistic criterion of truth, and in some of these the notion of self-evidence is, perhaps, obscurely suggested.

1. Hobbes says, "For the truth of a proposition is never evident, until we conceive the meaning of the words or terms whereof it consisteth, which are always conceptions of the mind; nor can we remember those conceptions, without the thing that produced the same by our senses. . . ." (I vi 4.) The significance of this last clause—"nor can we remember those conceptions, without the thing that produced the same by our senses"—is, it seems to me, a little obscure. Of course Hobbes has said that significant speech involves the occurrence of conceptions corresponding to the names used; that the conceptions caused by objects of sense do not completely vanish when the object is removed, but remain as images in imagination; and that remembrance is noticing that a conception is the same as some which we have had before (I iii 6). How, on Hobbes's account of thinking as a succession of images, we can *recognise* an image in imagination as the same as some previous image of perception is not altogether clear. Nevertheless it seems clear enough that he is saying that memories necessarily relate in some way to the objects which have caused the conceptions which, in a "decayed" form, are involved in remembering. But *why* does he say this here? One's first

impression might be that he is asserting that a proposition is evident to me only when I remember the experience which makes it true— that the proposition "Potassium cyanide is poisonous" is evident to me only when I remember the screams and convulsions which are the facts which establish its truth. But that would be a perverse inter- pretation, unless it were the only possible one, since in the first place such an account would fit only what Hobbes has called "knowledge original" and "prudence" and would be untrue of scientific proposi- tions, which have a universality which experience cannot guarantee, and in the second place, he has already defined "evidence" as "mean- ing with our words" (i vi 3)—that is, as a matter of significance, not of interpretation. Presumably, then the reference to objects is part of a criterion of significance; reference to objects as experienced is not enough to verify scientific propositions, but it is a necessary condition of their significance. This, then is compatible with the conventionalist view. But of course it is also compatible with the self-evidence view, which could, like the conventionalist view, incorporate this require- ment as part of a criterion of significance, though not of truth.

2. There is a passage in which there is just the hint of a suggestion of a doctrine of accidents like that of *De Corpore* (see Chapter Three, Section 3). Hobbes says, "The appellations that be universal, and common to many things, are not always given to all the particulars, (as they ought to be) for like conceptions and considerations in them all. . . ." (i v 7). It is the doctrine of accidents, with its denial of extreme nominalism, that was the first step in *De Corpore* towards a self-evidence theory and its occurrence here is enough to arouse the ghost of a suspicion, although not much more than that.

3. I suggested earlier in this section that when Hobbes talks about first principles which are "evident even to the meanest capacity", this could hardly be taken as an expression of a self-evidence view, since Hobbes goes on immediately to say that they are derived "from the imposition of names". That makes it look like the conventionalist view, especially considering the fact that in *The Elements of Law* the dominant stress is on linguistic criteria. Yet, it *could* be interpreted in a way that was compatible with a self-evidence view, if we de- parted from the account in *De Corpore* merely to the extent of distin- guishing between first principles and the logically precedent definitions which "imposed" the names, but required that names should be "imposed" in accordance with a "true conception" of the nature of

things. This is not a *completely* perverse speculation, because (i) the brief hint of a doctrine of accidents, considered in (2) above, lends a little weight to it; (ii) the expression "evident even to the meanest capacity" is one which, in a Hobbesian context, inevitably suggests a notion of self-evidence, because of its similarity to the expressions which Hobbes uses in *De Corpore* to describe the (self-evident) "primary propositions"; (iii) in the *Elements of Law* (I v 2) Hobbes defines a name as "the voice of a man, arbitrarily imposed", and there is a similar usage in *De Corpore* (I ii 4). This usage itself does not imply a conventionalist view, because what is arbitrary might be simply the choice of the word "king", for example, instead of the word "kong", to mean what "king" means. The use of the word "arbitrary" does not necessarily imply a denial of the view that the definitions of some fundamental terms express a true conception of the nature of things, yet a conventionalist view, which involves such a denial, does imply that words are "arbitrarily imposed", and it is perhaps a little surprising to find the word missing in this context. It may be—it probably is—a conventionalist view which is being presented; but it is expressed less clearly and less forcefully than one might expect.

4. I have argued in Chapter Three, Section 7, that in one passage in *The Elements of Law* (I v 10) Hobbes in effect gives a conventionalist account of truth and a correspondence account of falsity. His account of the falsity of "Every man is just" is not at all suggestive of a self-evidence theory, but neither is it at all clearly consistent with a conventionalist view.

There is a passage in *De Cive* in which Hobbes states a conventionalist view very clearly and sharply. He sums it up thus:

*Truth* is the same with a *true proposition*; but the *proposition is true* in which the *word consequent*, which by logicians is called *the predicate*, embraceth *the word antecedent* in its amplitude, which they call *the subject*. And to *know truth*, is the same thing as to *remember* that it was made by ourselves by the common use of words (XVIII 4).

A similar view is predominant in *The Elements of Law*, but it is at the very least stated less clearly and emphatically, and not with complete consistency. It is true that *The Elements of Law* is concerned with human nature and politics, and that topics of logic and method are only briefly discussed. That is true. But it cannot be argued that the deficiencies of Hobbes's account of method there are due merely to necessary or excusable brevity, for he is a great deal briefer about these matters in *De Cive*, yet states a conventionalist position very clearly. The deficiencies of what Hobbes says in *The Elements of Law*, then, must be attributed not to brevity of treatment but to vagueness, uncertainty and confusion in his thought.

## 3 A HYPOTHETICO-DEDUCTIVE THEORY OF PHYSICS (IN *DE CORPORE*)

The more-or-less-conventionalist account in *The Elements of Law* is presented as being true of all the sciences. But the self-evidence account in *De Corpore* is applied only to mathematics. A different account is given of physics. Here again, as always when Hobbes discusses method, there are confusions and inconsistencies.

At the beginning of *De Corpore* Hobbes divides philosophy into three chief parts: (1) natural philosophy, which is concerned with "bodies natural"; (2) ethics, or moral philosophy, which is concerned with "the dispositions and manners of men"; and (3) politics, which is concerned with "the civil duties of subjects" (119). Later Hobbes says that there are two different methods which are appropriate to politics. Firstly, it is possible to proceed by what he calls the "synthetical" method. This is a procedure of beginning with the simplest possible elements, defined in primary propositions, and going on, by means of further definitions and deduction, to reach complex, demonstrative conclusions. Thus it is possible to begin with primary propositions, derive from them first the propositions of *philosophia prima*, then the propositions of mathematics, then those of physics, then those of ethics, and so finally to the propositions of politics, in one, long, deductive chain. But secondly, it is possible to begin with a question of politics, and to proceed analytically. Thus we may begin with the question whether a certain action is just or unjust. Then "unjust" can be resolved or analysed into "fact against law", "law" into "command of him or them who have coercive power", and "power" derived from "the wills of men that constitute such power, to the end that they may live in peace"; and we arrive at last at the proposition that men's passions are such that, unrestrained, they will always be making war upon one another. And this is a proposition "which may be known to be so by any man's experience, that will but examine his own mind". Having reached this point it can then be used as a *beginning*, and a science of politics constructed synthetically on the basis of it. Politics, then, can be constructed without the necessity of going back to the first principles of *philosophia prima* (I vi 7).

Now this is just a special refinement of the self-evidence view. For (i) the analytical method is the method by which we arrive at the primary proposition of *philosophia prima*. We begin with conceptions of particular objects as experienced and analyse their natures until we arrive at the most universal conceptions of all. There analysis stops, and definitions at this level are manifest of themselves. In political science, however, analysis can stop long before it has reached *philosophia prima*: it can stop when it reaches propositions about human passions, because we know the truth of these propositions through our experience of the workings of our own minds. And (ii) the justification of these propositions by appeal to introspective experience is not to be regarded as just a special case of justification by appeal to experience, for then the propositions could not be necessary and universal, and therefore could not be principles of science, although of course this might be just another example of Hobbesian inconsistency. But it seems more probable that what Hobbes has in mind is that introspective experience gives us *insight* into the nature of the mind, just as at the foundation of *philosophia prima* we have insight into the nature of things generally.

On this view, then, the sciences form a progressive chain—*philosophia prima*, mathematics, physics, ethics, politics—with, however, a dividing line in ethics, marking the possibility of beginning demonstrations from a set of specifically human primary propositions. Nevertheless it is still a continuous chain, with demonstrative links from beginning to end.

Yet when Hobbes comes to discuss physics specifically, he adds a new complication. He concludes part III of *De Corpore* by remarking that what he has so far been considering is "motion and magnitude by themselves in the abstract" (III xxiv 9). He goes on to explain at the beginning of part IV that the previous parts have consisted of reasoning from definitions "made and constituted by ourselves", whereas in physics, which is expounded in part IV, the procedure must be different, since it is "the finding out by the appearances or effects of nature, which we know by sense, some ways and means by which they may be, I do not say they are, generated. The principles, therefore, . . . are not such as we ourselves make and pronounce in general terms, as definitions; but such, as being placed in the things themselves by the Author of Nature, are by us observed in them; and we make use of them in single and particular, not universal propositions" (IV xxv I). And at the end of part IV Hobbes says that his argument in it depends on *hypotheses*. He claims that his hypotheses are (i) possible and easily understood; and (ii) account for the phenomena; and he allows that if someone should produce other hypotheses which satisfy these conditions better, then "there will be greater praise and thanks due to him than I demand for myself" (IV xxx 15).

Now this fits very well with *some* things which Hobbes says elsewhere in *De Corpore*.

1. He says that all universal propositions—and therefore all the propositions of science—are *hypothetical* (I iii 11). Thus a proposition of the form, "Everything that is $\phi$ is $\psi$", does not assert that there *is* anything that is $\phi$ and $\psi$, but only that if anything is $\phi$, then it is also $\psi$.

2. Hobbes distinguishes between "knowledge of the causes of all things"—that is, "of such accidents as are common to all bodies"—and knowledge of "the cause of some determined appearance" (I vi 3-4).

3. It is the business of science to discover causes; and the notion of the cause of $X$ is the notion of the sum of all the accidents both in the thing acting and in the thing acted upon, such that it is inconceivable that this sum of accidents should occur and $X$ not occur (I vi 10 and II ix 1-5). Thus the notion of the cause of $X$ is the notion of some $C$ such that from the proposition "$C$ occurs" the proposition "$X$ occurs" necessarily follows. Thus we know that if a certain figure has been "made by the circumduction of a body whereof one end remained unmoved" then it is a circle (that is, all the radii are equal). That is a universal, hypothetical, and necessary proposition. But if what we are concerned with is some actual figure which we perceive, and which looks like a circle; and if we do not know how it was produced; then we cannot know, by perception, whether it is a true circle or not, but can only know that *if* it has been produced in a certain way then it is a circle (I i 5). What is known here is an

hypothetical proposition, "If $C$ then $X$". Such a proposition, if true, is true whether there are any $X$'s or not, and Hobbes later argues that mathematics does not presuppose the actual existence of objects in space (II vii I). But when we are concerned with actual $X$'s and trying to discover their causes, the discovery that a proposition of the form "If $C$ then $X$" is true does not assure us that $C$ is the actual cause of $X$, but only that it is a possible cause.

It is doubtful whether many scientists, or philosophers of science, would nowadays accept the view that science is a purely deductive system derived from either arbitrary or self-evident first principles. But they would find far less to object to in the account which we have been considering. For what it does is to draw a sharp dividing-line, not between mathematics plus physics on the one hand and politics on the other, but between mathematics and physics. It is worth noting that when Hobbes expounds the view that the physics consists of *possible* hypotheses he also talks in terms appropriate to a conventionalist theory of mathematics: he contrasts mathematical principles, which are "such as we ourselves make and pronounce in general terms, as definitions", with the principles of physics, which are "such, as being placed in the things themselves by the Author of Nature, are by us observed in them" (IV xxv I). This amounts to a twofold account. There is (i) mathematics, which is a demonstrative science derived from definitions, or arbitrarily chosen axioms; and (ii) physics, which is the construction of explanatory hypotheses which can only be established as *possibly* true. Physics, of course, uses mathematics, as Hobbes points out. But on this view it is constructed with the help of mathematics and not as a logical consequence of it. Once an hypothesis has been formulated, consequences can be deduced from it. The hypothesis, then, is not an hypothetical (and, for Hobbes, necessary) proposition of the form "If $A$ then $B$", but something much more complex. For it is the function of an hypothesis to explain some actual phenomenon or class of phenomena—for example, ($P$), a man's observable behaviour in grabbing, mouthwateringly, at an apple. Hobbes's hypothesis to explain $P$ is a complicated story. It is that, ($H_1$), there is a motion communicated from the apple to the man's heart, via his eyes, head and nerves, and involving certain minute and undetectable motions called "endeavours"; and if $H_1$ occurs then $P$ occurs. Now from "If $H_1$ occurs then $P$ occurs" and "$P$ occurs", it does not follow that $H_1$ occurs;

and Hobbes is quite clear about that. We are dealing with actual phenomena, and there are two respects in which an explanatory hypothesis goes beyond what is observed in the phenomena.

*a*. The hypotheses with which Hobbes is concerned—his own hypotheses about the causes of perceptions and desires—include the postulation of unobservables ("endeavours"). The only reason for accepting the proposition that $H_1$ occurs is that $P$ occurs, and that if $H_1$ occurs then $P$ occurs, so that the supposition that $H_1$ occurs *explains* the occurrence of $P$. But it is always possible that there is some $H_2$ such that if $H_2$ occurs then $P$ occurs, and if so, there is no more reason for supposing $H_1$ than $H_2$. We should then have to choose between alternative hypotheses. It might be that $H_2$ explained not only $P$ but also $Q$ while $H_1$ explained only $P$. That would be a reason for preferring $H_2$. Hobbes does not explore the question of what different sorts of grounds we might have for preferring one hypothesis to another. But what he insists on clearheadedly is that explanatory hypotheses are always to some extent *provisional*: there is always at least the logical possibility that they may be superseded.

*b*. Even if all the elements of $H_1$ were observed or observable, still, as Hume was later to point out, the *connexion* between $H_1$ and $P$, such that if $H_1$ occurs then $P$ occurs, is not observable: for the proposition that *if* $H_1$ occurs then $P$ occurs says more than is said in a report of the observed occurrence of $P$ *after* the occurrence of $H_1$. It is possible, then, that an occurrence of $H_1$ may not be followed by $P$, and then the proposition "If $H_1$ then $P$" would be falsified. Hobbes does not anticipate Hume's analysis of the concept of causation, but he does allow for the possibility of empirical falsification. Thus explanatory hypotheses, on his account, have the essential features of being *provisional* and *empirically falsifiable*.

What Hobbes has done, indeed, is to produce at least the outlines of an hypothetico-deductive analysis of scientific argument, and he has combined this appropriately with something like a conventionalist account of mathematics. It is not much more than an outline, but so far as it goes it is, of all the accounts which Hobbes has given, the one which comes nearest to being a true description of scientific procedures; and it compares none too badly with much that has been said by Hobbes's contemporaries and by some of his successors. It is, of course, completely inconsistent with the other accounts of his which have been discussed in the previous sections of this chapter.

It is only too obviously inconsistent with a conventionalist account of science, since it explicitly contrasts the construction of hypotheses in physics with the axiomatic system of mathematics. And it is inconsistent also with a self-evidence account of science, since if physical principles were self-evident, some at least of the hypotheses of physics would be certain and not merely possible. It is not inconsistent with a self-evidence account of mathematics. But since a self-evidence view, one presumes, derives some of its attractions from the fact that it gives some sort of account of how mathematical propositions come to be true of the world, and since, as Hobbes expounds it, physics *makes use of* mathematics, and itself relates to the world through observation, there is that much less temptation to postulate self-evidence at any point.

## 4 A MATHEMATICAL PARADIGM

So far I have distinguished elements of a number of different views of scientific method, all of which appear in Hobbes. It remains to discuss these, first in relation to each other, and second in relation to the arguments of *Leviathan*.

In Section 1 of this chapter I mentioned Hobbes's conviction (which he shared with many others) that mathematics was the most excellent of sciences, and that its methods and procedures provided a model which should be copied by all the sciences. This view was embodied in an extreme form in the conventionalist account of science in *The Elements of Law*. It is also present in *De Corpore*, when Hobbes claims that the propositions of political science are conclusions which are derived through a long series of deductions from the first principles of *philosophia prima*: whether those first principles are regarded as conventional or self-evident, on this view all the sciences are given the same methods and the same axioms as mathematics, and the latter is distinguished from the other sciences merely as being the earlier, compared with the later, links of the same deductive chain. I am inclined to think that one chief reason why he was prepared to take mathematics as the paradigm of the sciences was that, failing to distinguish between pure and applied mathematics, he thought that it could be taken for granted not only that mathematics was demonstrative but also that it *applied to* the world: it was therefore easy to suppose that physics also might be demonstrative, and yet also contain truths about the nature of things. The furthest away he got from this view was the hypothetico-deductive account of physics which we discussed in the last section. Yet that view depended on a distinction between propositions about universal characteristics of things, and propositions explaining how "singular things" come to have the specific characteristics which we discover in them. It was only the latter sort of proposition which required the special hypothetico-deductive account. The former sort belonged within mathematics conceived of as a demonstrative science, and yet also as a science which contained truths about the nature of things. He went about half way along the road to regarding mathematics as a purely formal system which could be applied within sciences which themselves contained propositions about the world: but he never went the whole way. He never succeeded in working out a single, consistent and adequate theory of mathematics.

His persistence with mathematics as a model for the sciences must lead him, one would think, to a very unreal, and sterile, conception of science. It is true, indeed, that he was not enthusiastic about the activities of some experimenters. Yet one must be cautious in one's judgments here. At the very least, Hobbes's mistakes are not the only mistakes that can be made about scientific method.

At the very beginning of *Leviathan*, referring to "the thoughts of man", Hobbes says: "The original of them all, is that which we call SENSE, for there is no conception in a man's mind, which hath not at first, totally, or by parts, been begotten upon the organs of sense. The rest are derived from that original" (1 7). That reads, of course, like the slogan for an Empiricist Manifesto. It would not be completely misleading, indeed, to describe Hobbes as a sort of empiricist. But the term "empiricist" is ambiguous in a complex way, and Hobbes's views are themselves by no means simple, so it is necessary to make some distinctions.

1. There is the view that sense experience provides us with a certain perceptual raw material, from which we derive all our concepts—deriving the idea of *red*, for example, from the perceptual experiences which are associated with ripe tomatoes, soviet flags, blood, and so forth. On this view, there is a certain order of logical (and even temporal) priority necessarily involved here: the

perceptual raw material must first be *"given"* so that concepts can be derived from it. This may be called *psychological empiricism*.

2. There is the view that concepts can be *validated* only by relating them to observations. This view does not require us to make a sharp distinction between concepts and perceptual raw material, nor to claim that the former can be derived only from the latter. It allows us to recognise that the way we perceive things, and what we perceive, depends to some extent on the concepts with which we are equipped. It makes no dubious claim about how concepts originate, but suggests a criterion for determining their validity. This view may be called *logical empiricism*.

Now Hobbes often seems to be expounding a doctrine of psychological empiricism, as in the passage which has already been quoted. Indeed, he takes this to absurd and extreme lengths, asserting that "we have no transition from one imagination to another, whereof we never had the like before in our senses" (*Leviathan*, III 13). But we have to be careful here, for it is not only the word "empiricist" that is ambiguous, but also the word "concept". This is a very convenient word, but it is not one of Hobbes's terms, and the empiricist views which I found it convenient to express as views about "concepts" can be related to Hobbes only if the ambiguity of the word "concept" has been allowed for. Sometimes the meaning of "concept" is tied fairly closely to uses of *words*, but dissociated from the use of actual words of a particular language, so that what is meant by "the concept *yellow*" may be just "the job which the word 'yellow' does in English (and which is the same as the job which the word 'gelb' does in German, and other words in other languages)". But sometimes what is meant by "the concept *yellow*" is some mental object which is occurrently in the mind of anyone who actually "has" the concept. Now when Hobbes talks about "conceptions" he is talking about mental objects —images in the mind, which are "really" residual bodily motions remaining after the grosser bodily motions of perception have somewhat subsided. When he talks about universals he is talking, as a nominalist, about *words*. If we combine his empiricist account of concepts with his nominalist account of universals, and if we add the conventionalist theory of the truth of universal propositions, which he sometimes expresses, and his standard criterion of significant language, what this adds up to is a complex doctrine. His empiricist account of concepts is partly a psychological statement about the source from which mental images originate. But in the sense of "concept" which is necessarily related to the use of universal words, what Hobbes has to say is not the statement of a psychological hypothesis, but a logical claim about the significant use of words: words are used significantly only if they can be related to conceptions (see Chapter Three, Section 4), and conceptions themselves relate necessarily to sense experience. Further, it is words that are universal (this is the nominalist account of universals), and it is we who use words who choose arbitrarily how to define their usage (this is part of the conventionalist theory of truth). What all that amounts to is a recipe for conceptual liberty without licence. Although concepts (in the sense of images) are all just the residue of sense experience, we have a large measure of freedom in the construction of concepts (in the sense of universals), limited only by the requirement that they can achieve significance only through being related to sense experience.

Of course I have been considering only one of the views which are to be found in Hobbes's works. He also developed another view in his doctrine of accidents and self-evidence. But although the two sets of views are incompatible, it is important to notice that one of them came near to stating, and at least to some extent implied, a logical empiricist position. It is important because in the first place the extreme empiricism of his psychological (and implausible) account of the origin of images has to be balanced by the logical empiricism of his account of the significance of universal terms. And in the second place, it is important because it left open a place for the sort of conceptual revision which had to be possible if science was to be given the freedom to make advances. Philosophers have sometimes tended to set forth conceptual schemes which could serve only as a straitjacket for scientific activity. It is to Hobbes's credit as a philosopher of science that at least one of the accounts which he gave did not have this fault.

Now so far I have distinguished two sorts of empiricism, or senses of the word "empiricism".

3. But there is yet another brand of empiricism, which had the support of many philosophers over a long period, and can be called *methodological empiricism*. This is the view that in scientific investigations it is necessary to begin at ground level with particular facts, deriving certain low-level generalisations from them (such as that all crows are black), and moving up to higher levels of generalisation,

employing more sophisticated concepts such as the concept of a molecule, an atom, and so forth. On this view even the lowest-level generalisations are somewhat uncertain (since no set of propositions about the colour of particular crows can entail any proposition about the colour of *all* crows), and the further reaches of scientific theory must become the more uncertain the further they are removed from the particular facts from which all the generalisations are derived.

The defect of methodological empiricism is that the actual practice of successful scientists has not conformed to it. Galileo made progress in mechanics, but he made it not so much by accumulating more facts about moving bodies, but by revising the fundamental concept of inertia and reducing the problems to terms of applied mathematics. A simple-minded empiricist would have sent a questionnaire round all the world's gun-layers, asking them to provide him with precise data about the trajectories of their projectiles at different elevations. What Galileo did was to hit on a new concept of inertia, and to draw some mathematical diagrams. Then he knew more about trajectories than the grimy gun-layers themselves. Of course he also did some experiments, rolling balls down inclined planes. But, in the first place, the relatively few facts which he gathered thereby, about a very small section of the class of relevant phenomena, could hardly, on empiricist grounds, support the weight of the conclusions which he drew, which constituted a general science of mechanics. And, in the second place, the new concept of inertia was not "derived" from the facts, except in the sense that it was the basis of a theory which was capable of explaining them.

Of course science depends on facts, which can only be discovered by observation. That may seem like a platitude, but to methodological empiricists like Francis Bacon it was a productive programme to substitute for the sterile fantasies of armchair physics. Yet if it was correct in its insistence on relating scientific generalisations to observed facts, it gave a much over-simplified account of that relation. Hobbes, in his inconsistency, avoided at least one element of over-simplification. For methodological empiricism, as I have expounded it, gave an account of the *verification* of general propositions: a general proposition of the form, "If anything is $\phi$ it is $\psi$", is verified by discovering that *this* thing which is $\phi$ is also $\psi$, *that* thing which is $\phi$ is also $\psi$, and so forth. Since no set of propositions of the form "This thing which is $\phi$ is also $\psi$" can ever entail the general proposition "If anything is $\phi$ it is also $\psi$", this process of verification, on which everything was to depend, seemed hardly strong enough to bear the weight that was put upon it. A more adequate account of scientific procedures, perhaps, would stress the importance of *falsification* and the role of hypotheses. There are three features of the use of hypotheses in science which are relevant to the discussion of Hobbes's views.

1. They are not "derived from the facts", but go beyond them. The scientist is free to employ bizarre and abstruse concepts, and to formulate extravagant and far-fetched hypotheses, so long as they are formulated in such a way as to make them susceptible of testing.

2. Confirmation of an hypothesis depends on the possibilities of falsification. Hence it is not of primary importance to construct a logically valid inference from singular positive premises to a general conclusion. What is important is to notice that some singular propositions entail the falsity of some general propositions.

3. The mathematical formulation of hypotheses enormously increases the possibilities of falsification and therefore of confirmation.

These three features are all to some extent recognised by Hobbes in his accounts of scientific method.

1. Even his insistence on a conventionalist theory of truth, which, if pressed far enough, could result in regarding science as a system of tautologies, did at least, once Hobbes had abandoned his extreme doctrine of psychological empiricism, allow the scientist freedom to construct concepts as he chose.

2. The logical empiricism, which he never abandoned, imposed limits on this freedom. I have already mentioned the curious fact that in *The Elements of Law* Hobbes at one point expounds a conventionalist account of truth and a correspondence theory of falsity. This, I think, was not merely a confusion. If one were disposed to be sympathetic to Hobbes, one might interpret the conventionalist account of truth as a denial that general propositions are logically derived from singular propositions, and the correspondence theory of falsity as asserting that general propositions, nevertheless, are subject to empirical falsification. (In fact, of course, as hypotheses survive the possibilities of falsification and gradually approach the status of laws of nature, some of the concepts involved may change their character, so that the propositions in which they are incorporated become rather like logical truths. The fact that this might occur makes Hobbes's conventionalist account of truth less absurd than it might seem to be, so

long as it is accompanied by an insistence on the possibility of falsification. It is the overstatement of an actual or possible feature of scientific discourse.) Certainly there are a number of places where Hobbes recognises the importance of falsification. There is the passage in *The Elements of Law* (I v 10) already referred to. Again, in chapter I of *Leviathan* he argues that *colours* cannot be properties of objects, and his argument is to mention certain facts, which, he claims, contradict the assumption that the colour is in the object—e.g., the fact that pressing my eyeball can make me see a light, although there is no object corresponding to the image, and the fact that if I look in a mirror I see colours in one place although the object is elsewhere. Whether this is a good or a bad argument, its pattern is to establish one proposition by rejecting the alternative because falsified by the facts. Again, in chapter XVII Hobbes discusses the social life of bees. This arises because he has claimed that a state of war would be inevitable in the absence of coercive institutions of law and order, and bees, which live at peace without kings, judges or policemen, may seem to be a counter-example. Hobbes agrees that this is a fact, but claims that the reason lies in a number of relevant differences between bees and humans. In other words, Hobbes argues that the facts are not contrary to his conclusions, but in doing this he admits the importance of falsification. These examples could be multiplied.

3. I do not know of any occasion on which Hobbes argued that the use of mathematics increased the possibilities of falsification. The most that can be said, if one thinks that this is a matter of any importance, is that Hobbes did insist on the importance of mathematics, and that science conducted according to his prescription would in fact have possessed this feature.

The directions in which Hobbes's philosophy of science might have developed is a very speculative matter. What is certain is that Hobbes always regarded mathematics as a model. What I have been arguing in this section is that so far from its being the case that this vitiated his philosophy of science, on the contrary, because he conceived of mathematics (no doubt wrongly) as a science which stated truths about the world, and because he never refused to allow for the possibility of empirical falsification, his philosophy of science avoided the mistakes and over-simplifications of methodological empiricism, and at times, and in some respects, provided the beginnings of an adequate account of scientific method.

## 5 A DEMONSTRATIVE SCIENCE OF POLITICS (IN *LEVIATHAN*)

Whatever virtues one may try to find in Hobbes's discussions of scientific method, the one virtue which it would be insane to look for is consistency. Thus even in *De Corpore*, the work in which Hobbes devotes a great deal of space to the matter, and in which the admirably lucid hypothetico-deductive account of physics is given, other and inconsistent views appear as well. What we discover in *The Elements of Law* and *De Corpore* is a mixture of insights, confusions and inconsistencies. At the very least Hobbes wavered uncertainly between a conventionalist and a self-evidence theory of mathematics, and between a conventionalist, a self-evidence and an hypothetico-deductive theory of physics. Consequently he was confused and uncertain about the relations of mathematics to physics and about the logical structure of moral and political science. And it is very difficult to see any clear pattern emerging out of the confusion. In some matters there seems to have been a definite development. Extreme psychological empiricism is most marked in *The Elements of Law*, an early work, and is largely replaced in later works by a doctrine of logical empiricism. And there are some constant features of importance: Hobbes always thought both that mathematics was the model for the sciences and that scientific propositions were in some sense propositions about the world, because he was always prepared to admit the relevance of testing them against the facts.

It may be that the hypothetico-deductive account of physics in *De Corpore* was a late development. *De Corpore* was published years after *Leviathan*, and the views of the latter may simply belong, along with those of *The Elements of Law*, to an earlier stage in the development of Hobbes's thought. But since Hobbes began work on *De Corpore* years *before* the publication of *Leviathan*, the matter may be much more complicated. Since in any case Hobbes seems never really to have resolved his confusions, since he produced incompatible views side by side with each other, the only safe course seems to be to allow *Leviathan* to speak for itself, bearing in mind only three things learned from his other works. These are (i) that we must not *expect* to be able to find a single and consistent doctrine. (ii) It is probable enough that, as elsewhere, Hobbes will be convinced that mathematics is of great importance to science, and will not admit that there is any difficulty in regarding science as derived from definitions and also as true of the world. And (iii) the unacknowledged difficulties of this view will create problems for Hobbes. (It is always possible, of course, that *Leviathan* will attempt its own distinctive solution to such problems, and in the remainder of this book I shall be arguing that that is indeed the case.)

Now *Leviathan*, like *The Elements of Law*, is chiefly occupied with political arguments. The discussion of logic and method is much briefer than in *De Corpore*. What Hobbes says—sometimes *very* briefly—has often a familiar ring about it, but with some variations that require attention. The self-evidence view hardly appears at all. Hobbes begins chapter 11 with a proposition "that no man doubts of". But on the whole there are even fewer traces of a self-evidence view in *Leviathan* than the occasional, vague and ambiguous traces which can be discovered in *The Elements of Law* (see Section 2 of this chapter). What Hobbes produces in *Leviathan* is (1) a clear statement of a conventionalist view of science (restricted to universal propositions); (2) an assumption that scientific propositions state important truths about the world; and (3) some mention of the possibilities of empirical confirmation and falsification.

### 1. *The conventionalist account of science*

According to Hobbes, reason is "nothing but *reckoning*, that is adding and subtracting, of the consequences of general names agreed upon for the *marking* and signifying of our thoughts" (v 25–26). Hobbes goes on to contrast science and prudence. Prudence is knowledge gained by experience, and in this field, in which we may "reckon" without words, *error* is possible—as when we conjecture, on the sight of one thing, what is likely to follow. But science is concerned with *general* propositions, and derives these, like geometry, from definitions.

By this it appears that reason is not, as sense and memory, born with us; nor gotten by experience only, as prudence is; but attained by industry; first in apt imposing of names; and secondly by getting a good and orderly method in proceeding from the elements, which are names, to assertions made by connexion of one of them to another; and so to syllogisms, which are the connexions of one assertion to another, till we come to a knowledge of all the consequences of names appertaining to the subject in hand; and that is it, men call SCIENCE (v 29).

In case there should be any doubt whether this is a conventionalist view of the truth of scientific propositions, Hobbes has already said that "when we make a general assertion, unless it be a true one, the possibility of it is inconceivable" (v 27), and he has contrasted *error* within the field of knowledge of experience with scientific error, which is not so much error as "absurdity, or senseless speech" (v 27; and also IV 24). This is certainly armchair science which Hobbes is defending: the criterion of truth is not correspondence with observed facts, but simply the logical criterion of significance—if a scientific (universal) proposition is significant it is true, and if it is not true it is "senseless". It is completely consistent with this view that Hobbes should devote a chapter of *Leviathan* (chapter IV) to the proper use of speech, and that he should repeatedly insist on the supreme importance of care in the use of words, and attention to definitions (see IV–V 21–30; VII 40–41; VIII 46–51; XI 67, etc.). In no other work of Hobbes's is the conventionalist view expounded with such clarity and persistence.

## 2. *Science and the world*

It would be quite wrong, however, to conclude that Hobbes regarded the propositions of science as we should regard straightforward tautologies. For not only did he allow of the possibility of empirical confirmation (which will be discussed presently), but he also conceived of science as providing technical knowledge which could be applied and used. Thus, having claimed that science is a knowledge of the consequences of *names*, Hobbes goes on: "Science is the knowledge of consequences, and dependence of one fact upon another: by which, out of that we can presently do, we know how to do something else when we will, or the like another time; because when we see how any thing comes about, upon what causes, and by what manner; when the like causes come into our power, we see how to make it produce the like effects" (v 29). Hobbes found no difficulty in believing both that scientific propositions were derived from definitions, and that they expressed knowledge of causes and effects. In *De Corpore* his notion of causal connexion was the notion of some $x$ and *y* such that *y necessarily* followed *x*, and there is no reason that I know of for supposing that his view of causation was different in any of his other works. It may seem obvious to us nowadays that causal propositions are not logically necessary propositions, but we have had the benefit of the discussions and analysis of the notion of causation which was initiated by Hume. Hobbes, however, lived before the time of Hume, and like most other pre-Humean philosophers he thought of the causal connexion as a logically necessary connexion. It makes, perhaps, for defects in his philosophy of science which simply have to be noticed and regretted but not too contemptuously deplored.

### 3. *Confirmation and falsification*

In *Leviathan* Hobbes gives a sharper and more consistent exposition of the conventionalist view of science than elsewhere. Nevertheless, there are some complications.

i. The hypothetico-deductive view of *De Corpore* is not expounded in *Leviathan*. Yet there is at least one place in which Hobbes talks in a way appropriate to it. This is his suggestion, in chapter VI, that pleasure "seems to be" a corroboration of vital motion. He suggests this *as* an hypothesis, and not as a conclusion derived from definitions. This, I think, is a fact of great significance in the interpretation of the account of the passions which Hobbes gives in *Leviathan*, and it is discussed at some length in a later chapter.

ii. Although science is represented as a single deductive chain proceeding from elementary definitions, via mathematics and physics, to the further reaches of political theory, Hobbes draws a dividing line, as in *De Corpore*, between mathematics and physics on the one hand, and morals and politics on the other. In *De Corpore* Hobbes says that either we may begin with *philosophia prima*, and proceed, through mathematics and physics, to a knowledge of the causes of human passions, and thence to a knowledge of political matters; or we may take a short cut, *beginning* with the knowledge of the passions and proceeding to the political conclusion. This short cut is possible because "the causes of the motions of the mind are known, not only by ratiocination, but also by the experience of every man that takes the pains to observe those motions within himself" (I vi 7). This well-known passage has its parallel in the Introduction to *Leviathan*, where Hobbes claims that by self-examination a man "shall thereby read and know, what are the thoughts and passions of all other men upon the like occasions" (Introduction, 6). Here again, then, we are told that experience of ourselves gives us the basis for the first principles of politics. Yet the parallel is not exact, for in fact Hobbes is very guarded in the claim that he makes here. The basis of the claim is "the similitude of the thoughts and passions of one man, to the thoughts and passions of another", but he insists immediately that the "similitude" is only in the thoughts and passions themselves and not in the *objects* of these, not in the *things desired*, which vary from man to man. This seems to limit the knowledge furnished by experience to knowledge that people do have thoughts, desires, fears, etc., and to fall short of allowing us to draw any specific conclusions about the particular nature of actual human motives. The very guarded nature of this claim should warn us to be very careful in the interpretation of Hobbes's account of human nature, and not to attribute to him any views which are not clearly stated. This again is a point which will be important in later chapters.

iii. Hobbes argues in chapter XIII of *Leviathan* that in the absence of any coercive power to keep order in society, there would be a state of virtual war between man and man. This, he says, may not convince everyone, and a man "may therefore, not trusting to this inference, made from the passions, desire perhaps to have the same confirmed by experience". Hobbes offers such confirmation by pointing out that people do not in fact behave as if they trusted each other: when a man goes on a journey, even in a society with laws and officers to protect him, he locks his house, takes his sword, and seeks the protection of companions on the way (XIII 82). This is a favourite argument of Hobbes's, which occurs also in *The Elements of Law* and *De Cive*. What Hobbes is doing here is presenting certain truths as already demonstrated and addressing himself to the man "that has not well weighed these things" and therefore has doubts, pointing out that the facts about human behaviour are in accordance with his claims. Hobbes is not claiming that the propositions he is asserting can be *established* by observing how people behave: he is claiming merely *confirmation*. Indeed, even at that his claim is a fairly weak one, for the context is not the establishing of the truth of the proposition, but the meeting of a doubt, and amounts to very little more than a claim that the proposition is not actually falsified.

What this all adds up to is a clearer and more consistent account of method than in the other works which have been considered. *The Elements of Law* presented a conventionalist account of science, but sometimes suggested a self-evidence view, and traced scientific deductions back to "first principles of sense", without explaining very clearly what these were. And in *De Corpore* different accounts were given, in flat contradiction of each other. In *Leviathan*, however, a conventionalist account of science predominates, and the notion of self-evidence is conspicuously absent. This single-minded attachment to the conventionalist view makes for consistency, of course, but it may be thought that it is not a very promising framework for a philosophy of *science*. It is impossible to discuss the account of method in *Leviathan* adequately without following out its application in the actual arguments of the book, and this will be done in later chapters. But before going on to do that it may be useful to summarise the argument so far and to present some provisional conclusions.


## 6 SUMMARY OF PART I

In reaction against what he regards as the meaningless verbalising of Scholastic metaphysicians Hobbes thinks that progress in knowledge depends primarily on a close and critical attention to the uses of language. There are four parts of his theory of logic and method which are dominated by this concern for the proper use of language.

### 1. *A criterion of significance*

In *The Elements of Law*, an early work, Hobbes insists that in all significant use of speech there must be a conception in the mind corresponding to every "name" (i.e., proper or common noun or noun-phrase) used, otherwise there is mere nonsense or parrot-"talk". There is very little trace of this impossibly extreme view in *Leviathan*, where Hobbes merely demands that words should be *capable* of being given a cash-value in terms of conceptions, which themselves relate necessarily to perceptions—a simple logical empiricist position.

### 2. *A nominalist theory of universals*

Hobbes insists that it is only words, and not things or ideas in the mind, which are universal. But the view which he presents is not always an extreme form of nominalism, for although in *The Elements* and *De Corpore* he sometimes claims that the imposition of names is "arbitrary", and does not depend on the nature of the *things*, what he says in *Leviathan* is—more acceptably—that a general word is applied to a class of things because of some common quality or "accident".

### 3. *A criterion of truth*

Hobbes produces a purely logical or linguistic criterion of the truth of the propositions of science, according to which such propositions can be true only by virtue of the definitions of their terms. Yet (i) it has to be noticed that this is offered as a criterion only of the *universal* propositions of "science": Hobbes never suggests that particular propositions about things can be verified except by experience. (ii) Hobbes sometimes combines this, inconsistently, with the claim that certain fundamental truths are self-evident. That is a view which is conspicuous in some parts of *De Corpore* but virtually absent from *Leviathan*. (iii) Although his obsession with language and his admiration for the precise formulations and rigorous methods of mathematics lead him to view science as a system of demonstrated truths, Hobbes does allow that scientific propositions are susceptible of empirical *falsification*.

### 4. *A doctrine of method*

In *The Elements* and *De Corpore* Hobbes's views on method, though showing many insights, are confused and inconsistent. Sometimes science is presented as a purely deductive system, resting either on definitions or on self-evident premisses. The model is mathematics. Failing to distinguish between pure and applied mathematics, Hobbes believes both that mathematical propositions are demonstrable and that they express truths about the nature of the world. But at one point in *De Corpore* Hobbes gives a sophisticated account of the role of hypotheses in physics, according to which the propositions of physics are provisional and never demonstrable.

In *Leviathan*, however, there is on the whole less confusion than in the other works. What I shall be suggesting in the following chapters is that although the deficiencies remaining in the account of method given in *Leviathan* are serious defects in a philosophy of *science*, they are of small importance in the context of Hobbes's particular purposes. Hobbes has succeeded in achieving a fairly high degree of consistency. But some confusions remain unresolved. In particular, he fails in *Leviathan*, as elsewhere, to distinguish between pure and applied mathematics. Consequently he finds it easy to believe that a demonstrative science can establish truths about the world. Further, he assumes that the causal connexion is a connexion which is logically necessary. These two blunders, however excusable, make it difficult for him to see the need to give any important place in science to observation and experiment. Nevertheless, in *De Corpore* he constructs a hypothetico-deductive account of physics, which is an admission of the limitations of any purely logical criterion of truth; and there is at least the suggestion of the presence of such a view in *Leviathan*. But some confusion still remains, because Hobbes suggests in *Leviathan* that a science of politics can be constructed on the basis of knowledge of experience (experience of our own inner states), but describes this possibility in terms that are brief, vague and ambiguous. The view which is consistently stressed is a conventionalist view, and the model is mathematics. But although in theory political science is derived from the principles (definitions) which are in the first instance the axioms of *philosophia prima*, in practice Hobbes's argument begins with his account of the passions. The discussions which precede this in *Leviathan* are represented as a summary statement of the physical foundations of the account of human nature, but in fact no real *use* is made of these at all. Hobbes simply defines some terms—"desire", "aversion", "good", etc.—which are to be the materials of an *a priori* analysis of some formal aspects of the structure of human relations. The statement that political science can be based on principles known through self-experience becomes intelligible when we remember the guarded way in which it was made—we know from the inside about human nature, about desire, hope, fear, and so forth, but not about *what* is desired and feared. The beginning is not, in other words, in some *generalisations about human nature*, but in the understanding of some psychological concepts. Now a "science" of human nature of which the conventionalist account is true would consist of a set of propositions whose truth was determined by the (arbitrary) definitions of the terms involved. It would be absurd to expect that these propositions should embody truths about human nature, just as it is absurd to suppose that the proposition, "If there are 52 sisters in Buenos Aires there are 52 people in Buenos Aires who are not male siblings", expresses a truth about the people of Buenos Aires. Then if *Leviathan* gives the clearest and most consistent exposition of a conventionalist account of science, and *if* Hobbes's actual arguments are in accordance with his methodological prescriptions, we should expect to find the moral and political propositions of *Leviathan* presented as a system of propositions which are *definitionally true*, which are not to be interpreted as purporting to state truths *about human nature*, and which would remain true, if well constructed, regardless of what we might suppose the actual nature of human motivation to be. This formal system, nevertheless, might have some use in the discussion of political issues, just as mathematics has a use within physics and elsewhere; and there would be room for empirical confirmation, not of the truth of the propositions themselves, but of the applicability of the system as a whole within the discussion of specific political issues. In further chapters I shall be claiming that this is the actual pattern of Hobbes's argument in *Leviathan*. And I shall be claiming that it is to be contrasted both with the account of human nature in *De Corpore*, which is appropriate to the hypothetico-deductive method expounded there, and with the account of human nature in *The Elements of Law*, which is as muddled and unclear as the discussion of method which accompanies it. This is important, because there are some views which are commonly regarded as typical of Hobbes which, if this argument is correct, are *not* typical of the Hobbes of *Leviathan*.

# Part Two

# MAN

# CHAPTER FIVE

# *Human Nature*

THE earlier chapters both of *The Elements* and of *Leviathan*, in which Hobbes discusses language and method and gives a brief account of sense and imagination, are only preparatory to the chief arguments. One conspicuous feature of these preliminaries is Hobbes's insistence that all mental occurrences, in sense and in thought or imagination, are explicable in terms of bodily motions. Since Hobbes is famous for his mechanistic materialism, it is only too easy to notice and remember that he regards his materialistic categories as applicable also to the passions, and, indeed, conceives of ethics (the science of the human passions) as a branch of *physics* (*Leviathan*, IX 54–55). I shall be suggesting that this materialism of Hobbes's is less important to his account of the passions than is sometimes supposed, and than he sometimes makes it out to be. A common view of his account of the passions is that it is materialistic and egoistic. In this chapter I shall be discussing the elements of Hobbes's account of the passions and I shall be trying to show, in detail, that the account given in *Leviathan* is, in the first place, as different in its methods and procedures from those given in *The Elements* and *De Corpore* as the discussion of method in *Leviathan* is from the discussions of method in the other works; and secondly, that mechanistic materialism plays no important part in the account of the passions in *Leviathan*; and thirdly, that this account is not predominantly egoistic, although an unambiguously egoistic account is given in other works.

These are important issues. For Hobbes claims that his political conclusions are based on his account of the passions. If they presuppose the truth of such doubtful—at least disputable—views as mechanism and egoism, his political conclusions must themselves be more doubtful than if they had no such presuppositions.

## 1 EGOISM AND HEDONISM

Since one of the questions at issue is whether Hobbes's account of the passions is egoistic, it is best to begin by discussing what egoism is.

It is a fact that people sometimes have disillusioning experiences. When you were stealing pennies out of the blind beggar's little tin, you told him funny stories to distract his attention. He thought that you were trying to cheer him up, out of kindness of heart. Later, when he found out what had happened, he was disillusioned. Your old aunt also was disillusioned when you promised to look after her and then deserted her as soon as you found out how little money she really had. Those who have numbered people like you among their circle of friends can readily become quite pessimistic, and leap to the general conclusion that every apparently kind or unselfish action conceals some hidden, self-regarding motive. Others may be equally pessimistic, not because of any specially disillusioning experiences, but merely because a naturally dismal or suspicious turn of mind disposes them that way. Such people tend to enjoy a gloomy triumph whenever they find hypocrisy unmasked, for this confirms their pessimistic view of people. There are three reasons why I call this "pessimism" and not egoism. In the first place, I want to reserve the term "egoism" for something which is a product of *theory*, rather than of experience or temperament. In the second place, this pessimism can allow of exceptions (but regards them as merely very rare), whereas what I call "egoism" does not allow of exceptions. Thirdly, to adopt a pessimistic view of human nature is to have *different expectations*: before you were a pessimist you were shocked to discover that although the vicar had embezzled the church funds he was still neglecting his many illegitimate children, but such news does not surprise you *now*.

Egoism, however, is something very different. (By "egoism" and "egoist" in this context I do not, of course, mean "self-centredness" and "self-centred person", but a certain theory about motives and one who holds such a theory.) In the first place, by "egoism" I mean a certain theory about human motives which is typically held by happy and innocent philosophers rather than by battered news-hounds and other disillusioned worldlings. In the second place, egoism does not allow of exceptions. It is not a generalisation based on, or at all events confirmed by, bitter experience. It is rather an analysis of the nature of a human motive as such, and the purported discovery of a pattern to which, it is thought, all human motivation must somehow conform. According to the egoist all human action, if motivated at all, is motivated by the agent's desire to promote his own advantage or interest. This has to be carefully stated, otherwise the egoist position becomes implausible or else vacuous. Normally one would distinguish between what one wants at some particular time and what is to one's advantage or in one's interests. The notion of prudence is based on such a distinction. What I want is to smoke, but there are a lot of petrol fumes around, and if I light my pipe I shall probably blow myself up. Prudence requires that I should abstain. I may *be* prudent; or I may rashly light up, knowing that it is imprudent, and preferring to gratify a pressing desire rather than defer to my own long-term interests. Now if egoism were the claim that all motivated action was motivated by the agent's desire to promote his own interest, and if the notion of interest were expounded in these terms, egoism would be too silly to be worth bothering about. For this notion of interest contrasts actions done from self-interest with imprudent actions which reject self-interest. Therefore *not* all motivated actions are motivated by the agent's desire to promote his own interest. And if one allows that some imprudent desires can be deliberately indulged, there seems no reason to suppose that some generous and kindly desires should not also occur and be indulged, even although they are not prudent. Indeed it would be difficult to find any *reason* for describing the action of a patriot, who deliberately gave himself up to a painful death in order to further his cause, as motivated by a desire to promote his own *interest*, for he might not believe in an after-life and could therefore not be aiming at any long-term advantage to himself. In order to make it plausible, the egoist position has to be restated. One might be tempted to restate it very simply, as the proposition that actions which are apparently altruistic are not *really* altruistic because a person *really* always just does what *he* most wants to do: the patriot endures torture and death because he wants to further the cause, even at the cost of a painful death, more than he wants to survive comfortably, at the cost of neglecting the cause. This, indeed, is the sort of proposition which often appeals to students of philosophy about five minutes after they have first become acquainted with the subject. But it does not survive another five minutes of careful examination. There is a sense of "want"—not

very precisely or clearly defined—in which what one *wants* to do is
contrasted with, and sometimes different from, what one thinks one
*ought* to do, or with what one thinks it would be *best* to do. After all,
we understand what someone means when he says, "I want to light
my pipe, but I'd better not", or "He wanted to withdraw, but he
knew that everyone was depending on him". "Want" in this sense
is a relatively limited concept. But in the restated egoist proposition
it is given an unlimited usage, and is applied even to those cases which
it is part of its normal meaning to exclude. Of course one may say, if
one chooses, that an isolated soldier in an exposed position, who is
permitted to withdraw, but who holds on heroically in order to protect the others, is just doing what he wants. It is unfortunate that this
obscures a distinction which the ordinary usage of "want" is well
adapted to express. There is on the one hand the case of the man who
enjoys and is thrilled by dangerous situations and who positively
seeks out opportunities for exposing himself to them. If the soldier in
question were a man like this, one might not hesitate to say that he
was doing what he wanted. And one might wish to distinguish this
from the different case of a man who normally *avoided* dangerous
situations if he could, and did not enjoy them at all when he was
unable (or unwilling) to avoid them. The soldier in question might
be *this* sort of man, holding on not because he enjoyed danger, but
because he thought he ought. And according to at least one normal
usage of "want", it would be correct to describe him as doing something which he did not want to do. Nevertheless, one may impoverish
one's language if one chooses, and insist on widening the sense of
"want" to cover both cases. But then saying that the fearful soldier
is still doing what he most wants to do is just saying that he has
*preferred* to hold on—that is, that he has chosen to hold on rather than
to withdraw. And the reason for saying this is that he *has* held on
although he could have withdrawn. Then when anyone does $X$ who
could have done $Y$, it will be correct to say that he wanted to do $X$
rather than $Y$, in the sense that he *preferred* $X$ to $Y$, chose $X$ when he
could have done $Y$. Now egoism is or purports to be a proposition
about human motivation; it purports to explain the choices that
people make. But on this analysis it is stating simply that when
people act in accordance with a choice, they do what they have
chosen to do. This proposition cannot be denied: but its explanatory
powers are very poor, because it says nothing.

What the egoist is concerned to say is that all human motivation is really self-regarding, however altruistic it may seem. Perhaps the most plausible expression of this, without falling into vacuity, would be the proposition that when someone chooses to do something it is always with a view to bringing about some state of himself which he prefers to any other state which he thinks it is possible for him to bring about. This still involves a preference, but it is not vacuous because it states that a person always chooses with a view to some future state of himself. On the egoist account, then, what the patriot who chooses between a painful death and betraying the cause is *really* choosing between is, on the one hand the state of dying painfully with the compensation of knowing that he has not betrayed the cause, and on the other hand the state of surviving, but with the knowledge that he has betrayed the cause. If the patriot chooses to die *because* he prefers the former state to the latter, then his choice conforms to the egoistic pattern. It is easy to see that this formulation of the egoist position is not a mere tautology. For one can imagine the secret police of an occupying power, with psychiatric weapons at their disposal, convincing some captured patriot that they could ensure both that if he betrayed the cause he would be made to forget his betrayal afterwards, and that if he refused he would be killed not only painfully but in such a state of induced confusion that he would be unaware that he had *not* yielded. On the egoist analysis the patriot would now have a *very* different choice to make, and at least the chief factor which had made death preferable (the awareness of not having betrayed) would now make betrayal preferable. But someone who denied the egoist position would hold that at least sometimes a person could choose something not merely with a view to bringing about some preferred state of himself. On this view the patriot might choose death with a view to promoting the interests of his fellow-countrymen. In such a case, the patriot's conviction that he would be unaware of his success or failure would not necessarily be relevant to his choice: if what he cared most about was promoting the cause, then he would be liable to choose *now* to die, because although he would know that his future beliefs about his own action would be both false and distressing, he would also know *now*, when choosing, that his choice of death would in fact promote the cause. On the egoist analysis, then, we should expect the patriot to yield to such psychiatric bullying, since it would deprive him of the reasons for his original preference, whereas on a non-egoist analysis we should not necessarily expect him to yield, since the threats would not necessarily affect his preference.

I must refuse to attempt the impossible task of convincing the reader that this egoistic account is true, because I believe it to be patently false. I have taken the trouble of devoting several pages to the exposition of it only because it is, I think, a little less *obviously* silly than some other possible statements of egoism, and because it at least has the merit of not being vacuous.

There is one special variant of egoism which ought to be mentioned here. It is sometimes held that every choice that any person makes aims at securing *pleasure* for himself, and this is called egoistic *hedonism*. This is merely a refinement—if such it can be called—of the egoist position already stated. It holds, with egoism, that choice is always with a view to bringing about some state of the agent which he prefers; and it adds that the preference is always for a more, rather than a less, pleasurable state. Thus the patriot chooses a painful death because he thinks that he will enjoy a painful death, accompanied by the gratification of knowing that he has promoted the cause, more than survival accompanied by torments of conscience. This is even more clearly not a vacuous statement, because if this account is true, then the patriot who is convinced that in dying he will be deprived of his gratification, while in survival he will be anaesthetised against the pangs of conscience, will inevitably choose survival; while on a non-egoistic account he may still feel that he has good reasons for choosing death, although it has been made more painful for him.

The question with which I am concerned in this chapter is not whether any variety of egoism is true; but, assuming that egoism is at least doubtful, whether Hobbes weakens his argument by including such a doubtful proposition as part of its foundations.

## 2 MECHANISTIC MATERIALISM AND THE PASSIONS

Some of the most famous of all Hobbesian quotations are expressions of the mechanistic materialism which is such an important feature of

his philosophy. He very cleverly places one of these
at the beginning of *Leviathan*:

For seeing life is but a motion of limbs, the beginnir
some principal part within; why may we not say, t
(engines that move themselves by springs and wh
watch) have an artificial life? For what is the *heart*, bt
the *nerves*, but so many *strings*; and the *joints*, but so many *wheels*,
giving motion to the whole body, such as was intended by the
artificer? (Introduction, 5.)

Hobbes thought that everything was explicable in terms of motions
of bodily particles, and this is a view which is expounded consistently
in *Leviathan* and elsewhere. Thus sense is the reaction of the human
body to a physical stimulus provided by an external object. This
reaction is an internal motion outwards, and Hobbes suggests, perhaps naïvely, that it is because this motion is *outwards* that the perception seems to be (as it is) of something external (*Leviathan*, I 7).
Of colours, sounds, etc., Hobbes says: "All which qualities, called
sensible, are in the object, that causeth them, but so many several
motions of the matter, by which it presseth our organs diversely.
Neither in us that are pressed, are they anything else, but divers
motions; for motion produceth nothing but motion" (I 7–8). Imagination is just "decaying sense"—that is, the motions of sense, diminished, like the rolling of waves which continues even after the wind
has stopped. "All fancies are motions within us" (III 14), and thought
in general, and understanding in particular, are just varieties of
imagination. Similarly, desire and aversion are *endeavours*, and endeavours are the "small beginnings of motion, within the body of man,
before they appear in walking, speaking, striking, and other visible
actions" (VI 31). Hobbes has explained that there are some animal
motions, such as breathing, the pulse, etc., which occur without the
help of imagination. But other motions, called "voluntary", are caused
by first imagining the action—a voluntary action is such "as to *go*,
to *speak*, to *move* any of our limbs, in such manner as is first fancied
in our minds" (VI 31). This is in turn *caused* by something, for
example, food, so that if the endeavour is towards what causes it it
is called "appetite" or "desire", and if away from it, "aversion".

Thus in *Leviathan*, as elsewhere, Hobbes consistently describes
perception, thought and desire as physical motions. That is what

ey *really are*, in Hobbes's view. But of course he is aware that that is not necessarily how they *appear* to us. When the motions in a ripe tomato "press" my eyes, I see something red, and I do not actually observe the motions in the tomato and in my sense organs which are what is *really* happening. And when I want to eat the tomato, I have the desire, but I do not actually observe the quiverings of my heart and nerves which is what is *really* happening. Thus I have already quoted part of the passage in which Hobbes declares of sensible qualities that neither in the object nor in the person affected by the object "are they anything else, but divers motions . . ." (1 7–8). But he goes on to say, "But their appearance to us is fancy. . . ." (1 8.) Thus Hobbes distinguishes between how things appear to us and how they really are: the reality is always bodily motions, although these may not be perceptible. He expounds this distinction at greatest length in a passage which draws an analogy between the application of the distinction to the senses and its application to the passions.

As, in sense, that which is really within us, is, as I have said before, only motion, caused by the action of external objects, but in appearance; to the sight, light and colour; to the ear, sound; to the nostril, odour, etc.: so, when the action of the same object is continued from the eyes, ears, and other organs to the heart, the real effect there is nothing but motion, or endeavour; which consisteth in appetite, or aversion, to or from the object moving. But the appearance, or sense of that motion, is that we either call *delight*, or *trouble of mind* (VI 33).

Now in his discussion of the uses of language in chapter IV of *Leviathan* Hobbes distinguishes several categories of language. The first category is names of matter, and the third category is "names of fancies" ("as when anything is seen by us, we reckon not the thing itself, but the sight, the colour, the idea of it in the fancy" (IV 23)). What Hobbes is saying, then, is that we can distinguish between categories of language—physical (first category) language and appearance (third category) language; but propositions expressed in appearance language are reducible to propositions expressed in physical language, and a true description of the world must be expressed in physical language.

Now one may be tempted to think that if Hobbes conceives of his theory of the passions as an account of human nature in physical terms, this theory cannot be an egoistic—nor any other kind of—

theory of motives. For it might be—and has been—argued by some, that the concept of a motive is not a physical concept and is not reducible to any physical concept, so that a physical theory, or a proposition in physical language, cannot be a theory, or proposition, about motives. If this issue were relevant to the study of Hobbes, it would be necessary to discuss it and come to a conclusion. I am convinced, however, that it is not relevant. For Hobbes thought—wrongly, perhaps—that propositions about motivation *could* be expressed in physical language. But what he was concerned with in the first instance was propositions about *motives*, and he had things to say about these which he thought could be represented as physical propositions. However wrong he may have been about this, the things he was saying were things about motives, and his theory may be a bad, muddled, or radically confused theory, but it is still a theory about motives.

Thus he distinguishes between *vital* and *voluntary* motion. The latter is that which depends on imagination, on "a precedent thought of *whither*, *which way*, and *what*" (VI 31). Hobbes's account, of course, maintains that such thoughts, like all thoughts, are *really* bodily motions. But what he is *talking about* is actions determined by thoughts. An egoist, after all, might also be a simple-minded materialist, and he might hold that the thought that a certain action would promote the agent's advantage was a physical occurrence. That would not make him any the less of an egoist, but would merely make him an egoist who was also a materialist. A materialist, indeed, might represent the issue between the egoist and the non-egoist as the question whether or not every physical motion which we call "motivated action" is determined by the sort of physical motions which we call "the thought that the action is to one's own advantage". The question of what sort of account Hobbes gives of human nature—whether egoistic or not, and so forth—remains to be answered after we have reminded ourselves of his mechanistic materialism. If part of his account is expressed in first category language (*and hardly any of it is*), then we have to ask what sort of third category proposition this is a rendering of. Happily, however, we shall have to spend very little time over that sort of question, because mechanistic materialism is merely one of Hobbes's battle-cries, but it is not among the troops whom he deploys when the actual fighting begins. What Hobbes is interested in (in chapter VI and later chapters of

*Leviathan*) is "voluntary motions". The first sentence of chapter VI, introducing the discussion of the passions, distinguishes between vital motions and voluntary motions. Vital motions are those, like breathing, the circulation of the blood, and so forth, which we do not need to think about, but which go on so long as we are alive. Voluntary motions are those which depend on our thinking of an action and then acting accordingly. This is a very rough and ready distinction which Hobbes makes, but it is more or less co-extensive with the distinction between actions which do not depend on a choice and actions which do, and with the distinction between actions which are not motivated and actions which are. It is only "more or less" co-extensive. There are a host of distinctions which Hobbes simply ignores. Not all motivated actions involve a conscious choice, and Hobbes has nothing to say about the relations between "voluntary", "intentional", "deliberate", "chosen", "unintentional", "involuntary", "thoughtless", and so forth. Complications are simply ignored. But that is not necessarily a criticism, because it remains to be seen whether the arguments of *Leviathan* require them to be taken into account. Having made this basic distinction in terms of third category, or psychological language, Hobbes now forgets about vital motion, which is of no importance to the further course of the argument, and makes some claims, in first category, or physical, language, about voluntary motions, with which exclusively he is concerned. A voluntary motion involves a thought followed by an action (that has already been said, in making the distinction between "vital" and "voluntary"), and now Hobbes suggests that the overt action is preceded by an imperceptible, internal bodily motion, which he calls "endeavour". When endeavour is towards what causes it it is called "appetite" or "desire", and when away from it, "aversion".

From this point on, first category language, and mechanistic materialism, are hardly ever mentioned again. And that is just as well, because while Hobbes attempts to make very little use of them, the little use that he does make involves him in a staggeringly large amount of vagueness and confusion. For to begin with, when he first distinguishes vital and voluntary motion he defines the latter as that which depends on *a thought of the action*. Then he suggests that an endeavour is the internal beginning of such a preconceived action. But when he distinguishes endeavours into desires and aversions he defines "desire" as "endeavour, when it is toward something which causes it", and "aversion" as endeavour away from its cause. In the one case the cause of an endeavour is a thought of an action, in the other case the cause seems to be an object. Perhaps this is just a clumsy exposition of a slightly fuller account which is given a page or two later. There Hobbes says that an object affects our senses, and that when the internal bodily motions which *are* our perception of the object reach the heart they bring about a further motion or endeavour there, which is appetite or aversion to or from the object (VI 33). On this account, however, the cause of an endeavour is, indeed, a "thought", but it is the "thought" of an object, and in perception, not in imagination. But where is the thought of the *action* to be fitted in? No doubt it *can* be fitted in: but Hobbes is leaving the reader to do his work for him. In the second place, what does Hobbes mean by an endeavour "towards" its cause? The endeavour is an internal bodily motion. Suppose that I see an apple, and seeing it causes a desire for it. Then that is an endeavour towards the apple. Suppose that the apple is to the north-west of me. Is the endeavour, then, a thoracic disturbance proceeding in a north-westerly direction? Or is the "towards" metaphorical here? Is it endeavour towards simply in the sense that it is the beginning of an action which will procure the apple for me? Thirdly, that sort of question is of some importance, because it would be useful to know just how precisely Hobbes's language is to be taken here, so as to know just how much importance he attaches to his account. Is it intended to be a true description of all desire and aversion, or all voluntary motion? One must hope not. For surely not all voluntary behaviour conforms to this pattern of reaction to a present external stimulus. What about ambition, and ambitious actions, for example: what are the objects to which these are reactions? But perhaps Hobbes did not intend his account to cover *all* voluntary motions but only those simple cases which are caused by the effect of a present object. Indeed, Hobbes devotes a paragraph to distinguishing endeavours which men are born with from those which are acquired by experience, but he explicitly limits his discussion of the latter to those "which are appetites of particular things" (VI 32).

The most important fact in this connexion, however, is that really Hobbes himself is fanatically uninterested in these elementary physiological explanations. What he is interested in is, in the first place, the general category of actions dependent on "a precedent thought of *whither*, *which way*, and *what*"; in the second place, on certain other concepts defined in terms of this, such as desire, aversion, good, pleasure, etc.; and, in the third place, in certain specific desires such as the desire for power. Desires stimulated by present objects are of no importance in his argument, but the desire for power is. The physiological account of "endeavour" disappears very quickly and is *never* used. The concept of "endeavour" which Hobbes actually uses is simply the concept of some state of a person such that, if unchecked, it will result in an overt action towards or away from some preconceived objective. That suggestion, of course, can be substantiated only gradually, in the process of following out the actual course of Hobbes's argument. What is a fact is that the physiological language *disappears*. I hope that it will become apparent that even its brief appearance is an irrelevance, and that the best thing that the reader of *Leviathan* can do with Hobbes's mechanistic materialism is to dismiss it from his mind as quickly as Hobbes dismisses it from his argument.

## 3 AN HYPOTHESIS ABOUT PLEASURE (IN *DE CORPORE*)

It must be admitted that reading Hobbes requires one to indulge in a good deal of mental gymnastics, which are pleasant or painful according to one's tastes. For while the intelligent Hobbes-reader closes his mind to mechanistic materialism when examining *Leviathan*, he must open it again when he turns to *De Corpore*. For there Hobbes produces an account of the passions in which his physiological hypotheses are actually used. This is not terribly surprising. It is in *De Corpore* that he produces his hypothetico-deductive account of physics, and the account of the passions is part of the physics. What we may expect to find is an *hypothesis* about pleasure and desire, offered as such, and expressed in physiological terms: and that is what we actually do find.

The first part of the physics of *De Corpore* is an account of sense and imagination similar to the account given in *Leviathan*. Sense is the occurrence of "phantasms" caused by (or, is the appearance to us of) internal motions from the heart outwards, caused by internal motions inwards to the heart, caused in turn by the effect of external objects on our sense organs; and imagination is decaying sense (IV xxv 1–7). Now, Hobbes argues, "the original of life being in the heart, that motion in the sentient, which is propagated to the heart, must necessarily make some alteration or diversion of vital motion, namely, by quickening or slackening, helping or hindering the same" (IV xxv 12). This proposition is one which Hobbes might regard as necessarily true. But he goes on in the next sentence:

Now when it helpeth, it is pleasure; and when it hindereth, it is pain, trouble, grief, etc. And as phantasms seem to be without, by reason of the endeavour outwards, so pleasure and pain, by reason of the endeavour of the organ inwards, seem to be within; namely, there where the first cause of the pleasure or pain is; as when the pain proceeds from a wound, we think the pain and the wound are both in the same place.

Hobbes has begun his discussion of physics by explaining that he will now not be arguing demonstratively from definitions, but suggesting *possible* causes of particular appearances in nature (IV xxv 1), and he ends the discussion by repeating this, and describing the fundamental propositions of his physics as "hypotheses" which are possible and comprehensible, but not necessary, and in a sense provisional (IV xxx 15). These propositions about pleasure and pain seem obviously to be offered as hypotheses. In *The Elements of Law* Hobbes gives an account of pleasure and pain which is in some respects similar to this account in *De Corpore*. But in *The Elements* what Hobbes says is "when it *helpeth*, it is called *delight, contentment*, or *pleasure*" (I vii 1), and the words "it is called" announce that what is being offered is a definition. But these words do not occur in the passage in *De Corpore*. Of course it might still be *intended* as a definition, although not explicitly presented as such. But this seems unlikely, for two reasons. The first is that Hobbes has described the procedures of physics in *De Corpore* as the production of hypotheses, and has explained why physics cannot argue from definitions. The second is that in *Leviathan* Hobbes says: "This motion, which is called appetite, and for the appearance of it *delight*, and *pleasure*, seemeth to be a corroboration of vital motion, and a help thereunto" (VI 33). The words "*seemeth* to be" indicate that what was presented in *The Elements* as a definition is regarded in *Leviathan* as an hypothesis. Thus if Hobbes in *Leviathan* did not regard this proposition as a definition, there is no reason for supposing that he would have produced it as a definition in the physics of *De Corpore*, which is *supposed* to consist of hypotheses. And of course the last sentence of the passage quoted from *De Corpore* is obviously an hypothesis offered as a likely explanation of why pleasure and pain seem to be "within".

Hobbes now identifies vital motion with the circulation of the blood.

Which motion, when it is hindered by some other motion made by the action of sensible objects, may be restored again either by bending or setting strait the parts of the body; which is done when the spirits are carried now into these, now into other nerves, till the pain, as far as is possible, be quite taken away (IV xxv 12).

Having asserted the existence of this nervous mechanism, Hobbes goes on to suggest how it may be expected to work. "But if vital motion be helped by motion made by sense, then the parts of the organ will be disposed to guide the spirits in such manner as conduceth most to the preservation and augmentation of that motion, by the help of the nerves." He goes on to incorporate some known facts which tend to confirm the hypothesis: "And in animal motion this is the very first endeavour, and found even in the embryo; which while it is in the womb, moveth its limbs with voluntary motion, for the avoidance of whatsoever troubleth it, or for the pursuing of what pleaseth it." He now goes on to distinguish endeavour into *appetite* and *aversion*. "And this first endeavour, when it tends towards such things as are known by experience to be pleasant, is called *appetite*, that is, an approaching; and when it shuns what is troublesome, *aversion*, or flying from it." Thus little children have few appetites or aversions, because they have little experience. Hobbes finally sums up the discussion: "To conclude, all the passions, called passions of the mind, consist of appetite and aversion, except pure pleasure and pain, which are a certain fruition of good or evil" (IV xxv 13).

There are several features of this account which are of importance.

1. The connexion between pleasure and pain on the one hand and endeavour on the other hand is not a *logical* one. "Pure pleasure and pain" are "a certain fruition of good or evil" (whatever that may mean: Hobbes does not explain these terms in *De Corpore*, and since their occurrences in other works are in the contexts of very different

theories it would be dangerous to use them as clues) and are distinguished from the other passions. The connexion indeed is straightforwardly causal: in the simplest pattern, pain is a certain state of the vital motion, while endeavour is a reaction of the nervous system to this state of the vital motion.

2. Hobbes seems to define "appetite" (and "aversion") as endeavour towards (and away from) things known by experience to be pleasant (and painful). There are two possible ways of regarding this. One way is to think that Hobbes is simply making it a definitional truth that all human desire is for the agent's own pleasure, or for the avoidance of pain to him. If this is what Hobbes is doing he is cheating, because he has said that physics is to construct hypotheses and not to rely on definitions. But it is quite unnecessary to adopt this interpretation. Hobbes has already told a long story about a bodily mechanism constructed so that endeavours tend towards the procuring of pleasure and the avoiding of pain. The hypothesis is that there are just these two sorts of endeavour, whose mechanism is as described. He then goes on to assert, as a fact about language, that what we call "appetite" and "aversion" can in fact be identified with these two classes of endeavour. That all endeavour is either for pleasure or for the avoidance of pain, stimulated by the effect of states of the vital motion on the nervous system, remains an hypothesis, and the statement of it precedes the remarks about "appetite" and "aversion".

3. Hobbes gives a detailed account of the mechanism which he supposes to be involved when the nervous system of an organism takes avoiding action against a present pain. But he is somewhat vague about the mechanism involved when the organism is pursuing some future possible pleasure (or avoiding some future possible pain) —something known by experience to be pleasant (or painful). Since when he comes to generalise, what he says is that endeavour is always for things known by experience to be pleasant, and away from things known by experience to be painful, the vagueness of his account of the mechanism of the pursuit of future pleasure is unfortunate. His hypothesis, perhaps, is not a very well-constructed hypothesis.

4. Nevertheless, even if it is not a terribly good hypothesis, it is very much an *hypothesis*, and not simply a definition or set of definitions. What Hobbes is doing is to describe in some detail a mechanism

whose operations could account for some general facts, such as that human beings suffer pleasure and pain, and have desires, and also for some particular facts, such as that infants have only a small *variety* of desires. It is much more than merely a statement that all desire is for pleasure and the avoidance of pain. It is much more, even, than a statement that all desire is for pleasure and pain, plus a statement that this is because of some (unspecified) effect of objects on the (physical) organism. It is an attempt at a fairly detailed *explanation* of why desire is always for pleasure and the avoidance of pain.

5. The adoption of the hypothesis commits Hobbes to the position of egoistic hedonism, because it states that what a person always desires is pleasure, or the avoidance of pain, for himself. This is not at all like the view which I called "pessimism" in Section 1 of this chapter. Pessimism is—or purports to be—a *generalisation* about people based on experience. But what Hobbes offers in *De Corpore* is a scientific hypothesis: it is a detailed account of the human organism which, if true, has, *as a consequence*, that all desire is for the agent's pleasure, or for the avoidance of pain. Hobbes connects his explanation with a respectable item of scientific theory, namely, Harvey's theory about the circulation of the blood. His method is as far as possible from either the uncertain sort of generalisation which is the most that pessimism can achieve, or the vacuity which is the result of an attempt to establish psychological propositions by deriving them from definitions. The theory of *De Corpore*, then, is an example of the strongest possible variety of egoistic hedonism.

## 4 A MUDDLE ABOUT PLEASURE (IN *THE ELEMENTS OF LAW*)

I have put the theory of *De Corpore* first in order of discussion, but that is not to say that it was the first of Hobbes's theories. *De Corpore* was, of course, published in 1655, while *Leviathan* was published in 1651, and *The Elements* printed publicly in 1650, having circulated in manuscript form since 1640. Hobbes had been at work on *De Corpore* before he began work on *Leviathan*, but I do not know whether the account of the passions in *De Corpore* should be counted as earlier or later than that of *Leviathan*. What *is* clear is that the account in *The*

*Elements* is earlier than both those of *Leviathan* and *De Corpore*. But for the purposes of exposition it has been convenient to discuss first the account in *De Corpore*. The reason is that what Hobbes says there is very clearly put and is presented explicitly in the familiar form of a recognisably scientific hypothesis. The clear features of its logical structure make a useful contrast with the very different, and trickier, structures of the theories of *The Elements of Law* and *Leviathan*.

In *The Elements* Hobbes begins his account of the passions by asserting that the motion in the head, which is what the "conceptions and apparitions" of sense and imagination *really* are, continues to the heart, and "of necessity must there either *help* or *hinder* the motion which is called *vital*; when it *helpeth*, it is called *delight, contentment*, or *pleasure*, which is nothing really but motion about the heart . . .: but when such motion *weakeneth* or hindereth the vital motion, then it is called *pain*" (I vii I). In contrast with *De Corpore*, where Hobbes constructs a quite detailed hypothesis about inner mechanisms, and is able to offer the hypothesis as an *explanation* of the phenomena of pleasure and desire, here he merely asserts that motion in the head continues to the heart, affecting the vital motion, but he does not make any attempt to describe *how* it operates. He goes on to say that when the motion coming from the head helps the vital motion it is called "pleasure". Then he goes on:

This motion, in which consisteth pleasure or pain, is also a solicitation or provocation either to draw near to the thing that pleaseth, or to retire from the thing that displeaseth. And this solicitation is the endeavour or internal beginning of animal motion, which when the object delighteth, is called APPETITE; when it displeaseth, it is called AVERSION, in respect of the displeasure present; but in respect of the displeasure expected, FEAR (I vii 2. See also I vii 7 and I x 2).

Now there are two different directions in which it is possible to develop an interpretation of this passage.

I. Remembering that in *The Elements* the predominant theory of method is a conventionalist account of science (see Chapter Four, Section 2) as a system of necessary truths derived from definitions; and noticing that most of the propositions in the section to which this passage belongs are offered *as* definitions; one may think that Hobbes is establishing certain *logical equivalences* by appealing to definitions.

Thus Hobbes is asserting that there is a connexion between "appe-tite" and "pleasure" because "appetite" *means* "endeavour towards that which pleases". "Being pleasurably affected by something", on this view, means the same as "being affected by something so as to have an endeavour towards it". Hobbes concludes a part of the dis-cussion here with the words, "So that pleasure, love, and appetite, which is also called desire, are divers names for divers considerations of the same thing" (I vii 2). That suggests, perhaps, that what Hobbes has in mind is a distinction in respect of two different ways of talking about the same thing. The phenomenon in question is a person's reaction to an object. This reaction can be described either as a *state* of the agent, in which case the word "pleasure" is used, or as an *activity*, in which case the appropriate word is "appetite" or "desire".

2. But such an interpretation is prompted more by a desire to make Hobbes's practice in *The Elements* conform with the views on method which he expounds there than by the actual details of his argument. For "pleasure" is initially defined by Hobbes as a certain state of the vital motion—its being "helped". "Endeavour" is an internal motion towards something, the "internal beginning of animal motion". This suggests that what Hobbes is saying is that the phenomenon of pleasure and desire is a *sequence* of motions: first, an internal motion from the head to the heart, caused by the perception of an object; *then* a quickening of the vital motion, which is called "pleasure"; *then* an internal motion "towards" the object, which is called "endeavour". That is a sequence of different and distinguishable motions, each caused by the preceding one, and there is an obvious logical gap be-tween the propositions "Bloggs's vital motion quickens" and "Bloggs has an internal motion towards an object". Of course the gap between "pleasure" and "endeavour" could be easily enough closed by, for example, defining "endeavour" as "motion towards an object caused by the pleasure caused by the perception of the object". Only some such heroic measure can preserve a necessary connexion between "pleasure" and "desire". But Hobbes has already seemed to define "endeavour" *simply* as "an internal motion towards something" ("the endeavour or internal beginning of animal motion"), and at all events he has given an account within which pleasure and the internal be-ginning of animal motion are different motions. If "endeavour" is *defined* as "the internal beginning of animal motion *caused by pleasure*"

then he leaves open the possibility of internal beginnings of animal motion *not* caused by pleasure; and he gives no reason for excluding these from consideration. It seems obvious that he does not believe that these *are* possible. But then the proposition that every internal beginning of animal motion is caused by pleasure is not a necessary proposition within Hobbes's system. That would raise no difficulty if we were dealing with *De Corpore*, but in *The Elements* Hobbes makes no allowance for hypotheses.

Further, the words" solicitation" and "provocation" raise problems. Hobbes's account of pleasure and desire, as so far considered, describes a sequence of internal motions, such that the perception of an object causes that motion which is called "pleasure", which in turn causes that motion which is called "endeavour". Thus what we are dealing with is the connexion between endeavour and some actual, present pleasure. A word like "solicitation", however, surely suggests *expected* rather than *present* pleasure. Soliciting is a matter of *inviting* or *enticing*, of holding out the promise or possibility of something agreeable. Hobbes, indeed, is aware of the difference, because he distinguishes explicitly here between "aversion", which is endeavour in respect of a *present* displeasure, and "fear", which is endeavour in respect of an *expected* displeasure (*Elements*, I vii 2). (In *Leviathan* the same distinction is made, except that "aversion" is substituted for "fear" and "hate" for "aversion"—see *Leviathan*, VI 32.) A similar distinction can also be made between present and expected pleasure, and in *Leviathan* Hobbes distinguishes these explicitly in terms of "love" and "desire". But this side of the distinction is simply omitted in *The Elements*.

Now Kant was later (in the *Anthropology* and elsewhere) to define taking pleasure in *x* in terms of the disposition to pursue *x*. There is some plausibility in this. At least a case can be made for arguing that to say that some present state of mine is pleasurable is the same as to say that I am disposed to preserve my present state in that respect, and to pursue its continuance. This is not altogether remote from some aspects of Hobbes's analysis. For the notion of an endeavour is the notion of the internal beginning of an overt action. But an endeavour does not necessarily result in an overt action: I may desire to drink and yet not actually drink—perhaps because I also desire to drive safely. In such a case no actual drinking follows my desire to drink. But it is still the case that I would have drunk if I had not wanted to drive safely. An important part, at least, of the concept of having an endeavour is that it is being in a state in which one is *disposed* to do something. Then when Hobbes asserts a connexion between pleasure and endeavour, he may be taken to be claiming that my presently finding *x* pleasurable is the same as my presently being disposed to act so as to preserve *x*.

But such an analysis is not so helpful when it comes to *expected* pleasure. For on this analysis, to say that I expect that *x* will be pleasurable will be the same as to say that I expect that when (or if) *x* is present I shall (or would) be disposed to preserve it; and there is no logical connexion between the propositions "I am now disposed to pursue *x*" and "when (or if) *x* is present I shall (or would) be disposed to preserve it", because there is no contradiction in saying that I am *not* now disposed to pursue *x*, although when (or if) *x* is present I shall (or would) be disposed to preserve it. The account that Hobbes has given, then, may on this interpretation establish a connexion between present pleasure and desire, but it fails to establish any necessary connexion between present desire and *expected* pleasure.

Yet one of the central propositions of his account is that pleasure is a "solicitation". It is not merely that as a matter of English usage this word suggests expected pleasure, so that Hobbes would seem to be implying that desire is necessarily self-regarding, since to endeavour *is* to be "solicited" by (the promise of) pleasure. The fact is that the later development of his argument presupposes such a view. For he goes on to argue that human beings are dominated by fear of death and desire for precedence—that is, that the dominant pattern of motivation is a person's desire *now* to bring about a future pleasure (in precedence) and to avert a future pain (in dying). His account of pleasure and desire, so far as we have considered it, fails to provide Hobbes with the premisses which he needs for the later steps in his argument.

The reason for this failure is, I think, that what Hobbes needs in *The Elements* is an *hypothesis* about human nature—that human beings are invariably self-regarding in their desires. But the conventionalist approach required by the methodological theory of *The Elements* limits him to working with and from definitions. So he disguises the hypothesis and hangs definitions all round it, and the reader is invited to accept it as if it had all the authority of a proposition which is true by virtue of the definitions of its terms.

## 5 A NEUTRAL ANALYSIS (IN *LEVIATHAN*)

The account of pleasure and desire which Hobbes gives in *Leviathan* is very different from those given in *The Elements* and *De Corpore*. His first step is to distinguish between *vital* and *voluntary* motions. Voluntary motions are those which are done "in such manner as is first fancied in our minds", while vital motions are those, such as breathing, excretion, the circulation of the blood, and so forth, "to which motions there needs no help of imagination" (VI 31). (This gives a different meaning to the term "vital motion" from its meaning in *The Elements* and *De Corpore*. There "vital motion" was the name specifically of a certain motion around the heart, with which pleasure could be identified. But in *Leviathan* at this point of the argument, it is the name for a class of many different kinds of bodily motions, which have nothing in common beyond their being bodily motions, except the fact that they are not voluntary.) Hobbes goes on to claim that voluntary motions are preceded by very small internal motions, which are the "small beginnings" of voluntary motion, and which are called "endeavours". I have argued in Section 2 of this chapter that Hobbes's account of "voluntary motion" and "endeavour" is not in all respects as clear as it might be, but that the concept of an endeavour which is developed in *Leviathan* is the concept of some state of a person such that, if unchecked, it will result in an overt action towards some preconceived objective.

Now nothing whatever is said or assumed by Hobbes about the *nature* of the objectives of human endeavours. Specifically, he does *not* say that what one desires is always some (present or expected) pleasure. What he does say about pleasure, once he has got round to discussing it, is something very different indeed from what he has said in *The Elements* and *De Corpore*. He says that to call something "good" is to express one's desire for it (VI 32), and he goes on to say that pleasure is "the appearance, or sense of good" (VI 33). This is because he has already defined "pleasure" as the name of the appearance of the internal motion called "appetite". This may or may not be a good account of "pleasure". What is quite clear about it is that pleasure is given no important part to play in the analysis of desire. On the contrary, on this account, a desire must already exist before it is possible to talk about pleasure.

It is at this point that Hobbes slips in a remark about vital motion which sums up in a single sentence all the differences between *Leviathan* and the other works. He says: "This motion, which is called appetite, and for the appearance of it *delight*, and *pleasure*, seemeth to be a corroboration of vital motion, and a help there-unto . . ." (VI 33). This seems to be the more restricted meaning of "vital motion" given to the term in *The Elements* and *De Corpore*. But whether that is so, or not, the important thing is that although Hobbes says that this motion, the appearance of which is called pleasure, seems to be a "help" to vital motion, he does not say that we seek such help. The connexion between vital motion and pleasure and desire, indeed, is offered as a speculation ("it seemeth to be a corroboration"), and as one which is so unimportant that it can be casually mentioned in a single sentence and then dismissed. It is, of course, precisely the sort of hypothesis which he was prepared to take great trouble constructing in *De Corpore*. This casual attitude towards an hypothesis is a piece of practice which is consistent with the absence of an hypothetico-deductive *theory*. There is a very marked contrast with *The Elements*. There Hobbes was committed to the demonstrative method required by his conventionalist theory. Hence he presented his argument as resting on definitions. But he smuggled in an egoistic hypothesis, without recognising that it was an hypothesis, with the result that his argument became confused and broken-backed. But here in *Leviathan*, where the production of hypotheses is precluded by the method which he has prescribed for himself, the hypothesis appears, but is hung around with red flags and warning signs which separate it off from the main flow of traffic. The language is hesitant, the suggestion is thrown out in a tiny paragraph which stands all on its own, and the hypothesis plays no part at all in the subsequent development of the argument.

The feature of Hobbes's argument which most calls for comment is the fact that there seems to be very little to comment *on*. In Section 2 of this chapter I have suggested that if Hobbes's account is regarded as a general analysis of the concept of a voluntary action it is not a very impressive piece of work, because it ignores a vast number of distinctions that would have to be allowed for; and further, that the detail of his account of voluntary action is confusing because some of what he says is appropriate only to the simplest case of reaction to a present physical stimulus, which causes an endeavour, whereas at other times an endeavour is conceived of as caused, not by the *perception* of an *actual object*, but by the *thought* of a *possible action*. Now what Hobbes is interested in in *Leviathan* is not at all the behaviour-patterns of solitary individuals faced by delectable apples, but the motives and deliberations of people in political contexts. The endeavours which matter are those which are based on long-term calculations about power and security, and assessments of the possibilities of conflict or co-operation. There is every justification, then, for rejecting those elements of Hobbes's account which represent motivation as a simple matter of stimulus and response, and for preferring the more generalised analysis of endeavour which also he offers. On this general analysis, then, voluntary actions are those which "depend upon a precedent thought of *whither, which way, and what*"; and an endeavour is the beginnings of a voluntary action—i.e., a state of a person which will, if unchecked, result in an overt action towards some preconceived objective. If the objective is conceived of positively as the bringing about of a state of affairs it is called "desire", and if negatively as the averting of a state of affairs it is called "aversion". What Hobbes has to say about pleasure is that it is the appearance of that state which is called "appetite" or "desire", and that, of course, is equivalent to saying that it is the appearance of "good", since to say that something is good is simply to express one's desire for it.

Thus all that Hobbes has done is to define one or two psychological concepts—the "endeavour"-family—in the most general terms. His account of "pleasure" may or may not be important, but its deficiencies can be measured only against the importance of the concept in his subsequent arguments, and that is negligible. What is important is that no hypothesis about the nature of the *objectives* of desires—neither an egoistic nor any other kind of hypothesis—is incorporated in, presupposed or implied by the account. And that is a fact which is of obvious significance, since at the correspondingly early stages of the discussion in *The Elements* and *De Corpore* an egoistic position had already been adopted.

## 6 THE PARTICULAR PASSIONS

Having completed his account of the fundamental psychological concepts, Hobbes goes on to provide a string of definitions of words for particular passions—"hope", "despair", "benevolence", "jealousy", and so forth. These are laid out systematically, and developed out of each other. Thus "hope" is defined as "appetite, with an opinion of attaining", "confidence" as "constant hope". There is not very much that is interesting in these definitions. But there are two of them which show a significant change from the corresponding accounts in *The Elements*.

Thus he takes "benevolence", "good will" and "charity" as synonyms, and defines them as "desire of good to another" (VI 34). That is all he has to say about them. In *The Elements*, by contrast, Hobbes discusses charity at greater length, and goes to some trouble to construct an egoistic account of it. He explains that helping his friends or family gives a man a great sense of his own power, while helping strangers is done either to placate them or to purchase their friendship (I ix 17). This egoistic element is completely absent from *Leviathan*, where Hobbes confines himself to a bare definition. Of course it would be a mistake to attach too much importance to that. Nevertheless it is a *fact*, which ought not to be completely ignored, that in *Leviathan* an egoistic account has been excluded from a place where it might have been expected to appear.

There are differences also in the accounts of "pity" given in *The Elements* and in *Leviathan*. In *The Elements* Hobbes writes: "*Pity* is *imagination* or *fiction* of *future* calamity to ourselves, proceeding from the sense of *another* man's calamity" (I ix 10). "Pity" here is *defined as* the imagining of a calamity to oneself that arises from perceiving another man's distress. Hobbes goes on: "But when it lighteth on such as we think have not deserved the same, the compassion is greater, because then there appeareth more probability that the same may happen to us: for, the evil that happeneth to an innocent man, may happen to every man." What Hobbes seems to be suggesting here is that pity is really the fear that a calamity may fall upon oneself: one is distressed by the distress of others just to the extent that the occurrence of calamity to another makes the occurrence of a similar calamity to oneself more "probable". Certainly such an account of pity is consistent with the egoistic account of the passions which is developed in *The Elements*. But although the account given in *Leviathan* is superficially similar, there are some substantial differences. In the first place, in *Leviathan* Hobbes writes: "*Grief*, for the calamity of another, is PITY; and ariseth from the imagination that the like

calamity may befall himself" (VI 37). Here "pity" is defined as
for the calamity of another", and it is asserted that it "ariseth f
the imagination that the like calamity may befall himself", wherea
in *The Elements* it was defined as "imagination or fiction of future
calamity to ourselves". I think that this may be more than merely a
trivial difference because, in the second place, Hobbes goes on in
*Leviathan* to say that pity "therefore is called also COMPASSION,
and in the phrase of this time a FELLOW-FEELING: and therefore
for calamity arising from great wickedness, the best men have the
least pity; and for the same calamity, those have least pity that think
themselves least obnoxious to the same". That passage is not entirely
unambiguous. It *could* be read just as a restatement of the position
expressed in *The Elements*. But if one were not already determined to
put an egoistic interpretation upon it, the more natural way to take
it would be as (i) a definition of "pity" (as "grief, for the calamity of
another"), and (ii) an account of how it is that we come to be able
to have such a feeling—namely, through being able to put ourselves
in the other person's shoes. There is nothing very shocking in saying
that we cannot feel compassion for another unless we can imagine his
distress as if it were our own. That is very different from saying that
pity for another is merely the *fear* that a similar calamity may fall on
oneself. The reference to "probability" in *The Elements* suggests the
egoistic account, but the different account in *Leviathan*, omitting any
reference to probability, is at least as susceptible of a non-egoistic as
of an egoistic interpretation. It is rather like Hume's concept of
"sympathy".

## 7 "GOOD" AND "EVIL"

In the middle of his exposition of the elementary psychological concepts in *Leviathan* Hobbes slips in a brief account of the use of the words
"good" and "evil":

But whatsoever is the object of any man's appetite or desire, that is it
which he for his part calleth *good*: and the object of his hate and
aversion, *evil*: and of his contempt, *vile* and *inconsiderable*. For these
words of good, evil and contemptible, are ever used with relation to
the person that useth them: there being nothing simply and absolutely so. . . . (*Leviathan*, VI 32.)

analysis of "good" and "bad" is an element of
Hobbes's argument, and it is a topic which he
to time. At this stage, however, there are only
ich need making.

subjectivism and egoism are obviously not the
hat the use of "good" and "bad" is to express the
ot to say anything at all about the objects of
these desires.

The second is that this is one place where Hobbes does actually try to make *use* of his materialistic account of life and the world. He precedes his subjectivist account of "good" and "evil" with the sentence: "And because the constitution of a man's body is in continual mutation, it is impossible that all the same things should always cause in him the same appetites, and aversions: much less can all men consent, in the desire of almost any one and the same object" (VI 32). This, combined with the assertion that the use of "good" and "evil" is to express the speaker's desires, gives the conclusion that people will tend to be inconsistent and in conflict in their opinions about "good" and "evil", which is important to the later development of Hobbes's argument. So this seems to be one place where Hobbes's materialism plays an actual and important part in the argument. It would be a mistake, however, to attach a great deal of significance to it. In the first place, it is a very *bad* argument. Even if Hobbes is correct in believing that the nature of a man's desires is determined by bodily factors, the "continual mutation" of his body would not necessarily involve any mutation in his desires. Men's bodies *are*, of course, in a state of continual mutation, with cells dying and being replaced by new ones, but this does not *necessarily* involve any change in the *functioning* of the body. In the second place, it is an unnecessary argument, because quite independently of any materialistic hypothesis one might expect that as a person lived through different situations and came to acquire and develop new beliefs, his pattern of desires and evaluations would change also, and would not always resemble those of other people whose experience was different. In any case, it is just a fact, however it is to be explained, that such differences do exist. And in the third place, when Hobbes later discusses the point in more detail he mentions a number of sources of the differences in desires and evaluations, and specifies "different tempers, customs, and doctrines of men", but he does not so much as mention bodily mutation (XV 104). And in an earlier discussion of the "inconstant signification" of value words, bodily mutation is only one of the factors which he mentions: "For though the nature of that we conceive, be the same; yet the diversity of our reception of it, in respect of different constitutions of body, and prejudices of opinion, gives every thing a tincture of our different passions" (IV 24). Hobbes's materialism is, as ever, a very dispensable part of his argument.

The third point about Hobbes's account of the use of "good" is that it differs typically from the account given in *The Elements*. The latter is very similar to what Hobbes says in *Leviathan*, except that in *The Elements* he says that a man calls "good" that which *pleases* him (I vii 3). It follows from that, of course, that a man calls the things which he desires "good"; but that follows only because in *The Elements* Hobbes claims that men desire things because they please. But in *Leviathan* no such intermediate step is necessary, because Hobbes's claim is simply that the use of "good" is to express desires directly. Thus the difference between the account of "desire" given in *The Elements*, which depends on a prior definition of "pleasure", and the account given in *Leviathan*, in which "pleasure" is a derivative and subsidiary notion, is reflected also in the analysis of "good" and "evil". An egoistic view is, in fact, embodied in the account of "good" given in *The Elements* but not in the *Leviathan* account.

## 8 DELIBERATION AND THE WILL

The next stage of Hobbes's argument is an account of deliberation and the will, which, like his account of the fundamental psychological concepts, is very brief and very general. It is remarkable for the number of questions which it leaves unanswered. Regarded as a contribution to the philosophical analysis of "volition" it has very few merits. Hobbes begins with a general account of deliberation:

When in the mind of man, appetites, and aversions, hopes, and fears, concerning one and the same thing, arise alternately; and divers good and evil consequences of the doing, or omitting the thing propounded, come successively into our thoughts; so that sometimes we have an appetite to it; sometimes an aversion from it; sometimes hope to be able to do it; sometimes despair, or fear to attempt it; the whole sum of desires, aversions, hopes and fears continued till the thing be either done, or thought impossible, is that we call DELIBERATION (*Leviathan*, VI 37).

Of things known or thought to be impossible there can be no deliberation (and therefore none of the past, which it is impossible to change). "And it is called *deliberation*; because it is a putting an end to the *liberty* we had of doing, or omitting, according to our own appetite, or aversion." Hobbes now introduces the concepts of "act of will" and "voluntary act". Philosophers (and others too) have sometimes constructed the notion of "will" either as something distinct from desire or as a special kind of desire. Thus a person who very much *wants* to do something which he ought not to do—take more than his fair share of pudding, or desert from the field of battle —may be exhorted to overcome his desires by an "act of will". It has sometimes been suggested that although we may be pushed this way or that by our desires, we are also rational beings who are able to reflect, so that sometimes we can reason about our desires and conclude that, for moral or prudential reasons, we ought not to yield to them. On this view an act of will is simply resisting one's desires in accordance with rational reflection. Some have thought that no one could do *x* reflectively unless he had a desire to do *x*. That still leaves a place for the notion of will, so long as it is possible to distinguish rational from non-rational desires, for the opposition between will and desire is then the opposition between rational and non-rational desire. Hobbes, however, rejects such views. The will is simply the last appetite or aversion in a deliberation—the endeavour "immediately adhering to the action, or to the omission thereof" (VI 38). "Will" cannot be defined as "rational appetite", Hobbes argues, because a voluntary act is one which proceeds from the will and if "will" meant "rational appetite" a voluntary act against reason would then be impossible. "But if instead of a rational appetite, we shall say an appetite resulting from a precedent deliberation, then the definition is the same that I have given here. *Will* therefore *is the last appetite in deliberating*" (VI 38).

That is what Hobbes has to say about deliberation and the will in *Leviathan*, and it is not very much. In the first place, it is at first sight a little surprising that Hobbes should assert that deliberation ends when "the thing be either done, or thought impossible". Suppose that I am sitting at a desk in the evening, working. I may think of going for a walk before sunset, and the thought of this may make me have an "appetite" to go. I may think, further, that the interruption to my work will compel me to stay up late, and then I may have an "aversion". I may think of this and that, veering between appetite and aversion as Hobbes describes. Then a friend may come in and divert me with brilliant conversation, so that I just forget all about going for a walk. My deliberation will have ended, but not either in my going for the walk or in my thinking it impossible. Presumably what Hobbes means by the "end" of a deliberation is not so much merely the (chronologically) last point of the process but something which is also a *conclusion*. If deliberation is merely interrupted or abandoned, then in a sense it has ended, but it has not been concluded. Yet this does not remove the whole difficulty. My work may be so urgent to me that although the thought of a walk momentarily tempts me, knowledge of the disastrous consequences of interruption may give rise to an overwhelming aversion. I may then give the matter of a walk no further attention. In such a case I have not abandoned my deliberating but have brought it to a negative conclusion. Yet according to Hobbes the deliberation cannot *end* until either I go for the walk before sunset or else my thinking that the sun has set makes me think that it is impossible for me to go for a walk before sunset. What Hobbes says is that "it is called *deliberation*; because it is an end to the *liberty* we had of doing, or omitting, according to our own appetite, or aversion" (VI 37). One thing that he has altogether left out of his account is *decision*. It might seem more natural to say that what concludes deliberation about doing or not doing *x* is a decision either to do or not to do *x*. "Deliberating about *x*" might be defined as "trying to reach a decision either to do or not to do *x*". Such a definition would be in accordance with much common usage. *Being undecided* typically calls for deliberation, and deliberation is *concluded* by a decision in a way in which it is not concluded merely by being interrupted or abandoned. But deciding to do *x* is not the same as doing *x*, since I may make decisions in advance, still less is deciding not to do *x* the same thing as thinking *x* impossible. Hobbes, then, is departing from the usual meaning of "deliberation", and extending it to cover the whole process which is terminated only by doing the thing in question or coming to think it impossible. But there is perhaps some justification for the artificial definition which he insists on. For although deliberation may aim at decision, yet a decision terminates deliberation only *provisionally*. After deliberating, I may decide *now* to go to the dentist tomorrow. But later today my toothache abates and my mind is filled with visions of the dental torture chamber. So I develop an overwhelming aversion to going to the dentist tomorrow and desire to put off the visit as long as possible. Once again I am undecided, and deliberating, and my decision to go to the dentist tomorrow is as if it had never been. Such a thing always *may* happen, although often it does not. But because always it *may*, there is some justification for regarding a deliberation as not *finally* concluded until there is no longer anything to deliberate about, either because the thing has been done or has come to be thought impossible.

In *The Elements* there is just one sentence in which Hobbes takes account of *interrupted* deliberation. "In *deliberations* interrupted, as they may be by *diversion* of other business, or by *sleep*, the last *appetite* of such part of the deliberation is called *intention*, or *purpose*" (I xii 9). That is all he has to say about it, and in *Leviathan* he does not say even as much as that.

Secondly, there are a great many distinctions which Hobbes completely ignores. It is not merely that he does not mention decisions, but that he gives a brief and simple account of "voluntary" without discussing "involuntary", "intentional", "unintentional", "deliberate" (the adjective), and other related expressions. An involuntary act is not the same as an unintentional act, for example, and any discussion of *excuses* might have to take account of the difference. Although Hobbes does discuss excuses at a later stage (in chapter XXVII of *Leviathan*), the main line of his argument does not require him to engage in a detailed analysis of volition and deliberation. His chief concern is to reach conclusions about political obligation. What Hobbes is going to be arguing is that there are certain rules of conduct, embodied in the "Law of Nature", which are relevant to all human deliberations, and which are necessary for avoiding the calamities of a state of nature. The adequacy of his account of deliberation depends only on whether it makes possible the discussion of these issues, and not on whether it provides a satisfactory general theory of volition.

## 9 APPARENT GOOD

The account of deliberation in *Leviathan* is followed by a brief and uninteresting digression on "the forms of speech by which the passions are expressed", and that is followed by a discussion of *apparent* good and evil, the considerable significance of which lies in what is omitted.

Hobbes begins by saying that "in deliberation, the appetites, and aversions, are raised by foresight of the good and evil consequences, and sequels of the action whereof we deliberate" (VI 39). Therefore deliberation involves "the foresight of a long chain of consequences, of which very seldom any man is able to see to the end. But for so far as a man seeth, if the good in those consequences be greater than the evil, the whole chain is that which writers call *apparent*, or *seeming good*." So, Hobbes concludes, the man who is best at deliberating, and at advising others, is he who through experience and reason is best at calculating consequences. There is nothing very exciting about this as it stands. Hobbes raises and dismisses the matter in a single paragraph. What he says, within the context of the definitions already provided in *Leviathan*, amounts to little more than a few tautologies. Since "good" has been defined as a word which a person applies to *X* to express his desire for *X*, *of course* appetites are raised by foresight of good consequences. If Hobbes had not already defined "good" in terms of desire, then this little story about apparent good would be a *theory* about the determination of desire. Of course it might be that Hobbes had failed to recognise the tautologous nature of these propositions, and intended them to be taken as a theory. But he attaches no apparent importance to them, and presents the notion of apparent good, not as a concept which is needed within his own system, but as a concept employed by others, which can in fact be related to his own system—"the whole chain is *that which writers call* apparent, or seeming good". What Hobbes is doing, in fact, is to *reduce* a certain concept, for which he himself is not responsible, to terms of the elements of his own system.

That point needs emphasising, because it is one more of the respects in which the account given in *Leviathan* diverges from accounts given by Hobbes elsewhere. In *The Elements* Hobbes discusses deliberation without specifically mentioning apparent good.

But a rather similar notion does appear at an earlier stage of the discussion in *The Elements*. Hobbes points out that usually we cannot choose things singly, taking the good and leaving the bad. What we have to accept is something more like a chain, with inseparable links, some good and some bad—"as for example, the pleasures of sin, and the bitterness of punishment, are inseparable; as is also labour and honour, for the most part. Now when in the *whole chain*, the *greater part* is good, the *whole* is called *good* . . ." (I vii 7). Hobbes has already defined "good", not in terms of "desire", as in *Leviathan*, but in terms of what pleases. On *this* account, then, calculations about the goodness on balance (or in the language of *Leviathan*, the apparent goodness) of chains of consequences are essentially self-regarding, because they are calculations not merely about what one on the whole prefers, but about what one on the whole prefers *because* promising the greater pleasure on balance. Hobbes's example here fits this pattern of self-regarding calculation—the pleasures of sin weighed against the bitterness of punishment. Similarly, when he comes to discuss the will in *The Elements*, Hobbes talks about the *cause* of appetite and will, and says: "the propounding of the benefits and of harms, that is to say, of reward and punishment, is the cause of our appetite, and of our fears, and therefore also of our wills, so far forth as we believe that such rewards and benefits as are propounded, shall arrive unto us . . ." (I xii 6). In *Leviathan* the discussion of the will wholly omits any mention of the self-regarding notions of reward, benefit and punishment. Again, the description of deliberation in *The Elements* is very like that given in *Leviathan*, except in one respect. In both accounts deliberation is described as an alternation of appetites and aversions (or "fears"), and "will" is identified with the last appetite or aversion. In *The Elements*, however, referring to the conception of evil consequences which can be an element in deliberation, Hobbes writes of "some conception of evil *to happen to us* by such actions" (I xii 1), whereas in *Leviathan* he refers merely to "evil consequences" (VI 37).

Thus in *The Elements* the account which is given of deliberation, of the will, and of "good on balance", presents deliberation as essentially self-regarding—as the calculating of how best to procure pleasures, benefits, rewards for oneself, and how to avoid pain, punishment, and evil *happening to oneself*. But in *Leviathan* the account is completely generalised. Deliberation is merely about good and evil, and there is nothing in the description of deliberation, nor in the definitions of the terms involved, which entails any theory about how the good and the evil are to be conceived.

Nevertheless, that is not to say that Hobbes has changed his own view of human nature. There are passages in *Leviathan* in which an egoistic view is quite clearly expressed. One which it is relevant to consider in this context occurs in a later chapter of *Leviathan*. Hobbes argues that in a state of nature everyone would have a natural right to everything. The consequence of this would be universal misery and frustration. Therefore one ought to be prepared to lay down one's natural right to everything and be content merely with as much liberty against others as they will allow against oneself. That is Hobbes's second law of nature. The whole of his arguments about the nature of political obligation and the powers of the sovereign depend on this requirement that the individual should renounce certain rights. Nevertheless some rights, he argues, *cannot* be renounced:

. . . of the voluntary acts of every man, the object is some *good to himself*. And therefore there be some rights, which no man can be understood by any words, or other signs, to have abandoned or transferred. As first a man cannot lay down the right of resisting them, that assault him by force, to take away his life; because he cannot be understood to aim thereby, at any good to himself (XIV 86–87).

This argument relies on an egoistic assumption about human nature, similar to the view expressed consistently in *The Elements* and *De Cive*. One might be tempted to regard this as a simple inconsistency—to contrast, on the one hand, some particular arguments which presuppose an egoistic view of human nature, with, on the other hand, the general account of the passions, and the main line of political argument, which are not egoistic. But that would be an over-simplification. The account of the passions given in *Leviathan* is non-egoistic, not in being contrary to all possible egoistic views, but in being abstracted from all consideration of the specific nature of actual human objectives. It is compatible with an egoistic account of motivation, as it is also with non-egoistic accounts. It leaves Hobbes free to argue that in some particular respects—or, for that matter, that in all respects—desires are essentially self-regarding. It leaves him *free* to argue thus, but it does not give him any justification for so doing. His position, then, is very different from his position in *The Elements* or in *De Corpore*. For in *De Corpore* an egoistic view is presented as the only hypothesis which is adequate to explain the facts, while in *The Elements* it is built into a structure of necessary propositions derived from some rather doubtful definitions (see Chapter Five, Section 4). But in *Leviathan*, I have been arguing, the definitions are so generalised that they abstract altogether from consideration of the objectives of desires. Consequently the system of definitions in *Leviathan* does not allow Hobbes to present any egoistic view in the form of a set of necessary propositions. The logical status of propositions expressing an egoistic view in *Leviathan* is therefore doubtful and uncertain, and there would be an inconsistency, not in his views about human nature, but in the implied status of the propositions expressing these views, if egoistic views were to be expressed in propositions which were presented as logically necessary.

Then how does Hobbes present those propositions in *Leviathan* which embody an egoistic view? There is no general answer to that question. There is one place where Hobbes advances a sort of egoistic view as a tentative, empirical generalisation. Discussing "the natural condition of mankind", Hobbes says: "And therefore if any two men desire the same thing, which nevertheless they cannot both enjoy, they become enemies; and in the way to their end, which is principally their own conservation, and sometimes their delectation only, endeavour to destroy, or subdue one another" (XIII 81). An egoistic view is expressed here, but with heavy qualifications—"principally" and "sometimes". That is not language appropriate to necessary propositions. It is perfectly consistent for Hobbes to construct a generalised theory of the passions and then to present an egoistic view as something which is not derived from, and could not be derived from, the generalised account, but is a cautious, empirical generalisation *added* to the latter. The only inconsistency here is between the practice of incorporating such a proposition in his arguments, and the methodological theory of *Leviathan*, which limits "science" to necessary propositions. That will be an important inconsistency only if the offending proposition is itself an indispensable part of the argument. We shall see, however, that it need be regarded as nothing more than an aside.

His statement that the object of every voluntary act is some good to oneself is not similarly qualified and looks much more like a proposition which, if true at all, is necessarily true. For in the account given in *The Elements* it *is* a necessary proposition, and Hobbes seems simply to have transported it into *Leviathan*, to meet the needs of a particular argument, without recognising that it simply does not fit into the generalised account in *Leviathan*.

It remains true, nevertheless, that the account of deliberation and "good" in *Leviathan* differs from that given in *The Elements* in excluding any commitment to an egoistic view.


## 10 TWO CONCEPTS OF FELICITY

Hobbes concludes his discussion of deliberation with a brief account of what he calls "felicity", which, roughly, is the notion of the greatest good which a person can strive after. He discusses it in two places, one of which is a short paragraph at the end of chapter VI and the other a slightly longer paragraph at the beginning of chapter XI. On neither occasion has he very much to say, on neither occasion does he say it very satisfactorily, and what he says in the one place is not quite the same as what he says in the other.

On both occasions he restricts his discussion and its conclusions to the felicity of "this life", conceding that there is no knowing how different life in the hereafter may not be. "What kind of felicity God hath ordained to them that devoutly honour Him, a man shall no sooner know, than enjoy, being joys, that now are incomprehensible, as the word of Schoolmen *beatifical vision* is unintelligible" (VI 39). If Hobbes's religious protestations are taken seriously, this is to be regarded as an expression of simple piety.

On both occasions also, part of what he has to say is *negative*. Some had thought that it was possible to conceive of a *summum bonum* to which everyone could aspire for himself, such that, having attained it, a man would be completely satisfied—something, therefore, which would give him "perpetual tranquillity of mind". Hobbes consistently rejects this conception of felicity, and sometimes he gives reasons for rejecting it which do not depend simply on his own positive account of felicity. His argument in chapter VI is that "life itself is but motion, and can never be without desire, nor without fear, no more than without sense" (VI 39). Hobbes seems here to be harking back to his earlier argument that a man's desires must be unstable because his body is in a state of "continual mutation" (VI 32. See Section 2 of this chapter). In chapter XI, however, he says: "Nor can a man any more live, whose desires are at an end, than he, whose senses and imaginations are at a stand" (XI 63). Hobbes does not actually say here that the reason for this assertion is his belief that "life itself is but motion". It may be that that is what he had in mind. Or it may be that he is arguing, more generally, that life is inconceivable without change and activity (whether or not in the form of physical *motion*), and that to every change there must be a reaction of either desire or aversion. Some of the Buddha's followers once suggested to him that Nirvana was just a sort of nothing, and what Hobbes intends to express here may be some such view as that. He says so little that it is difficult to know exactly how to take it. What is more important is the positive account he gives of felicity, and the conclusions he draws. In fact he gives two positive accounts, one in chapter VI and one in chapter XI.

1. In chapter VI he says: "*Continual success* in obtaining those things which a man from time to time desireth, that is to say, continual prospering, is that men call FELICITY" (VI 39). There is no reason for supposing that the expression "success in obtaining those things" should be taken in a very narrow sense, to refer only to those desires which are for the obtaining of *things*, that is, physical objects. Hobbes recognises the existence of many desires which are not desires for material objects—benevolence, for example, which is desire of good to another, or curiosity, which is desire to know. Presumably "continual success in obtaining those things which a man from time to time desireth" means the same as "the continual realisation of the objectives of those desires which a man has from time to time". Now the question with which this discussion of Hobbes's account of the passions in *Leviathan* has been chiefly concerned is the question of how far, if at all, that account amounts to an egoistic theory. The description of felicity in terms of "continual success" does not seem to incorporate any egoistic notions, since it specifies merely the realisation of objectives but not their nature. If your objectives are predominantly non-self-regarding, then your pursuit of felicity will be the pursuit of non-self-regarding objectives.

Nevertheless, it is possible to imagine some difficult cases. People sometimes change very much as a result, for example, of physical conditions like brain tumours. Someone may change from being well-disposed to being ill-disposed to others. Suppose that you now desire the happiness of others but believe that you suffer from a diseased condition which is going to have the effect of making you want other people to be miserable. If you make felicity an over-riding objective, and secure for yourself now the power that will enable you to realise your future objectives, then in that case your pursuit of felicity is going to lead you to a course of action contrary to the direction of your present benevolent desires. In that case you would be subordinating the good of others (the objective of your present benevolent desires) to the pursuit of "your own" felicity. But of course there is nothing in the notion of felicity itself which would necessitate such a decision. Felicity is the continual realisation of *all* one's objectives, and that includes one's present objectives. If now you really care about the good of others, and foresee that something is going to make you ill-disposed towards them, you will not desire that your future objectives should be realised: you will desire that you should not change, that your future objectives should be consistent with your present objectives, and be realised. (That last proposition is not a psychological *generalisation*, but rather an analysis of what is implied in the statement that someone really cares about other people: if you foresaw that you would come to desire misfortune for others, and yet did not desire that this should not happen, we would not be entitled to say that now you really desired the good of others.) Felicity for you, then, consists in the realisation of your present objectives, including the objective of not changing so much as to come to have objectives incompatible with your present objectives; and in all of your objectives then being realised. If some of your objectives cannot be realised, then to that extent complete felicity is unattainable by you. If it is impossible for all of your objectives to be realised *because* some are incompatible with others, then you have to decide which to pursue. If the concept of felicity required you to make such a decision on the basis of aiming at those objectives the pursuit or realisation of which would give you the greatest pleasure or happiness, then to that extent an egoistic view would have been incorporated in the concept of felicity. But the concept of felicity which we are considering does not require that a decision between incompatible objectives should be made on the basis of pleasure or happiness, or indeed on any other specific basis. Felicity is the realisation of all of one's objectives, and if all of one's objectives cannot be realised then presumably the next best thing is the greatest possible degree of realisation. But nothing is implied about what the greatest degree of realisation consists in. It surely does not consist in merely the realisation of the greatest possible *number* of objectives, because this might be achieved by realising a lot of minor objectives at the cost of forgoing a few major objectives. One would not choose to forgo the realisation of major objectives for the sake of realising a few more minor objectives, because at least an important part of what one could mean by saying that something was a major objective for someone would be that he would not readily forgo its realisation.

This concept of felicity, then, is a very empty one. It amounts to nothing more than the realisation to the greatest extent possible of all one's objectives, and the proposition that a person, so far as he has objectives, will aim at felicity is a necessary, but not a very informative, proposition.

2. But in chapter XI of *Leviathan* a very different account is given. There he says:

Felicity is a continual progress of the desire, from one object to another; the attaining of the former, being still but the way to the latter. The cause whereof is, that the object of man's desire, is not to enjoy once only, and for one instant of time; but to assure for ever, the way of his future desire (XI 63).

In the first place, according to this formulation felicity requires not merely that *if* I have objectives they should be realised, but also that I should in fact continue to have objectives. "Continual success" (the formula of chapter VI) might mean no more than consistent and *uninterrupted* success in realising whatever objectives one had; so that if one of one's objectives involved the sacrifice of one's life, the process would then come to an end but would be felicity if it had been uninterruptedly successful. But if felicity is a "continual progress", so that the realisation of one objective is "still but the way" to another; and if "the object of man's desire is . . . to assure for ever the way of his future desire"; then *complete* felicity is achieved only in an *everlasting* life of uninterrupted success, and everyone must necessarily seek not only the realisation of whatever objectives he may come to have, but the indefinite prolongation of his own life.

But, secondly, Hobbes goes on also to draw a conclusion:

And therefore the voluntary actions, and inclinations of all men, tend, not only to the procuring, but also to the assuring of a contented life; and differ only in the way: which ariseth partly from the diversity of passions, in divers men; and partly from the difference of the knowledge, or opinion each one has of the causes, which produce the effect desired (XI 63).

The notion of contentment, or "a contented life", is not at all the same as the notion of the realisation of objectives. If my objective is your happiness, then when you become happy my objective is realised. But your becoming happy, although it is the realisation of my objective, may not make me contented, because I may not know that you are happy. Nor is aiming at the realisation of my objectives the same as aiming at my contentment. For I might think that the world was a bad place and desire that it should be a good place. If you then offered me a euphoric drug, and if I believed your claim that its effect would be to make me feel that the world was a good place, then I might either accept the drug, on the grounds that it was easier to take the drug than to attempt to make the world a good place, or reject it, on the grounds that what I desired was the improvement of the world and not merely the easing of my mind. If I took the drug, that would tend to show that all that I was aiming at was my own contentment. *What* I was aiming at, of course, was something complex: namely, to come to be in a state of believing (whether truly or falsely) that a certain objective of mine had been realised. If one feels that one's objectives have been, or are being, realised, then to that extent one has achieved contentment, and this does not depend on the actual realisation of the objectives, but simply on the state of mind of the person involved.

That, at least, is what is involved in the ordinary use of "contented". But perhaps Hobbes was using it in some special sense? That is always possible. It is a word which he seldom uses, and although in chapter VI he defines an enormous number of psychological terms, "contented" is not among them. But there is no reason for supposing that he is using it in any extraordinary way. What he asserts is that all voluntary actions of all men tend towards the same end, "and differ only in the way". Different sorts of people have different passions, and therefore different specific objectives, but in all cases the specific objectives are "ways" to, and are subordinated to, the over-riding objective of a contented life. That has very different implications from those of the account given in chapter VI. The concept of felicity defined in chapter VI is a formal concept—simply the notion of the greatest possible realisation of whatever objectives a person may have. But felicity, in the sense of contentment, is a *specific* objective. To pursue felicity, in the formal sense, is simply to pursue the objectives one happens to have, whatever these may be. To pursue felicity, in the sense of contentment, is to pursue a specific objective, namely a certain state of mind of oneself. Felicity in the formal sense can be achieved only through the achievement of the specific objectives one has, while felicity in the sense of contentment does not require the actual realisation of one's other objectives but merely the *feeling* that one's objectives have been realised. If one came to believe that one's major objectives could not be realised in one's lifetime, then the pursuit of them would not be incompatible with the pursuit of felicity in the formal sense, but it would be incompatible with the pursuit of felicity in the sense of contentment. Of course the sharp edges of this distinction can become blurred. If someone has objectives which he believes will not be realised in his lifetime—like the defeat of capitalism, or the defeat of communism—then the pursuit of these objectives will involve the pursuit of intermediate objectives, like the building up of a strong communist party on the one hand, or the discrediting of communism on the other. These intermediate objectives are steps on the way, and presumably contentment will be achieved in the feeling that they are being realised. Yet the distinction becomes sharp again if we think of a suitable case. Someone might have an objective which was very important to him —say, the well-being of his children. He might believe that only two courses were open to him, one of which would result in the happiness of his children, although it would result in his coming to feel that they were miserable, and the other of which would result in their misery, although it would also result in his coming to feel that they were happy. Such an extreme situation is very improbable, but it is not impossible. Your children believe that you are dead, and have adjusted themselves to it. You are in the hands of the secret police, who have an interest in sophisticated psychological experiments. They have graduated beyond the stage of merely making baby monkeys miserable in order to see how they react. They offer you a choice: they will either send your children abroad to grow up in a happy environment and then dose you with depressive and delusional drugs, or put your children in a concentration camp and dose you with delusional but euphoric drugs. They offer you convincing guarantees that your choice will in fact be implemented. They produce evidence that they have conducted this experiment before and have always kept to its terms. They are interested in collecting data about the reactions of different kinds of people to this sort of stimulus. (Of course this is a nightmare situation. But life with the secret police *is* a nightmare. The situation is unusual rather than improbable.) Now if felicity, in the sense of contentment, is an over-riding objective which it is *reasonable* for anyone, or, alternatively, *inevitable* for anyone, to prefer, then in this situation it is reasonable, or inevitable, that you should choose misery for your children and euphoria for yourself. But it is not at all clear that that choice *is* reasonable, and it is certainly not inevitable. If what Hobbes means by asserting that all voluntary actions tend towards a contented life, "and differ only in the way", is that people always choose what they believe will lead to contentment, then what he is saying is clearly untrue.

It is not merely untrue, however. It also has no business to be appearing in the pages of *Leviathan*. Hobbes makes no serious attempt to derive it from what has gone before, and, having produced it, he subsequently makes little use of it, and certainly no important use. The only argument he produces to support his first concept of felicity is in the words "because life itself is but motion, and can never be without desire, nor without fear, no more than without sense" (VI 39). All that that argument even purports to show is that so long as people are alive they are going to have objectives of some sort, but it does not show that these objectives are going even to include, still less to be dominated by, the objective of preserving one's own life. Since this "argument" is produced in the context of the merely formal concept of felicity it is not surprising, perhaps, that it supports nothing more than a vacuous conclusion. The argument, however, is different in the account of the second concept of felicity. There Hobbes says: "The cause whereof is, that the object of man's desire, is not to enjoy once only, and for one instant of time; but to assure for ever, the way of his future desire" (XI 63). It is difficult to tell which is the more shocking: Hobbes's brazen refusal even to attempt to connect this (patently false) proposition with his preceding arguments, or its irrelevance to the important political arguments which follow. The irrelevance of this concept of felicity is something which will be discussed in later chapters. But first there are two final elements of the foundations of Hobbes's political theory which need examining—the concepts of power and glory which, to some extent, mark the transition from Hobbes's account of *individual* human nature to his account of political relationships.

# CHAPTER SIX

# Power and Glory

THE concepts of power and glory are important elements of Hobbes's account of human nature as a basis of his political theory. Hobbes defines "power" in *Leviathan* as a man's "present means, to obtain some future apparent good" (x 56). If someone has any objectives at all, then, he cannot be indifferent to power, which is just the means to realising them. The exercise of power, however, may well involve one in conflict with others, because the exercise of power by one person may, and sometimes does, interfere with the exercise of power by another. (Communists, for example, cannot seek means to realise their objectives without directly or in effect preventing liberals from seeking the means to realise liberal objectives—and vice versa.) The concept of power, then, arises naturally in the discussion of individual desires, and also is politically significant. So much is obvious. What is not so obvious is the importance of "glory" and its connexion with power. Glory—in Hobbes's use of the word—is a certain state of mind of an individual which tends to bring him into conflict with others. Precisely what Hobbes means by it, and its relation to power, is a complex matter, because Hobbes says different and inconsistent things. The differences are important not merely because they do as a matter of fact exist but because if one fails to notice them and their significance one inevitably misinterprets an important part of the argument of *Leviathan*. Hobbes's discussion of power and glory in *Leviathan* is different from his discussions of them in *De Cive* and in *The Elements* both in what he actually says and in his manner of saying it. I think that it is possible to trace a pattern of development from the earliest view, in *The Elements*, through the account given in *De Cive*, to the latest version in *Leviathan*, and I shall consider each of these in turn. This development is of some importance in its own right, since it occurs in a concept of Hobbes's which both is interesting and is specially associated with Hobbes.

But it also has a further significance, in relation to Hobbes's *method*, both in theory and in practice.

## 1 LIFE AS A RACE

When Hobbes comes to discuss the state of nature in *The Elements* the essentials of his argument are apparently simple. Men are more or less equal in power with each other, because even the strongest is vulnerable and may easily be killed by the weakest. Therefore no man can rely simply on his own strength for security. Yet there is a need for some means of security, for there are certain aspects of human nature which lead inevitably to violent contention. Everyone wants to be "pre-eminent", out of a natural desire for glory; and many often desire the same thing, which "can neither be enjoyed in common, nor divided". And "moderate" men, who do not strive after pre-eminence but would be content with equality, are "obnoxious" to the vainly glorious, who hope to attain superiority even when they are inferior in power. Hence arises "mutual fear one of another", and a state of hopeless, perpetual war (I xiv 2–5).

Hobbes seems to have arrived here at a fairly sensible view of human nature. Apart from competition for scarce goods, which arises not so much from the limitations of human nature as from the limitations of the environment, the source of violence is the human capacity for glory. But Hobbes is allowing that there are moderate men who are willing to accord equality to others, and whose reasonable approach is defeated only by the existence of vainglorious men. Unfortunately, however, Hobbes has already discussed glory, and also power, at some length, and in very different terms.

In an earlier discussion Hobbes argues that *human* power is essentially relative: "because the power of one man resisteth and hindereth the effects of the power of another, *power* simply is no more, but the *excess* of the power of one above that of another: for equal powers opposed, destroy one another" (I viii 4). What Hobbes might mean by this is that since the power of another is always *potentially* a hindrance to one's own power, the latter cannot be safely and surely relied on unless it exceeds the former. In fact, of course, Hobbes neither expresses nor implies such a restriction, and the discussion of glory which follows in the next chapter of *The Elements*, along with the simile of the race in which he sums up his whole account of the passions, commit him clearly to the view that the power of one person is not merely potentially, but actually, invariably and necessarily, a hindrance to the exercise of the power of others. For Hobbes goes on to define "glory" in these terms: "Glory, or internal gloriation or triumph of the mind, is the passion which proceedeth from the imagination or conception of our *own power* above the power of him that contendeth with us" (I ix I). Now he has already distinguished just two kinds of pleasure. There is *"sensual"* pleasure specifically associated with the body, and *"joy"* or "delight of the mind", which is pleasure "not particular to any part of the body" (I vii 8). In I ix Hobbes discusses a number of passions which fall under the second head, but they are all variants of glory, for he says of them that they consist "in the pleasure men have, or displeasure from the signs of honour or dishonour done unto them" (I viii 8), and honour is "the acknowledgement of power" (I viii 5). He discusses glory and its variants (for example, *laughter*, which is *"sudden glory* arising from some sudden *conception* of some *eminency* in ourselves, by *comparison* with the *infirmity* of others, or with our own formerly" (I ix 13); or *charity*, of which Hobbes says that "there can be no greater argument to a man, of his own power, than to find himself able not only to accomplish his own desires, but also to assist other men in theirs" (I ix 16)), and finally ends the discussion appropriately with the famous simile of the race. He likens the life of man to a race, which "we must suppose to have no other *goal*, nor other *garland*, but being foremost" (I ix 21). He defines a number of passions in terms of progress in the race—"To see another fall, is disposition to *laugh*"—and ends:

> Continually to be out-gone is *misery*.
> Continually to out-go the next before, is *felicity*.
> And to forsake the course, is to die.

There are, I think, a number of points of interest here. In the first place, according to the view expressed in *Leviathan* felicity involves a constant striving after objectives, but the nature of these objectives is not in any way specified or limited, but according to the doctrine of *The Elements* it consists in the successful pursuit of one particular objective, pre-eminence over others.

In the second place, there is no foundation in the detailed account of the passions in general, or of glory in particular, for the notion of the "moderate" man who willingly accepts equality with others. Power is essentially power in excess of the power of others, and glory is the conception of superior power. Vain glory, on this account, is not *excessive* glory but *unreal* glory—"the *fiction*, which is also imagination, of actions done by ourselves, which never were done, is *glorying*; but because it begetteth no appetite nor endeavour to any further attempt, it is merely *vain* and unprofitable; as when a man imagineth himself to do the actions whereof he readeth in some *romance* . . . and this is called *vain glory*" (I ix I). Every man, on this account, inevitably strives to be, and to be admitted as, superior to others. There is, of course, room for some sort of concept of a moderate man, within the structure of Hobbes's argument as a whole. The only alternatives are either to accept the restraints of society, limiting the pursuit of power, or else to seek power without limitation, and lapse into the state of nature. Since the state of nature is above all a state of insecurity in which no power can be effectively exercised or relied on, the man who refuses to adopt the policy of moderation is a fool who is refusing to abandon the pursuit of something which he can never obtain. Moderation on this understanding, however, is simply coming to terms with disagreeable reality: the moderate man is not the man who has a taste for moderation, but the realist who has learned to swallow bread because cake is impossibly expensive. And society must for each of us be a source of limited gratifications, but also continual frustration—like a community of drug-addicts which has somehow succeeded in preventing the sale and use of drugs.

Thirdly, Hobbes has claimed that all voluntary human behaviour is in the pursuit of pleasure, which may be either of the body ("sensual") or of the mind ("joy"). The pleasures of the mind he reduces all to terms of glory and he gives this a dominant place in his account of motivation. Yet although this part of *The Elements* is supposed to be giving a "scientific" account of human nature—by careful, logical steps, deriving conclusions from definitions—the concept of glory is based on an obscure argument which is given the most cursory attention. The distinction between sensual pleasure and joy is drawn clearly enough, in terms of pleasures which are or are not specifically associated with an organ of the body. But when he comes to discussing joy itself Hobbes's argument seems to be merely that all joy involves conception of the future, and that conception of the future involves conception of a power able to produce something. Hobbes makes a show of giving reasons for the second of these propositions, but the first, which is as necessary for his argument, and no less in need of justification, is left wholly unsupported. Perhaps it is not completely surprising that at this stage of his argument eloquence, and all the signs of a sense of conviction, are in inverse proportion to considerations of system and logic. The significance of this is discussed in the next section, in connexion with the account given in *De Cive*.

Finally, it is not merely that this conception of glory is dragged into the account of human nature. When Hobbes comes later to discuss the state of nature, glory is the chief of the causes which lead to violent competition. This also has special significance in relation to the account given in *De Cive*.

## 2 "ALL THE PLEASURE AND JOLLITY OF THE MIND"

Whereas in *The Elements* and *Leviathan* Hobbes produces a more or less systematic theory of the passions as the explicit foundation of his political theories, in *De Cive* he makes no attempt to elaborate a systematic doctrine of human nature, for *De Cive* is intentionally limited to only the last part of the great three-fold philosophy of body, man and society. But he does begin the first chapter with a very pungent description of human behaviour, which embodies the concept of glory expounded in *The Elements*. The Greeks, Hobbes says, thought of man as essentially a political being, by nature fitted for society. But that, he says, is a mistake:

For if by nature one man should love another, that is, as man, there could no reason be returned why every man should not equally love every man, as being equally man; or why he should rather frequent those, whose society affords him honour or profit. We do not therefore by nature seek society for its own sake, but that we may receive some honour or profit from it; these we desire primarily, that secondarily. How, by what advice men do meet, will be best known by observing those things which they do when they are met. For if they meet for traffic, it is plain every man regards not his fellow, but his business; if to discharge some office, a certain market-friendship is begotten, which hath more of jealousy in it than true love, and whence factions sometimes may arise, but good will never; if for pleasure and recreation of mind, every man is wont to please himself most with those things which stir up laughter, whence he may, according to the nature of that which is ridiculous, by comparison of another man's defects and infirmities, pass the more current in his own opinion. . . . So clear is it by experience to all men who a little more narrowly consider human affairs, that all free congress ariseth either from mutual poverty, or from vain glory, whence the parties met endeavour to carry with them either some benefit, or to leave behind them that same εὐδοκιμεῖν, some esteem and honour with those, with whom they have been conversant. The same is also collected by reason out of the definitions themselves of *will*, *good*, *honour*, *profitable*. For when we voluntarily contract society, in all manner of society we look after the object of the will, that is, that which every one of those who gather together, propounds to himself for good. Now whatsoever seems good, is pleasant, and relates either to the senses, or the mind. But all the mind's pleasure is either glory, (or to have a good opinion of one's self), or refers to glory in the end; the rest are sensual, or conducing to sensuality, which may be all comprehended under the word *conveniences*. All society therefore is either for gain, or for glory; that is, not so much for love of our fellows, as for the love of ourselves. But no society can be great or lasting, which begins from vain glory. Because that glory is like honour; if all men have it no man hath it, for they consist in comparison and precellence (1 2).

I have quoted Hobbes at length here, not merely because some details of the discussion are interesting but because the sheer length of it is significant. What Hobbes does is to set out in loving detail the way in which the behaviour of people towards each other always follows the same pattern—the pursuit of either gain or glory. That, Hobbes claims, is evident "by experience" of human affairs. But it can also be demonstrated, by resorting to the definitions of "will", "good", etc. By contrast with the detailed *description* of social intercourse, based on experience of affairs, the *derivation* of the conclusion from definitions is very perfunctory. One of the vital steps, for example, is the assertion that "all the mind's pleasure is either glory, (or to have a good opinion of one's self), or refers to glory in the end". Hobbes does not suggest that this is a definition (of the term "the mind's pleasure"), nor does he give any indication of how it could be derived from or otherwise related to a definition of any of the terms involved. Presumably Hobbes thinks that the details of such a demonstration belong to the philosophy of human nature which *De Cive* presupposes but does not contain. He had already, of course, expounded a theory of human nature in *The Elements*, but I have argued in Section 1 of this chapter that even in *The Elements*, which gave a similar account of glory, Hobbes provided very little demonstrative backing for his position.

But the most interesting feature of Hobbes's discussion of glory in *De Cive* is its great length. There are several pages of it, including the passage which I have quoted. Hobbes then turns briefly to a discussion of natural equality—it is possible for even the weakest man to kill the strongest, therefore no man can rely for security simply on his own strength. In the state of nature, therefore, there is permanent insecurity. Having argued that point briefly Hobbes turns to the sources of violence—"whence the will of mischieving each other ariseth". He distinguishes two chief sources. The first is glory, and Hobbes seizes the excuse to write happily about it for another page or so, concluding even more pungently than before:

And since all the pleasure and jollity of the mind consists in this, even to get some, with whom comparing, it may find somewhat wherein to triumph and vaunt itself; it is impossible but men must declare sometimes some mutual scorn and contempt, either by laughter, or by words, or by gesture, or some sign or other; than which there is no greater vexation of mind, and than from which there cannot possibly arise a greater desire to do hurt (1 5).

The second source of violence is competition for scarce goods. Hobbes says that this is "the most frequent reason why men desire to hurt each other" (1 6). Yet although it is as important as that, Hobbes devotes just a single sentence to it. It is perhaps an odd feature, and it is certainly a prominent one, of his discussion of glory in *De Cive* that Hobbes should *say* that competition for scarce goods is a more frequent cause of violence than glory, and yet should only mention competition while producing a lengthy and vivid discussion of glory.

The accounts of glory in *The Elements* and *De Cive* have some obvious common features. It is common to both that the concept of glory is logically a weak link in the chain of argument. In spite of that, however, it is obvious that it dominated Hobbes's view of human nature, because it is a topic which he discusses at great length, and with eloquence and gloomy relish. But there are also at least two important differences. The first is that whereas in *The Elements* the concept of glory is linked with a conception of power as essentially relative, this is omitted from *De Cive*. It is not that it is renounced or contradicted, because Hobbes has very little to say about power, but it is omitted. The second, and remarkable, difference is that in *The Elements* Hobbes gives glory and competition for scarce goods as the two sources of violence between men, and gives pride of place to glory, which is discussed first: competition for scarce goods is then briefly mentioned under the depreciating heading of "Moreover, . . ." (I xiv 5). In *De Cive*, however, although Hobbes pays much greater attention to glory, and very little to competition for scarce goods, he does say that it is a more frequent cause of violence. Although Hobbes's view of human nature in *The Elements* and *De Cive* is dominated by the notion of glory, there are some signs of change and development within this part of his philosophy. These are small enough, and might hardly be considered significant, if it were not that a further and very marked change along the same lines can be discovered in *Leviathan*.

## 3 POWER AND GLORY IN *LEVIATHAN*

Whereas in *The Elements* Hobbes's account of power is that it is essentially relative—"power simply is no more, but the *excess* of the power of one above that of another" (I viii 4)—in *Leviathan* he says simply: "The power *of a man*, to take it universally, is his present means, to obtain some future apparent good" (x 56). Hobbes goes on a few pages later to draw a conclusion from his account of the passions: "So that in the first place, I put for a general inclination of all mankind, a perpetual and restless desire of power after power, that ceaseth only in death" (xi 64). There is nothing very surprising in this. The notion of "some future apparent good" is just the notion of some objective that one happens to have, and power, therefore, has been defined merely as the means to realising objectives. In imputing "a perpetual and restless desire of power after power" to all men Hobbes is not implying that this power is necessarily competitive. What he says, indeed, is largely innocuous. Power is not presented as some special, dominating objective. On the contrary, although it is specially important, still it is logically derivative, because it is merely a means to some other primary objective, which is presupposed. The desire for power, as defined by Hobbes in *Leviathan*, is logically connected with the desire for any objective whatever, because to the extent that there were grounds for supposing that someone was indifferent to the means for realising an objective, to that extent there would be grounds for doubting that he really desired the objective. Nevertheless, there is something more to it than that. The account of the desire for power immediately follows and is connected with the exposition of the concept of felicity as contentment. The argument is not merely that the desire for some power is necessarily a part of the desire for any objective, but that quite apart from any desire that a man may have to *improve* his lot, he cannot even assure his present state of well-being without seeking more power. What Hobbes is arguing, then, is not merely that a man necessarily seeks power to realise his objectives (which might be altruistic ones), but that he also seeks power now as a means to further *self-regarding* objectives—"the power and means to live well". That looks like an egoistic doctrine, and it is supported by nothing better than the very dubious concept of felicity as contentment. It might be argued that these further self-regarding objectives are given by Hobbes merely as *examples*, and not as the universal pattern, of the further objectives a man may have. But that would make little difference, because then Hobbes would be saying that a man always desires power, not merely as a means to his present objectives, but as a means to future possible and indeterminate objectives. To desire power to realise certain objectives, not because in fact they *are* my objectives, nor because of the sort of objectives they are, but merely because, whatever they may turn out to be, they are going to be *mine*, is a self-regarding desire.

Yet what Hobbes says here falls short of being a clear and outright statement of egoism. For he describes the desire for power merely as "a general inclination of all mankind"—a self-regarding desire which everyone has (or merely *tends* to have?)—and he does not say nor imply that it is a wholly dominating desire. Nor does the further course of his argument presuppose any dominant, self-regarding desire for power. His discussion of the state of nature in *Leviathan* is going to depend chiefly on the concepts of diffidence and anticipation, and this "perpetual and restless desire of power after power" is largely irrelevant to it.

That, however, is a topic for my next chapter. What concerns me here is that Hobbes's discussion of power in *Leviathan* is different from the account given in *The Elements*. In *Leviathan* Hobbes is going to argue that certain aspects of relations between men bring one man's power into conflict with that of another, but he does not, as he does in *The Elements*, build a relative concept of power into his account of *individual* human nature as such.

And that is a difference which works through his whole account of power and glory. In *Leviathan* there is nothing corresponding to the cynical description of social intercourse in *De Cive* or the simile of the race in *The Elements*. The definition of glory in *The Elements* was the conception of our own power "above the power of him that contendeth with us" (I ix I), but in *Leviathan* it is merely " *Joy*, arising from imagination of a man's own power and ability" (VI 35), and there is nothing comparative about it. That this is no mere accidental omission is obvious not only from the fact that this difference in the definition of glory corresponds to the difference in the concept of power which we have already discussed, but also from the fact that certain particular passions are also treated differently. Thus in *The Elements* an account of "good will" or "charity" is a part of the long discussion of glory and its varieties, and Hobbes's account of good will is that "there can be no greater argument to a man, of his own power, than to find himself able not only to accomplish his own desires, but also to assist other men in theirs" (I ix 17), but in *Leviathan* "good will" is mentioned before the topic of glory has come up for discussion at all, and it is defined very briefly as "desire of good to another" (VI 34). There are somewhat similar changes also in the accounts given of pity, laughter, lust, indignation and magnanimity.

It would hardly be an exaggeration to say that in *Leviathan* Hobbes does not miss an opportunity of diminishing the importance of glory in his psychological and political arguments. In his book on Hobbes, Richard Peters writes: "Social life, for Hobbes, was a race for precedence which had no final termination except death" (*Hobbes*, p. 148).

Peters goes on to expound the "perpetual and restless desire of power after power" in *Leviathan* in terms of the *relative* concept of power in *The Elements* (pp. 148-9). Laird makes a similar mistake, giving an exposition of the desire for power which is a marvellous omelette made up of broken eggs from *The Elements, De Cive* and *Leviathan* (*Hobbes*, pp. 171-2). But it is simply untrue to say that *for* Hobbes life was a race for precedence, unless one qualifies that carefully and says "for Hobbes in *The Elements* but not in *Leviathan*". There is no single Hobbesian doctrine of power and glory but two sharply different accounts. Nor is it merely an insignificant difference. Hobbes always, so far as I know, regarded his political conclusions as derived from his account of the passions. It *is* true that in *The Elements* and *De Cive* he regarded life as a race for precedence because the dominant human passion was the desire for pre-eminence. The abandoning of this view —or at least the exclusion of it from his actual arguments—represents a major change in the foundations of his political theory.

## 4 "THIS INFERENCE, MADE FROM THE PASSIONS"

In chapter XIV of *Leviathan* Hobbes, having completed his discussion of the passions, argues that there are certain features of human nature which are "causes of quarrel", so that unless there is some coercive power imposing order there must be a state of nature, with every man at war with every man. Hobbes describes this conclusion as an "inference, made from the passions" (XIV 82). That, of course, is what one would expect from his reiterated assertions of the inter-connectedness of the different parts of his philosophy. In the Introduction to his edition of *Leviathan*, Plamenatz describes Hobbes's method:

He seeks first to determine the strongest and most recurrent of men's appetites and passions, he then considers their situation and their needs as creatures who cannot avoid contact with one another and who have to compete for the wherewithal to satisfy their appetites, and finally seeks to explain the rules they observe and their institutions as arising from their appetites and passions, their situation and their needs (Introduction to *Leviathan*, Fontana edition, pp. 9-10).

The interesting thing about that is that part of what Plamenatz says is true of *Leviathan* and part of it true of *The Elements* and *De Cive*, but taken as a whole it is not a true description of Hobbes's procedure in any single one of his works. It is true that in *The Elements* and in *De Cive* it is important to Hobbes to "determine the strongest and most recurrent of men's appetites and passions": he represents glory as the dominant passion and is able to draw obvious conclusions about the political difficulties posed by it. But his procedure in *Leviathan* is quite different. He runs through a catalogue of the passions, as he did in *The Elements*, with definitions of "hope", "fear", "indignation", "good will", "glory", "laughter", and a great many others. But his treatment of them in *Leviathan* is perfunctory. In *The Elements* there is an extended discussion of a number of them, going into considerable detail to show that they are varieties of glory and involve comparison with the power of others. In *Leviathan* precisely this detail is omitted, and glory is given an unimportant part as merely one among a great number of passions. There are two concepts to which Hobbes does attach special importance—felicity and the desire for power. These, however, are "dominant" only in the sense of being second-order concepts: *if* one has any desires at all, and whatever they may be, one must desire the means to realising them, and one may be continually successful in pursuing them. (What I have distinguished as the concept of felicity as contentment goes beyond this, because the present pursuit of it does not presuppose that currently one has, but merely that in the future one may come to have, other desires. But it is not clear that Hobbes realised that, and in any case I shall be arguing that he makes no important use of it.) On the other hand, while it may be true that in *Leviathan* Hobbes represents men as "creatures who cannot avoid contact with one another", that would be a very odd way of describing men as Hobbes depicts them in *The Elements* and *De Cive*. If what Hobbes says there is true, then it is not that men are pitched willy-nilly into a contact with each other for which they are not very well adapted by nature, but that although men indeed are not naturally fitted for social life they do and must cultivate relations with others because their dominant passion of glory is essentially a social passion—a man seeking glory is frustrated as much by withdrawal as by failure.

Now I am not suggesting that Hobbes simply changed his view of human nature. For "Hobbes's view of human nature" is an ambiguous expression. It could mean either "Hobbes's (private) beliefs and feelings about people generally" or "Hobbes's (public) exposition of a theory about people generally". I do claim that his public view changed, because by his public view I mean just the views which actually appear in his books. But no one can ever put everything which he thinks into anything which he writes, however copiously; and we may go beyond a philosopher's writings and speculate about his private view. It may be, indeed, that sometimes what is of most value to us in an author is not so much what he explicitly says as what, deviously, we can gather about the view which lies behind. In the case of Euclid, for example, I suspect that it is his theorems rather than his private views which have the most value for us. On the other hand it is sometimes suggested that it is wrong to take the sayings of Jesus, for example, and treat them as a body of explicit doctrine, and that what we have to do is to try to penetrate beyond what he is recorded as saying to the person behind it. That may be true of some, but I do not think that it is true of Hobbes, who regarded himself as a political teacher but not as a second Jesus. Hobbes thought—and persisted in thinking when he was writing *Leviathan*—that his psychological and political theories were scientific and that science consisted of a body of very clearly articulated propositions demonstrated within a system. Hence the most deeply Hobbesian of Hobbes's thoughts are those which are to be found floating on the public surface of his published works and not buried in the private depths beneath.

Earlier (in Chapter Five, Section 1) I tried to distinguish between pessimism, which arises from temperament or experience, and egoism, which is a product of theory. I argued that pessimism involves a wide range of specific expectations about human nature, although admitting of rare exceptions. Thus the pessimist expects civil servants to accept bribes and ministers of religion to embezzle church funds if they think they can escape detection. The pessimist thinks that most apparent acts of self-sacrifice are really motivated by some benefit which is their ulterior aim. The egoist, however, does not have to offer a (falsifiable) hypothesis of further benefit but asserts merely that the self-sacrificer enjoys the sacrifice itself more than anything else open to him in the situation. Egoism is in danger of becoming vacuous, and can be saved from vacuity only by being restated as a simple, and manifestly untrue, proposition, such as that everyone always and necessarily seeks to promote only states of himself, and therefore always seeks self-preservation. The distinctions between public and private view, and between pessimism and egoism, are readily applicable to the differences between the accounts of human nature in *The Elements* and *De Cive* and *Leviathan*. The account of glory in *The Elements* and *De Cive* is of course a part of Hobbes's public view—as expressed in these works. I think that it was also a part of his private view. The *way* in which he writes about glory, the way in which he dwells on the disreputable inner springs of men's behaviour, the length at which he writes, and the eloquence which he devotes to it, all suggest that he is expressing a deeply held conviction. The fact that he makes such a good job of spelling out the details of glory, and attaches such importance to it, along with the fact that he makes such a poor and half-hearted attempt at *supporting* it with rational arguments, suggests that it appears in his theoretical system not so much because it belongs there as because he could not keep it out. I think that it is to be described also as pessimism rather than as egoism, because it is a view which leads to, or consists in, having certain specific expectations about human nature. The egoist is not on the whole committed to expecting people to behave in this way rather than that, because egoism does not of itself specify the things which people can be expected to like doing. But Hobbes expects people to laugh at his infirmities, he expects strangers to help him only if they fear him, and so forth. In *The Elements* and *De Cive* he is imputing a specific and identifiable sort of motive to people generally. Hobbes of *The Elements* and *De Cive* then, was privately as well as publicly a pessimist. I should imagine that it is probable that privately he never changed, and that he remained a pessimist when he wrote *Leviathan*. What changed was the extent to which he thought that his pessimism could be incorporated in a "scientific" system. In *The Elements*, as I have argued in Chapter Five, Section 4, his account of pleasure and desire was confused, and he presented an hypothesis about pleasure in the trappings of theoretical egoism; while his account of glory was almost a straightforward (and "unscientific") expression of a variety of pessimism. Now Hobbes was later—in *De Corpore*—to construct an account of the use of hypotheses in science (see Chapter Four, Section 3), but according to that account the explanatory hypotheses were not capable of demonstration. In his political works, however, he ignores that account and represents his theories of human nature and politics as a system of demonstrated truths. The intrusion of a pessimistic view into the foundations of his political science in *The Elements* and *De Cive* must be attributed to confusion about method, and in Chapters Three and Four I have suggested that there is evidence that for a long period Hobbes's views on method were in a state of confusion and flux. In *Leviathan*, however, there is a fairly clear and unambiguous adherence to a demonstrative and conventionalist view of method, and the exclusion of a pessimistic view from its pages is simply a case of his practice coming into conformity with a theory which has, at least temporarily, become clarified.

Yet in the Introduction to *Leviathan* Hobbes says that because of:

the similitude of the thoughts and passions of one man, to the thoughts and passions of another, whosoever looketh into himself, and considereth what he doth, when he does *think, opine, reason, hope, fear, etc.* and upon what grounds; he shall thereby read and know, what are the thoughts and passions of all other men upon the like occasions (Introduction, 6).

If that has to be taken as a claim that some sort of descriptive psychology can be based on generalisation from introspective experience, then it is not consistent with the interpretation of *Leviathan* which I have been attempting. But I do not think that it is obvious that that is precisely what Hobbes is claiming, and indeed I do not think that anything at all is clear about it except that whatever the claim is it is a very severely qualified one, because Hobbes goes on to add: "I say the similitude of *passions*, which are the same in all men, *desire, fear, hope, etc.*; not the similitude of the *objects* of the passions, which are the things *desired, feared, hoped, etc.*" (Introduction, 6). At the very least that seems to exclude the pessimistic view of *The Elements* and *De Cive*, which alleges that there is a certain standard object of human desire, namely pre-eminence over others. And it is consistent with this that in *Leviathan* Hobbes should attempt to specify only two necessary objects of human desire, power and felicity, and that he should represent these as second-order, derivative objectives— successfully in the case of power and the formal concept of felicity, and not so successfully in the case of felicity as contentment. In fact the passions which he mentions in the Introduction—desire, fear, hope—are not so much specific passions (like greed or lust) as inter-related formal concepts which can be used as a framework within which an account of the passions could be placed. In *Leviathan* Hobbes does not attempt to describe the passions. He merely elaborates a conceptual framework for psychological concepts, by means of a series of interrelated formal definitions. Everything extraneous to that—the materialistic metaphysics, the mechanistic hypothesis, the account of vital motion, and so forth—is not only dispensable but very quickly dispensed with.

An apt example of confused commentary resulting from the failure to make necessary distinctions about Hobbes occurs in Laird. Discussing the proposition in *Leviathan* about "a perpetual and restless desire of power after power" Laird says:

This statement was much more than an account of what Hobbes had learned by observation. It was a metaphysical assertion to the effect that power *had to be* the mainspring of every man's action; and Hobbes connected this metaphysical assertion with his pleasure-theory by saying that "whosoever expecteth pleasure to come must conceive withal some power in himself by which the same may be attained" (*Hobbes*, 171).

Laird, I think, has made at least two serious mistakes here.

1. He has connected together (attributing the connexion to Hobbes) two views of Hobbes's, one—on power—drawn from *Leviathan* and the other—on pleasure to come—from *The Elements*.

2. The "metaphysical" conception of power may well be part of Hobbes's private view, or his public view in some other work, but it is not part of the actual doctrine of *Leviathan*. It *may* lie behind the doctrine of *Leviathan*, but it is neither in it nor required by it.

What I am suggesting here is that Hobbes is making a serious attempt to construct his science of human nature and politics on the analogy of mathematics. Now mathematics can be regarded as a purely formal system, but when it is so regarded it is necessary to distinguish the formal system, with its logical relations and derivations, from its application to the real world. As a formal system Euclidean geometry has to satisfy purely logical criteria of consistency and rigour in deductions. But if the question arises of the applicability of Euclidean geometry to the real world, purely logical criteria are no longer adequate and the question can be answered only by examining the real world. I have discussed these matters in Chapter Four, where I argued that Hobbes—like his contemporaries and like many also of his successors—failed to make this distinction between the pure and the applied. Yet I think that his construction of a quasi-mathematical theory of man and society not only requires such a distinction but *readily admits of it*, and that he comes very near to explicitly acknowledging it. Thus in his argument about introspective experience, which I have been discussing, he concludes by saying:

But let one man read another by his actions never so perfectly, it serves him only with his acquaintance, which are but few. He that is to govern a whole nation, must read in himself, not this or that particular man; but mankind: which though it be hard to do, harder than to learn any language or science; yet when I shall have set down my own reading orderly, and perspicuously, the pains left another, will be only to consider, if he also find not the same in himself. For this kind of doctrine admitteth no other demonstration (Introduction, 6).

Hobbes seems to be asserting unambiguously here that the science expounded in *Leviathan* is to be derived from, and can only be derived from, introspective experience. If that is what he is asserting then it raises a problem not only on my interpretation but on any interpretation of the rest of the text, where Hobbes goes on to contrast science, as a body of universal propositions derived from definitions, with prudence, the product of experience (see above, Chapter Four, Section 5). The appearance of blank contradiction is avoided, however, if we regard this passage as an admission by Hobbes that his propositions require "demonstration" along two different lines.

1. They require demonstration, in the strict sense of "demonstration", by being given a place within a formal, deductive system. Much of *Leviathan* consists in constructing such a system.

2. The system is constructed, however, not just for the pure joy of system-building, but as something applicable to political relations between people. It has therefore to be shown that it is capable of being so applied. A rough analogy would be someone regarding Euclidean geometry as a purely formal system and then turning to consider whether there were in the real world any objects which could be described as more or less triangular, circular, etc. So the Hobbesian political scientist does not turn to experience to enable him to construct his formal system, but, having within it constructed

a formal concept of a human being as a being having certain (unde-termined) desires, fears and hopes, who can calculate rationally about these, and who is capable of entering into relations with other such beings, he is assured by experience that people and their relationships are such that the facts about them can be accommodated within that formal structure.

Now that is an interpretation of what Hobbes says and does in *Leviathan*, and it is not a *rendering* of anything which he explicitly says. It is an interpretation which I am *reading into Leviathan*. But I think that there is a great deal of justification for it.

1. It is to a large extent consistent with what Hobbes actually *does* in *Leviathan*—with the way in which he actually uses his arguments. That is something which I shall be developing in the next chapter.

2. It copes with some apparent inconsistencies in *Leviathan*, such as the apparent inconsistency of "demonstrating" political science from experience and also insisting that experience gives rise only to prudence.

3. It interprets *Leviathan* according to a conception of political science to which Hobbes had in fact been progressively approaching, because the difference between the accounts of human nature in *The Elements*, *De Cive* and *Leviathan* is precisely that the latter is con-structed as a formal system, excluding those elements in the earlier works which were not consistent with such an undertaking. In this connexion there is an illuminating passage in *De Cive*. It had been objected that his doctrines implied not only that all men are wicked but that they are wicked by nature. But Hobbes argues that this does not follow from his doctrines: "For though the wicked were fewer than the righteous, yet because we cannot distinguish them, there is a necessity of suspecting, heeding, anticipating, subjugating, self-defending, ever incident to the most honest and fairest conditioned" (Preface to the 2nd edition, xvi). What is illuminating about this is not just the argument itself but the fact that it occurs in the Preface to the *second* edition of *De Cive*, published in 1647. The argument is put in terms of the wickedness or righteousness of men, because it is meeting an objection raised in these terms. But the force of the argu-ment is that Hobbes's political arguments do not depend on men being positively characterised in any particular way. Thus in the state of nature a man does not know that some other man has any hostile intentions towards him, or ambitions of glory, and Hobbes has

realised at last that it is not necessary for him to presuppose such knowledge. All that is necessary is that there should be a range of possibilities, and that this should require certain kinds of calculation.

That brings us to a discussion of Hobbes's arguments about the state of nature.

# Part Three

# SOCIETY

## CHAPTER SEVEN

# *The State of Nature*

AT THE centre of Hobbes's political theory lies the concept of the state of nature. Although there are many differences in the arguments in his different works on politics, the superficial structure of the argument, in its broad outlines remains the same. There is an account of individual human nature, which is worked out systematically in *The Elements* and *Leviathan*, although only some conclusions are produced in *De Cive*, and this is used as the foundation of an argument to the effect that when human beings enter into relations with each other there is the possibility of perpetual war of all against all—the state of nature —which can be averted only by the existence of an ordered society governed by a coercive sovereign. And there is a law of nature which is such that if people follow it they will be led to take all the steps necessary for the institution or maintenance of such a society. This law of nature has a hold on us just because it is grounded in the hope of averting the awful calamity of a state of nature.

Thus on the one hand the notion of a state of nature leads the argument towards the development of the law of nature, and on the other hand it rests on the preceding theory of human nature—in *Leviathan* Hobbes describes it as an "inference, made from the passions" (XIII 82). In this chapter I shall be discussing first the notion of the state of nature itself, and what is to be understood by describing it as an inference from the theory of human nature, and then the foundations of the notion of natural law.

## 1 THE PRIMARY SOURCES OF QUARREL

The state of nature is a state of war of all against all, but Hobbes makes it clear that he does not conceive of the state of nature as a state of continual and overt violence:

For as the nature of foul weather, lieth not in a shower or two of rain; but in an inclination thereto of many days together: so the nature of war, consisteth not in actual fighting; but in the known disposition thereto, during all the time there is no assurance to the contrary (*Leviathan*, XIII 82. See also *The Elements*, I xiv 11 and *De Cive*, I 12).

Hobbes traces the sources of this violence and insecurity through a number of stages.

### 1. *Equality of ability*

Although some men are stronger or cleverer than others, when it comes to violent contention they are substantially equal to each other. For the strong man who easily vanquishes some weaker man is hardly more secure than weaker men generally, because he might almost as readily himself have been conquered by the weaker creeping up behind him unawares. No single man can, unaided, have such power as to give him much greater security than any other.

### 2. *Equality of hope*

Since men are roughly equal in ability each has equal reason to hope that he may realise his objectives, and therefore to strive actively towards them.

### 3. *Incompatible objectives*

Given equality in ability and hope, "if any two men desire the same thing, which nevertheless they cannot both enjoy, they become enemies . . ." (XIII 81). When a student whose mind has not been completely debauched by philosophy reads that proposition of Hobbes's he is liable to reject it as manifestly false and silly. For although people do sometimes quarrel over things they also frequently defer willingly and with pleasure to each other: some degree of social capacity is as natural to men as self-seeking drives. But of course Hobbes is not denying that, and he has already defined "benevolence" or "good will" as "desire of good to another" (*Leviathan*, VI 34). What is wrong is that Hobbes has not expressed himself very precisely. We saw earlier that he sometimes tended to write as if all desire were for things (specific physical objects), although many desires, whose existence he not only acknowledged but even considered important, such as the desire for power, or, for that matter, benevolence itself, were *not* desires simply for (the possession of) physical objects. He is, I think, guilty here of using the same oversimplified language. The point of the argument is that it is incompatibility of objectives that leads to quarrel. If you and I both desire the same object but cannot both have it, then a quarrel is at least possible. But there are many similar occasions of quarrel which do not arise out of desire of *the same object.* If you and I are sitting together in the train we may quarrel not only over the newspaper which someone else has left behind but also over whether the window should be open or shut. It is the same kind of quarrel, arising from the fact that each of us pursues an objective (in my case, *my* having the newspaper and the window being shut) which is incompatible with an objective pursued by the other. It seems, then, to be by no means false to the force of Hobbes's argument to render it more generally in terms of pursuit of incompatible objectives than to restrict it to the terms merely of that particular variety of pursuit of incompatible objectives which consists in competition for scarce resources. Now as Hobbes did not deny, and, indeed, often enough asserted, people do pursue a great variety of different objectives. If you and I both desire the same thing—the newspaper—then one of your objectives may also be the pleasure of Hobbes-studying fellow-travellers, and that may be a very important objective to you—much more important than merely the possession of the newspaper for yourself. In such a case your objectives and mine are *not* incompatible, taking all the relevant features of the situation into account.

### 4. *Competitive violence*

It may well be, then, that in a situation which prima facie is one of incompatible objectives there is no occasion for quarrel. It may be that you desire my pleasure, or that I desire to act according to some moral ideal of self-sacrifice: in either case our objectives, after all, are not incompatible. Or it may be that one of us fears the other. But that is different. The sort of people who engage in the study of Hobbes are in fact a pretty timorous lot, but—as Hobbes has pointed out in his propositions about equality of ability and of hope—you cannot (especially in a state of nature) place any general and firm reliance on your ability to discourage or repel hostilities from me, so that even if my fear of you restrains me from overt quarrel, you cannot afford to rely on such restraint. Therefore when our objectives really are incompatible we are in a state of enmity. That does not mean that necessarily we must come to blows. Hobbes is careful to point out that war is not necessarily a state of continual violence but consists in "the known disposition thereto" (see the quotation at the beginning of this section). Hobbes is arguing that when the incompatibility of objectives is unresolved there is no security against violence, and his argument seems sound enough when put in these terms. Of course there are all sorts of moral considerations which *may* inhibit people from acts of violence, but that is not to be relied on, because different people have different moral ideas, and there is no criminal more violent and dangerous than the altruist with a bomb.

### 5. *Self-glorying violence*

Further, men desire to be respected by others, and if they feel that they are not sufficiently respected they will assert themselves not only against those who have offended them but against others also; and there are some who pursue power for no other purpose than merely the enjoyment of power. Thus glory also is a source of violence.

### 6. *Diffidence*

When there is no assurance of defence against competitive violence and self-glorying violence the consequence is *diffidence* of one another. Diffidence in turn gives rise to (7) *anticipatory violence*. But although anticipatory violence is, I believe, the most important of the elements of the concept of the state of nature expounded in *Leviathan*, it is logically derivative, and I shall limit the discussion in this section to the primary sources of violence, which are incompatible objectives, leading to competitive violence, and glory, leading to self-glorying violence. ("Competitive violence", "self-glorying violence", and "anticipatory violence" are terms which I have adopted for convenience of reference in discussion of the concepts involved. Although they are not Hobbes's terms they derive from terms used by Hobbes in the appropriate contexts—"competition", "glory" and "anticipation". "Diffidence" is, of course, Hobbes's own word.)

Although Hobbes's argument about the state of nature is roughly similar in the different works in which it occurs, nevertheless there are some differences that are not unimportant, and which are consistent with the other differences which have already been explored in previous chapters.

1. In *The Elements* and in *De Cive* the concept of glory is given a prominent place in the argument. As we have seen in Chapter Six, it is hardly an exaggeration to say that Hobbes's account of the passions in *The Elements* comes ultimately to be dominated by the notion of glory. Consistently with that, when he comes to the state of nature he begins, as in *Leviathan*, with arguing that men are substantially equal in ability (and vulnerability), but then goes on immediately to discuss glory as a source of violence. The reason for "diffidence" is that "moderate" men, who are willing to accept others as equals, are "obnoxious" to the vainglorious, so that there is general diffidence, while the pursuit of glory by one and all leads to self-glorying violence. Having introduced the "moderate" man in one paragraph Hobbes in the next dismisses him summarily, arguing that "every man" provokes others "by words, and other signs of contempt and hatred" (*The Elements*, I xiv 3–4). In *De Cive* Hobbes is incoherent. It is the concept of glory which dominates the discussion, and yet he says that the "most frequent" source of violence is incompatible objectives (*De Cive*, I 6). Having said that briefly, however, he yields again to his obsessive concern with glory, and sums it up a few paragraphs later by asserting that it is *glory* which is the chief source of violence (I 12). In *Leviathan*, by contrast, diffidence is a consequence of competitive violence, and glory is given a rather unimportant place; it is merely the third of three "causes of quarrel" —competition, diffidence, glory.

2. In *The Elements* the notion of the "moderate" man is introduced at the very beginning of the discussion of the state of nature, in the course of Hobbes's exposition of natural equality of ability. Considering how easily the stronger may be overcome by the weaker "we may conclude, that men considered in mere nature, ought to admit amongst themselves equality; and that he that claimeth no more, may be esteemed moderate" (*The Elements*, I xiv 2). A similar argument, of course, is used in *Leviathan*, but it is used in a different context and in a different way. In *Leviathan*, having established— without using the concept of the moderate man—that in a state of

nature, equality of ability and hope, plus incompatible objectives, and the rest, lead to diffidence, anticipatory violence, and a general state of war, Hobbes argues that it is reasonable to aim at peace and that admission of equality is a necessary condition of the effective pursuit of peace. The moderate man of *The Elements* is simply the concept of natural law displaced into the foundations of the prior argument about the state of nature.

3. In all the versions of the argument the assertion of equality of ability is the first step. In *Leviathan*, but not in *The Elements* or *De Cive*, there is a second step, which is equality of hope. Again, in *Leviathan*, but not in *The Elements* or *De Cive*, one of the foundations of the argument is the notion of *anticipatory* violence.

## 2 ANTICIPATORY VIOLENCE

Hobbes's argument in *Leviathan* is that equality of ability gives rise to "equality of hope in the attaining of our ends". So incompatible objectives give rise to competitive violence and glory to self-glorying violence, and the possibility of these creates general diffidence. "And from this diffidence of one another, there is no way for any man to secure himself, so reasonable, as anticipation; that is, by force, or wiles, to master the persons of all men he can, so long, till he see no other power great enough to endanger him" (*Leviathan*, XIII 81). Therefore the state of nature is a state of war. There is a profound difference between the course of the argument in *Leviathan* and the versions in *The Elements* and *De Cive*. In the latter Hobbes's argument is primarily that because of the nature of his passions as an individual a man is driven into conflict with others, so that even if violence did not arise from the incompatibility of objectives it would be caused by every man's relentless drive for glory, which is the *chief* cause of conflict. But just as in *Leviathan* the account of human nature has become formalised, to the (almost total) exclusion of any theories about actual human motives, so also the argument about the state of nature has become formalised. Even the argument about incompatible objectives is put in hypothetical terms: in *The Elements* Hobbes states it as a fact that "many men's appetites carry them to one and the same end", *therefore* . . . (I xiv 5. See also *De Cive*, I 6); whereas in *Levia-*

*than* what Hobbes says is that "if any two men desire the same thing, which nevertheless they cannot both enjoy, they become enemies . . ." (XIII 81). What is important about this is not merely that the hypothetical form is appropriate, because science consists of universal propositions which are hypothetical. It is that the whole nature of the argument has been transformed. The argument no longer depends on any specific characterisation of human motives. What Hobbes is doing, rather, is to work out the structure of the reasonable calculations which an individual could make about relations with other beings such as himself, when the specific nature of these others is left indeterminate, and even the guide-lines of all elements of social order are removed. Even Hobbes's argument about equality of ability is not so much a statement of known facts about people—that they are equal in this or that respect—as merely the denial that any individual could have reason to rely on his own power for security. The introduction in *Leviathan* of the notion of equality of *hope* underlines the fact that what is important to the argument is not facts about men's passions and abilities but the form of rational *deliberation*, for hope is "appetite, with an *opinion* of attaining" (VI 34). From this equality it follows that *if* there are incompatible objectives then there is violence, and in the *Leviathan* argument general diffidence is a consequence of this *possibility* of competitive violence, so that anticipatory violence becomes a *reasonable policy*. In the argument of *The Elements* a certain human motive is specified—namely, glory—so that the observer can predict that when a group of men come together in the state of nature there will be violence. In the argument of *Leviathan* Hobbes is not an observer predicting on the basis of the known, but an analyst of the deliberations of a *participator* faced with the unknown. All that is postulated is a reasoning being having a number of objectives and in contact with similar beings. If he is to deliberate reasonably he must consider a range of possibilities—the objectives of others may be compatible with his own or they may be more or less incompatible. The more they are incompatible the more danger there is of violence. He may be tempted to decide to limit himself merely to resisting attacks from others, in the hope that others may similarly restrain themselves. Then there will be conflict only if an irresoluble incompatibility of objectives should arise. That might seem a reasonable decision. But it will be liable to leave him defenceless against any stealthy assault. The only way to secure himself against violence from others is to anticipate the possibility by securing power over them. The argument, of course, is hypothetical: it does not assert that it *is* reasonable to make precautionary war, but only that if there should be an opportunity of making precautionary war it would be reasonable to take it. It may seem, however, that it would be more reasonable to take the risk of being surprised and defeated, in the hope of avoiding any conflict except that which arises from incompatible objectives, and in the hope that others will see the need for similar restraint. And of course there *is* a need for restraint, because without it there is simply a perpetual state of war. The trouble is that this restraint has to be mutual. From the point of view of the individual— which is what is being analysed—a merely one-sided restraint is simply the acceptance of defeat. And even if he thinks that others might consider the possibility of restraining themselves, he must—if he is reasoning it through—reflect that *they* must have doubts about whether *he* will feel justified in restraining himself. Sometimes the only good reason—but still a good one—why you should attack someone else whom otherwise you do not want to attack is your knowledge that he may be afraid that you will attack him out of fear of his attacking you out of fear of your attacking him. . . . The point of the argument of anticipation, then, is not so much merely that each individual must face the possibility of competitive violence, and the only security against this is for him to anticipate if there should be an opportunity of successful anticipation, as rather that each individual must face the possibility of others contemplating anticipatory violence, so that his own reason for anticipating derives not merely from the possibility of competitive violence but from the possibility of the anticipatory violence of others.

This may all seem like typical philosopher's paradoxes and fantasies. The question of the *application* of this formal scheme of deliberation will be discussed more fully later, but it may be briefly remarked that it is by no means mere fantasy. If you have to have dealings with a dangerous wild beast and do not know how to re-assure it you have to overpower it, anticipating violence from it although you know that it will attack you only out of fear. We do not *usually* treat other people like wild beasts, of course, but that may be only because we do not normally meet them in a state of nature and are therefore not making our calculations in the vacuum pre-supposed by the argument of the state of nature. What Hobbes is saying is that the nearer a situation approaches to a state of nature the more force the argument of anticipation has.

What I am concerned with here, however, is not so much the merits as just the structure of Hobbes's arguments about the state of nature. Those elements of it which we have considered so far, I have been suggesting, are presented in *Leviathan* as a formal analysis of a piece of rational deliberation, whereas in *The Elements* they are presented as inferences about probable human behaviour from certain facts about human motivation. In *De Cive*, however, the *Leviathan* version is foreshadowed in at least two places.

1. The notion of anticipation appears at the end of the discussion of the state of nature. By right of nature, Hobbes argues, the conqueror can compel the conquered "to give caution of his future obedience", because it is reasonable to secure ourselves in advance (1 14). But unlike *Leviathan* the version of *De Cive* does not incorporate the notion of anticipation within the foundations of the argument of the state of nature—that is, it does not represent diffidence and anticipation as a prime source of violence.

2. As has been noted already, in the Preface to the second edition of *De Cive* Hobbes argues that "though the wicked were fewer than the righteous, yet because we cannot distinguish them, there is a necessity of suspecting, heeding, anticipating, subjugating, self-defending, ever incident to the most honest and fairest conditioned" (Preface, xvi). The force of that is clearly that what is important is not the nature of human motives, whether fair or foul conditioned, but the bearing of the *unknown* on rational deliberation. It is this passage, from the 1647 edition of *De Cive* (published at about the time at which Hobbes began work on *Leviathan*), which marks the transition from the earlier version of Hobbes's political science in *The Elements* to the later and formalised version of *Leviathan*.

What Hobbes has done at this stage of *Leviathan* is to establish a certain proposition about power. So long as a man has any objectives at all he has an interest in seeking some measure of power, because "power" has been defined as the means to realising objectives. When people come into contact with each other, then unless they have the basis for some firm assurance to the contrary, which they cannot have in the state of nature, they face the possibility of a threat to the realisation of their objectives, and they have reason for seeking power over others, *if* that can be achieved, as an alternative to falling under their power. Whatever one's objectives may be, there is the possibility that they will all be threatened. If self-preservation is my chief value, then the only security for my own life is the exercise of power over others. If my chief value is the happiness of my children, then except through an *excess* of power I cannot guarantee that someone else may not in the pursuit of his objectives inflict misery or death on my children. *Whatever* my objectives may be they are vulnerable to the exercise of power by others, and therefore in being committed to seek power as a means to my objectives I am committed to seeking power over others if the opportunity of seizing such power should offer. Thus Hobbes seems to have arrived at last, after a long argument, at a proposition which occurred much earlier in the system of *The Elements* —that power is essentially relative to the power of others. The similarity is only superficial, however. In the first place in *The Elements* the proposition is part of a description of individual human nature as essentially glory-seeking, whereas in *Leviathan* the relativity of power is not a consequence of one particular objective which all people seek, and therefore of one specific human passion, but a consequence of the bearing upon human deliberations in general of the existence of unregulated social relations. And secondly, not only does Hobbes arrive at his destination by a different route, but it is not in any case really the same destination. For if the theory of *The Elements* were true, then an individual in the state of nature who found himself in the happy situation of having subjected to his power the few others whom he had come across would necessarily be anxious to look for more people to place under subjection, not merely to increase his amenities by their labour but in order to honour him by the mere fact of their subjection. But according to the *Leviathan* argument this individual might be well advised to concentrate on increasing the productivity of those whom he had already subjected, before embarking on fresh conquests, and would not be impelled to the latter merely by a driving desire for glory.

## 3 LIBERTY

Hobbes now goes on to argue that a state in which everyone has reason to seize power over others whenever the opportunity should

offer is a state of general and perpetual war—not necessarily of continual and overt violence, but of a general will and tendency towards
it. He goes on to describe "the incommodities of such a war": none
of the benefits of civilisation would be available, "and the life of man,
solitary, poor, nasty, brutish, and short" (XIII 82). What Hobbes
seems to be doing here is appealing to and using certain empirical
facts—that men would be poor if each had to rely on his own efforts
to provide for himself without the benefit of organised society, and
so forth. But his argument does not *depend* on those facts. It is reasonable for each man to take any opportunity of successful anticipation,
but there is no assurance that such opportunities will occur. Each
man must calculate that the possibility is that he faces an endless
series of conflicts. The chances are that he will encounter a number of
enemies, and *a priori* his chances of surviving all of these encounters,
or of realising whatever objectives he may have, are small. The state
of nature, then, is a state in which a man can see little chance of promoting his objectives. Or, putting it in the language of "good" and
"evil", which has already been defined in terms of objectives, whatever a man may conceive of as good and evil, whether his own survival, or anything else which he can strive to promote, the chances
of good are small and the chances of evil are large.

Hobbes immediately draws some conclusions. The first is that in
the state of nature there is no justice and injustice. I leave over discussion of that, however, until the fundamental law of nature has
been examined, because some of the issues which it raises can best be
discussed in the light of an understanding of Hobbes's conception of
natural law. Another conclusion is that in the state of nature "every
man has a right to every thing; even to one another's body" (XIV 85),
and this depends on a prior definition of "right of nature" and
"liberty".

"The right of nature . . . is the liberty each man hath, to use his
own power, as he will himself, for the preservation of his own nature;
that is to say, of his own life; and consequently, of doing anything,
which in his own judgment, and reason, he shall conceive to be the
aptest means thereunto." "Liberty", Hobbes immediately goes on to
explain, means, strictly, "the absence of external impediments". Now
a law of nature is "a precept or general rule, found out by reason, by
which a man is forbidden to do that, which is destructive of his life,
or taketh away the means of preserving the same; and to omit that,

by which he thinketh it may be best preserved." *Right* and *law*, therefore, are to be clearly distinguished from each other, because right consists in liberty, whereas law obliges, and liberty and obligation "in one and the same matter are inconsistent" (XIV 84). Now, Hobbes concludes, in the state of nature every man is "governed by his own reason", and there is nothing that may not help him to preserve his life, therefore every man has a right to everything (XIV 85).

One thing which is puzzling about that, and which has received some attention from commentators, is the definition of "liberty". The mere absence of external impediments is not itself a very satisfactory criterion, because it would imply that a man who fell accidentally from an aeroplane was free because nothing was impeding his descent to the earth. Hobbes puts it more accurately later when he comes to discussing liberty in some detail, and the criterion then is that a man should not be hindered by external impediments in doing *what he has a will to do* (XXI 137). Such an account, of course, is consistent with his mechanical determinism. Will is the last appetite in deliberating, and appetites are explicable in physical terms as bodily motions caused by other bodily motions. Freedom, then, cannot be defined in terms of the absence of physical determining causes, and the criterion of the absence of external impediments to doing what one wills is a viable alternative. Hobbes had a controversy with Bishop Bramhall about freedom of the will, and an understanding of the metaphysical foundations of Hobbes's views on freedom and necessity is helpful in grasping his position in that controversy. There is an interesting discussion of it in Watkins's *Hobbes's System of Ideas*, chapter VII. Yet I doubt whether that has much, if any, relevance to the concept of liberty in Hobbes's *political* theory, and in that of *Leviathan* in particular, because I think that the concept which is *used* there is one which is adapted to and determined by its political context.

Hobbes's formal definition of "liberty" in *Leviathan* is, indeed, "absence of external impediments in doing what one wills". But when Hobbes discusses it more fully the matter is much less simple. He gives some examples. One of these is a free gift, which, he explains, is a gift which the giver was free to give—that is, not obliged to give by law or covenant. The criterion here is that one does X freely if there is no obligation to do X. Another example, however, is free speech, which is the speech "of the man, whom no law hath obliged to speak otherwise than he did" (XXI 137). The criterion has now become that there should not be an obligation to omit $X$. Perhaps what we have to do (as Professor A. G. Wernham has suggested in "Liberty and Obligation in Hobbes", *Hobbes Studies*, ed. Brown, pp. 120–1) is to take these criteria together, which gives us a concept of freedom as the absence of obligation (either to do, or to omit), which may be distinguished from the different concept of freedom as absence of external impediments. Yet I think that that is perhaps to be too severe on Hobbes. It is not that his two examples together suggest a single all-embracing criterion, but that each suggests a *different* criterion. And in any case, the example of a free gift would be a very bad example of the general criterion of absence of obligation, for it would imply that a gift was not free unless the giver had no obligation to give or to omit giving, so that a gift made *in breach* of an obligation not to give would not be a free gift. I know of no reason for supposing that Hobbes would have been prepared to agree to so silly a proposition. Yet he goes on in the next paragraph to argue that liberty and fear (of the law, for example) are consistent: he says that an action done from fear of the law is one done freely, and which the man also was free to omit. So where there is an obligation I act freely if I keep it and freely also if I break it, for there is nothing hindering me from keeping or breaking it at will. Whatever may have been the exact form of the criterion of no-obligation, Hobbes seems to be abandoning it here.

In fact, however, the confusion and complexity is not nearly so bad as it seems. Hobbes has failed to make sufficiently explicit distinctions within the concept of freedom which he is using, and has therefore got into some muddles.

It is necessary to distinguish three different, though related, things that may be referred to by the term "freedom" in connexion with obligation. I shall call them *being free to do something*, *doing something freely*, and *having freedom of*. Being free to do something is a simpler notion than doing something freely, because doing something freely entails doing it, and freely, whereas being free to do something does not entail doing it. Being free to seems the simplest notion, and it is the appropriate one to begin with. Deliberation involves the contemplation of a range of different possible actions—a number of paths which the person deliberating has to choose between taking. Sometimes there is an external impediment to some of the paths: the prisoner might choose to go for a ramble, but the prison walls bar the way. That path is blocked, and choice is limited to the other paths. To say that someone is free to do something is to point to an unblocked path. But of course physical obstacles like prison walls, chains and unbridgeable chasms are not the only kind of impediment there can be. Obligations also are impediments, because if I have an obligation to do something then all other paths but one are blocked. But does that analogy justify Hobbes in passing so happily from physical impediments to obligations? Surely *any* consideration which leads one to exclude an alternative blocks a path, just as an obligation does? Are we to say that the only thing which a person is free to do is that which ultimately he does in fact choose? Certainly Hobbes would not accept that conclusion: he believes that we act by necessity but also that necessity does not exclude freedom. But of course there is no need for Hobbes to be drawn towards such a conclusion, because obligations are path-blocking in a very special way. The fact that the rain may get through my leaky shoes if I go to the pictures may block the cinema-path in my deliberation about how to spend the evening, but there is only a contingent connexion between facts about leaky shoes and path-blocking—it may rule out picture-going for me, but you might not mind wet feet so much, or at all, and it would not therefore rule out picture-going for you. But the connexion between obligation and path-blocking is not contingent, for you cannot understand what an obligation is without understanding that it is a path-blocker—and still a path-blocker even when not a completely effective one. Not to be free to do something, then, is to have a path blocked—by an impediment such as a physical obstacle or an obligation not to do the thing. Since physical obstacles are of no importance to the arguments with which Hobbes is concerned he can afford to ignore them and to give exclusive attention to the other sort of obstacle, which is important. So a man is free to do something provided he does not have an obligation not to do it.

Doing something freely is, however, something like the converse of doing something which one is free to do, for I can be said to be doing it freely if I do not believe myself to have an obligation to do it. Such a usage—which so far I have been merely stipulating—is not very far removed from common usage, and it does at all events make a distinction which needs making. Hobbes's example of a free gift is an apt one, because he says that a gift is free if the giver had liberty (I should say, "gave freely"); and his criterion is *not* that the giver had no obligation either to give or not to give, but merely that the giver had no obligation to give. After all, a gift which the giver gave without obligation to give (or, more strictly, not believing himself to have an obligation to give), and in breach of an obligation not to give, may be naughty but is perhaps all the freer for that. When Robin Hood gave stolen money to the poor it might be argued that he was not free to give it, but surely it could not be said that he did not give it freely. Hobbes's example of free speech is also an apt example, but not of the same thing. I think that what is usually important when issues of free speech arise is the question of freedom *of* speech. To make a free gift is to make a gift freely in the sense of making it without regarding oneself as obliged to make it. The issue is whether there was or was not an obligation to make *that specific gift*. But the question whether I have freedom of speech is not the question whether merely there is or is not an obligation on me to say some specific thing, but whether there is a *general* absence of obligations to say or not to say a wide range of different kinds of things. To be free to express one's opinion is not to be free to express one's opinion that the world is flat, but to be able to express one's opinion, whatever it may be, unlimited by obligations. Such freedom is, of course, relative. We say we have a free press, but there are still some legal limitations—an obligation not to publish seditious libels, for example. Unless either one admitted no obligations of any kind whatever, or could hold that nothing one could say *could* ever contravene *any* obligation (e.g., a moral obligation not to hurt people gratuitously), then one could never claim *absolute* freedom of speech. Sometimes when one claims freedom of speech one is claiming merely absence of *legal* obligations, and even then one may be claiming only that there are not, or should not be, an *excessive* number of obligations specifically relating to speech-acts.

Although I have claimed that discussion of freedom of speech usually relates to what I have called *freedom of*, all three senses of "free" are, of course, applicable to speaking. (i) I am free to say "The monarch is wise" if there is no obligation *not* to say it. (ii) I say "The monarch is wise" freely if I say it, not believing myself to have an obligation to say it. Freedom in Sense (ii) is reducible to terms of a belief about freedom in Sense (i), because to say freely "The monarch is wise" is the same as to say "The monarch is wise", believing that one is free not to say it. (iii) I have freedom of speech in respect of my opinions of the monarch if I am not under any obligations either to say or not to say any particular things about the monarch. I have inaccurately referred to these as three different senses of "free" or "freedom". But of course this is not a matter of simple ambiguity. All three are related to each other, and relate back to the same fundamental concept of blocked or unblocked paths in deliberation.

Whatever interpretation one gives of, or imposes on, Hobbes's examples of "free gift" and "free speech", and however successful the interpretation which I have suggested may be in relating these both to each other and to the criterion of no external impediment, there remains the difficulty of accommodating what he goes on to say about freedom and fear. When Hobbes asserts that liberty and fear are consistent with each other, and that a man is still at liberty when he acts for fear of the law, because he has liberty not to do it, this freedom of a man to do or not to do something in respect of which he *has* a legal obligation clearly does not fall under any of the no-obligation criteria. Hobbes is simply reverting to the criterion of no external impediment. There is no reason why he should not, and what he says is, I believe, arguably true. The context in which it may be important to decide about a man's freedom in something which he has done is when a question of blame arises: "I was not free to do otherwise" is a typical *excuse*. If a man has kept an obligation then, so far as *that* obligation is concerned, no question of blame arises, and the criteria which we have discussed do allow us to say that a man is free to do something which he has an obligation to do, provided there is no obligation on him not to do it. If he has acted contrary to an obligation then he might seek to excuse himself by claiming that he was not free not to break it, and if there were external impediments to his keeping it this claim would be allowed by Hobbes. Hobbes, however, is asserting in the first place that *generally* there are no impediments either to keeping or (apart from the law itself) to breaking an obligation. But, in the second place and more importantly, he is touching on the question whether an obligation which a man has entered into out of fear is binding on him. For I might promise a gunman to give him some money tomorrow if he would spare my life today and then meet him tomorrow with no money but a coat of bullet-proof armour, laughing at his reproaches of me for breaking my promise, and claiming that I had no obligation to keep a promise made out of fear.

It may be that Hobbes is prepared to concede that no obligation arises out of an act which one is not free not to do, or it may be that he is not prepared to make that concession, but he certainly is refusing to concede either that because an act is done out of fear it is not free or that because it is done out of fear it cannot give rise to an obligation. And clearly he is right about that. It might be that we should think that a promise *extorted* under *threat* is not binding, but on the other hand if I need some medicine urgently, with possibly fatal results if I fail to get it, and promise a taxi-driver the standard fare to take me quickly to a chemist, I could hardly claim that I had no obligation to pay him, although I entered into the obligation only out of fear for my life. Therefore if the promise made to the gunman does not oblige me, it is not because it was a promise made out of fear.

The matter of excuses cannot be pursued here, because at this stage Hobbes only touches on it. But at all events what he says about freedom is not at all points very clearly expressed, but the concept which he is *using* seems to me to be capable of being formulated clearly enough to do the jobs which he requires it to do, and the discussion of freedom and fear says very little, but what there is of it is unexceptionable.

## 4 THE RIGHT OF EVERY MAN TO EVERY THING

It is possible now to return to Hobbes's account of "the right of nature": it is the absence of external impediments to the use of a man's power, as he wills, for the preservation of his own nature (that is, his life), and to his doing whatever reason tells him is the best means of achieving that. Hobbes seems here to be saying that in the state of nature a man has a right to act as he thinks best for the preservation of his own life—that is, that there are no external impediments to his so acting. Whatever meaning is attached to "external impediments" he can hardly have believed that to be true, and it would certainly make nonsense of the whole of his argument about the state of nature. For it is crucial to his argument to hold that in a state of nature a man can have no reasonable hope of achieving *anything*, and the chances must be that his probably short life will be dominated by encounters with external impediments. But he goes on to say, expounding the notions of "liberty" and "external impediments": "which impediments, may oft take away part of a man's power to do what he would; but cannot hinder him from using the power left him, according as his judgment, and reason shall dictate to him" (XIV 84). Thus of course there *are* going to be impediments to the exercise of one's power—natural obstacles, but also, more importantly, the competing activities of others—but such effective power as is left to a man he has freedom (that is, from contrary obligation) to use as he thinks fit. Thus a man does not, according to the right of nature, have an *unqualified* right to anything and everything —only the right to whatever his judgment and reason tells him is necessary to preserve his life.

Hobbes goes on to argue that in the state of nature every man has a right to everything, even another man's body. That is because he has a natural right to do whatever he thinks necessary to his preservation, and in a state of nature there is nothing that one can use that may not be of use in preserving one's life. This is an apparently simple argument, starting with the premisses, that by right of nature each man has the right to do whatever his reason tells him will conduce to his preservation, and that there is nothing which a man can use that may not be of use in preserving his life, and deriving from these the conclusion that every man has a right to every thing. The form in which Hobbes states the conclusion leads Professor J. R. Pennock, in his article, "Hobbes's Confusing 'Clarity'—The Case of Liberty", to contrast *De Cive* with *Leviathan*. In *De Cive*, Pennock points out, Hobbes argues that if someone claims that something is necessary to his self-preservation without really believing it, then he offends against the law of nature, whereas in *Leviathan* there is no such qualification of the right of every man to every thing (*Hobbes Studies*, p. 110). And of course it is a fact that this qualification does appear in the premisses from which, in *Leviathan*, the proposition about the right of every man to every thing is derived.

Yet I do not think that in this part of the argument of *Leviathan* there is either any confusion or any difference from the corresponding part of *De Cive*. For the point is that the qualification in question *does* appear in *Leviathan*, at least in the premisses of the argument. The fact that it does not appear explicitly in the conclusion of the argument is explicable if one attends to the form of the argument itself.

For one of the premises—the proposition about the right of nature—
is stated as a proposition about what a man has a right *to do*: he does
not have an unlimited right to do anything he pleases, but merely to
do what his reason tells him will help to preserve his life. Now that is
a proposition which is, as it were, addressed to an individual as a
rational, *deliberating* being: it tells *you* that (in the state of nature)
*you* may do anything that you rationally decide on as a means to self-
preservation. Hobbes is going to infer some further propositions—
about the law of nature and its derivatives—which, again, are addressed to the deliberating individual, telling him this time not what
he *may* do but what he *ought* as a rational being to do. In order to make
the transition from "may" to "ought" he has to point to the consequences of the right of nature being exercised by a number of individuals having relations with each other. He does this by narrowing his
attention to *things* which may be sought after by people exercising
the right of nature. There is nothing, Hobbes argues, that might not
conceivably be of use to man for preserving his life, therefore there is
nothing—not even the bodies of other men—that *could* not legiti-
mately be claimed by someone by right of nature. This is merely a
very concise way of expressing the whole of Hobbes's previous arguments and conclusions about violence, diffidence and the general
"incommodities" of the state of nature. The contrast between what
*is* necessary and what an individual *thinks* is necessary to his survival
is simply not relevant here. What is important in the transition from
the right of nature to natural law, both of which incorporate the
limitation to what the individual thinks is necessary for his survival,
is not that limitation but the fact that there is no restriction on what
may possibly be claimed under the right of nature. When I am thinking merely of my own exercise of the right I have to regard it as
restricted to what I think necessary for my own preservation, so in
the formulation of the right Hobbes explicitly expresses the restriction. But in arguing towards the law of nature the argument depends
on the consequences of the exercise of the right of nature by everyone.
That introduces into my deliberations the need to allow for the exercise by others of the right of nature, and what is important is not the
restriction to what each thinks is necessary for his preservation, because there is nothing that *may* not possibly be claimed under the
right, but the fact that there is nothing which I can regard as im-
mune from (rightful) interference by others. From the point of view

of the deliberating agent, then, there is nothing which cannot be claimed by others by right of nature, and Hobbes's formula of the right of every man to every thing is a very apt expression of this and is not the abandoning of the restriction expressed in the original formula.

## 5 "THE TERRIBLE ENEMY OF NATURE, DEATH"

The right of nature is the right to do what one thinks necessary for preserving one's life, and a law of nature is a rational precept forbidding one to do that which is destructive of one's life. It is clear that the notions of self-preservation and the avoidance of death occupy a central position in this stage of Hobbes's argument, but it is not so clear what right they have to be there. Watkins has summarised Hobbes's argument thus:

. . . men are restless egocentrics whose desires for self-advancement would generate something approaching the maximum amount of conflict in a state of nature; in such a state, each individual would face the near-certainty of eventually getting killed, but their desire not to be killed is stronger than all their other desires; so, when men in such a situation came to appraise it realistically—to recognise their basic equality and to acknowledge the futility of each trying to dominate the others—they would unanimously decide to try to extricate themselves from it (*Hobbes's System of Ideas*, p. 119).

But why should an "egocentric" fear death above all? Why might he not prefer death to living in pain? Watkins's answer is that according to Hobbes's "physiological theory of pleasure and pain" pain results from the hindering of the vital motion; the more the vital motion is hindered the more pain there is, until finally the vital motion is stopped and death ensues; so that being killed is necessarily the most painful thing that can happen to a man. The central position occupied by self-preservation in the formulation of natural right and natural law is justified within Hobbes's system, then, because Hobbes's theory of the passions has given a special and dominant place to the fear of death.   .

That rendering of Hobbes's argument finds some support, of

course, in *The Elements* and *De Cive*, for there glory is represented as the dominant object of desire and death as the dominant object of aversion. In *The Elements* Hobbes refers to "the terrible enemy of nature, death, from whom we expect both the loss of all power, and also the greatest of all bodily pains in the losing" (I xiv 6). Watkins has made a brave attempt to represent this as belonging within a systematic theory of the passions, and his interpretation is probably the best that can be made of the collection of bits and pieces which Hobbes throws at his readers in *The Elements*. Hobbes's whole account of human nature there is so incoherent that there is no knowing what to make of it, except that there is no doubt that it is intended to express and embody a pessimistic view of human nature. Thus Hobbes clearly regards death as a very great evil. But *how* great? What he actually says, in the words quoted above, is that in dying we expect the greatest of *bodily* pains. He has previously, however, distinguished between bodily and non-bodily pains (I vii 8), but has failed to give any account of how bodily are to be measured against non-bodily pains or of why death, the greatest of bodily pains, is necessarily the greatest of all pains. Hobbes's theory can be accommodated within Watkins's rendering by simply rejecting the distinction between bodily and non-bodily pleasures and pains. But then something would have to be done about the non-bodily pleasure of glory, the desire of which is as important a part of the account of the state of nature as is the fear of death. In *De Cive*, of course, Hobbes says: "Every man is desirous of what is good for him and shuns what is evil, but chiefly the chiefest of natural evils, which is death; and this he doth by a certain impulsion of nature, no less than that whereby a stone moves downward" (I 7). Watkins's interpretation of this passage is that in it Hobbes is asserting that fear of death has priority over all other considerations. But it is not clear that that *is* what Hobbes means. For there is nothing that is very clear about this passage. What are *"natural"* evils? Is death merely the chiefest of natural (but not necessarily of all, including non-natural) evils? In what sense is death the *"chiefest"* of natural evils? In a sense which would, or would not, permit of two other lesser evils together being greater than it? Hobbes is going to go on to use the notion of fear of death in something like the sense expounded by Watkins, but no clear and adequate foundation for it has been laid in the theory of human nature, and I suspect that the vagueness and ambiguity of

Hobbes's formula helps to conceal from him the weakness of its foundations.

There is even less justification for its appearance in *Leviathan*, whose formalised method and argument leave no place for propositions about the actual objects of human desires and aversions and dispense with hypotheses about pleasure and pain. In *The Elements* and *De Cive* Hobbes does at least go so far as to produce some unconvincing reasons for accepting his propositions about self-preservation, but in *Leviathan* he hardly goes so far even as that. The nearest he gets to it is in his confused and unwarranted conclusions about felicity as contentment. Certainly on the interpretation which I have been suggesting of the argument of *Leviathan* the concept of an overriding desire for self-preservation is not merely unsupported but incapable of being supported within the system. Yet it is used in the crucial arguments about the state of nature. Nevertheless the position is not so bad as it may seem, for the truth is that the offending concept *occurs* rather than that it plays an indispensable part in the argument. What *is* indispensable to Hobbes's argument is the concept of *despair*. Hobbes defines this as "appetite, without the hope of attaining" (VI 34). The notion could be extended, however, to cover the case of aversion without the hope of avoiding. I shall use "despair" in this extended sense: a man is in a state of despair when he has no hope of achieving the objects of his desires (what he values, regards as good) or of averting the things to which he has aversion (what he disvalues, or regards as evil). (There is no harm in my so extending the sense of the term, for it is not a word which Hobbes actually uses in his argument, so that there is no possibility of confusion between this use of the word and Hobbes's own use of it. But I shall be arguing that it is the concept of despair in this extended sense which Hobbes actually uses in his argument.) What Hobbes's argument about the state of nature shows is that in the state of nature a man has reason to despair. *Whatever* his desires and values may be there is no reason for him to expect anything but frustration. Now Hobbes thinks that death is the greatest evil that can befall any man—that is, that everyone does regard death as the greatest evil. He may or may not be entitled to that opinion, but there is no justification for incorporating it in the formal system of *Leviathan*. The fact is, however, that he *does* incorporate it. But as it appears in his argument the notion of the fear of death has two aspects. One aspect is formal. Hobbes thinks that death is the greatest evil that can happen to a man, and it is therefore the frustration of all his desires. The formal aspect of the notion of the fear of death is the notion of the fear of the frustration of all one's desires. The other aspect is the material aspect, the specific content which this formal notion must have for any particular man. Hobbes thinks that death is the content of this notion for all men. And surely he is wrong about that, for someone who willingly sacrifices his own life for a cause, or for his children, clearly regards the failure of the cause, or the destruction of his children, as a greater evil, a greater frustration of *his* desires, than his own death, and for him the content of the notion of frustration of all one's desires consists largely in the failure of the cause, or the destruction of his children. *What* the specific content is will vary from man to man, depending on his specific desires, or values. What is the same for every man is the possibility that all that he regards as good will fail, and all that he regards as evil be realised.

Fear of death, then, has this double aspect in Hobbes's argument. But although the material aspect is that which attracts the attention, and seduces commentators into speculations about Hobbes's views on death and pain, it is the formal aspect which does all the work, which carries the whole argument along. For Hobbes has to show both that in a state of nature a man has reason to despair—to have no hope of avoiding the frustration of all his desires—and therefore to be willing, necessarily, so long as he deliberates reasonably, to take any opportunity that may offer of putting an end to the state of nature. But fear of death is necessarily a reason for a man to seek a way out of a situation which threatens his life only if his own death is for him the frustration of all his desires. If it were not, then conceivably there could be a situation which threatened a man's life but did not threaten other more important objectives of his, and then such a man would not *necessarily* have a reason for attempting to end the situation. Similarly, what Hobbes's arguments about competition, anticipation and the rest show is not merely that these threaten a man's life but that they make impossible the rational pursuit of any coherent set of objectives.

What needs to be done with Hobbes's argument, then, is to restate it, substituting explicitly the formal concept of frustration of all one's desires for the material concept of death. That is to take a liberty with the text. But it is a very *small* liberty. For in the first place, the distinctive feature of *Leviathan* compared with other works is that so much of Hobbes's argument has been quite *explicitly* formalised, and this merely brings the arguments using fear of death into line with the rest. And in the second place, the change I am proposing is more apparent than real, because although it is the material aspect which gets Hobbes's attention, it is the formal aspect which does his work for him.

# CHAPTER EIGHT

# Natural Law

THE point of Hobbes's discussion of the state of nature is to lay a foundation for his account of natural law, on which the whole of his political theory is based. Natural law, like natural right, is expounded in terms of self-preservation, but it remains true that the very doubtful status of this concept does not invalidate Hobbes's argument, which depends only on the form of the concept and not on the content which Hobbes insists on giving it.

The course of Hobbes's argument is complex, and a number of issues arise from it which clamour loudly and simultaneously for discussion. Things have to be taken one at a time, and sometimes in this chapter I shall seem to be taking a very great deal too much for granted. Thus I shall sometimes describe some of Hobbes's propositions as "necessarily true within the system", and yet these propositions are presented by Hobbes as laws, precepts or maxims. It ought not to be too readily assumed that a precept can properly be described as "true", and later in the discussion I attempt to justify the usage. Again, in the last chapter I have discussed the state of nature, and in this chapter I shall be discussing natural law as a body of precepts which deliver us from the calamities of a state of nature. Much of the discussion is concerned with the measures which have to be adopted in order to bring an end to the state of nature and bring about the existence of an ordered society. That raises immediately some very obvious and pressing questions. Firstly, to what extent does Hobbes think that the state of nature is a situation which has ever actually existed? Does he think that, and does his argument require him to? Secondly, if the laws of nature merely prescribe for people the best way of getting out of a disagreeable situation which none of us ever actually encounters, of what interest are they to us? These are questions, I think, which need answering. But it is pointless to try to answer them before one has explored the detail of what Hobbes actually says about the state of nature and natural law. There is no point in discussing whether it is a good thing to play a certain game until one has examined the game itself and its rules.

## 1 THE FUNDAMENTAL LAW OF NATURE

A law of nature, Hobbes says, "is a precept or general rule, found out by reason, by which a man is forbidden to do that, which is destructive of his life, or taketh away the means of preserving the same; and to omit that, by which he thinketh it may be best preserved" (XIV 84). In chapters XIV and XV of *Leviathan* Hobbes produces a number of such precepts, all of which are laws of nature. Thus it is a law of nature "that all men that mediate peace, be allowed safe conduct" (XV 102). Another law of nature is "that no man by deed, word, countenance or gesture, declare hatred, or contempt of another" (XV 100). Hobbes produces detailed arguments to show that the various precepts are indeed laws of nature. Thus it is against natural law to "declare hatred or contempt of another" because it makes for violence "insomuch as most men choose rather to hazard their life, than not to be revenged" (XV 100). The proposition that most (but presumably not all) men prefer revenge to safety is not the sort of proposition which Hobbes in *Leviathan*, or elsewhere, would regard as scientific, because it is not universal: it depends on our experience, which teaches us (or at least, taught Hobbes) that *most* men prefer revenge to safety. Thus the "scientific" status of at least some of Hobbes's natural laws is questionable. His arguments in establishing them, however, depend not only on empirical facts, in some cases, but also in deriving them, with the help of these facts, from what he calls "the fundamental law of nature" (XIV 85).

A precept forbidding a man to do that which is destructive of his life is a rational precept, commanding assent necessarily from every man so long as he is rational, if and only if every man must, as a rational being, regard death as the frustration of all his desires. Hobbes does think that that condition is fulfilled. I have been arguing that Hobbes is wrong about that. If he is wrong, or even if it is merely possible that he is wrong, then it is necessary to apply again the distinction between the formal and the material: Hobbes is saying, formally, that a law of nature is a rational precept forbidding a man to do that which would lead to the frustration of all his desires (values) or would prevent him from realising them, and to omit that which would lead to their realisation; and, materially, that death is the frustration of a man's desires. The material proposition, of course, is, I have argued, both false and also, within the system of *Leviathan*, baseless. But the formal proposition embodies a defensible and useful concept of natural law. For it simply spells out what is involved in acting reasonably, or consistently, if there are some things that one desires—that is, if there are some things that one regards as good and some as evil. One may, of course, refuse to be reasonable, and if one does then one will not make contact with any of Hobbes's arguments. He has nothing to say to the irrational man. But of course he is not trying to do that. Nor is he describing how men necessarily *do* deliberate, because he knows that men can be mad, but merely laying out the formal structure of a rational deliberation.

Having explained what a law of nature is, Hobbes goes on to derive the first and fundamental law of nature from his account of the state of nature. In the state of nature there is a natural right of every man to every thing. But "as long as this natural right of every man to every thing endureth, there can be no security to any man, how strong or wise soever he be, of living out the time, which nature ordinarily alloweth men to live" (XIV 85). The formal rendering of that proposition is: so long as natural right continues no man can reasonably expect anything but the frustration of his desires—that is, has grounds for despair. Hobbes draws the conclusion:

And consequently it is a precept, or general rule of reason, *that every man, ought to endeavour peace, as far as he has hope of obtaining it; and when he cannot obtain it, that he may seek, and use, all helps, and advantages of war.* The first branch of which rule, containeth the first, and fundamental law of nature; which is, *to seek peace, and follow it.* The second, the sum of the right of nature; which is, *by all means we can, to defend ourselves* (XIV 85).

In order to see that that, as it stands, is a necessary proposition within Hobbes's system one has to revert to his account of peace and war. Peace is simply that state of affairs in which there is not war, and war consists not necessarily "in actual fighting; but in the known disposition thereto" (XIII 82). Hobbes does not define "fighting", but I think that an adequate definition of it would be "For $X$ to fight with $Y$ is for $X$ actively to exercise power over $Y$ in such a way as to prevent $Y$ from exercising his own power as he wills." That is a very general definition, and it would mean that some distant person who cornered the supply of some material which was necessary for my survival would be fighting with me. If my condition was very rare, and the monopolist did not know either about the curative properties of the material or about my need for it, it would be a very strained use of English to describe him as *fighting* with me. But I do not think that that matters at all in this context. The reason why Hobbes is able to represent war as *necessarily* evil is that it threatens the realisation of one's objectives, including, of course, one's own survival. A time of war is a time in which there is no restriction on each individual's pursuit of whatever objectives he has in the way which seems to him most effective—no restriction, that is, on the exercise of the right of nature—and it has already been argued that in such a situation no man has reasonable grounds for anything but despair, no matter what his objectives may be. Peace, then, is a situation in which there exist sufficient restrictions on the general exercise of the right of nature to give a man a reasonable hope of success in the pursuit of his objectives.

Now Hobbes thinks that such restrictions can exist effectively only if imposed coercively by a political authority: men are in a state of war "during the time men live without a common power to keep them all in awe" (XIII 82). That looks like merely the reflection of Hobbes's pessimistic view of human nature, so that only the effective threat of punishment, including death, can restrain men from violence against each other. But I think that Hobbes's argument is much more powerful than that. Whatever my objectives may be I can have reasonable hope of pursuing them effectively only if I can have reasonable hope that my endeavours will not be frustrated by the activities of others. In order that I should be able to place some reliance on that it is necessary that people's behaviour generally should conform more or less to some ascertainable rules, otherwise it will be unpredictable, and to that extent my situation will be insecure. Now it may be supposed that there could be a society in which people willingly conformed to certain rules and were prepared to continue conforming even although the rules were not in any way enforced. If that were possible then the proposition that when there is no "common power" there is a state of war would clearly not be a necessary proposition. I think, however, that Hobbes not only *could* meet this argument but has in fact gone a good deal of the way to meeting it. What is in question is whether there could be a society in which there was no coercive order but a non-coercive order sufficient to permit security in the pursuit of objectives. Either there is some *logical* reason for rejecting the notion of such a society, or the proposition that without a "common power" there is a state of war cannot be *necessarily* true. Just how much is involved in the notion of a "common power"? The function of the common power is to compel conformity with those rules which make it possible for people to have some reasonable hope of success in pursuing their objectives. The nature of that power, and how exercised, must depend on many variable factors—the size of a society, its homogeneity, its level of sophistication, and so forth. A small, developed, stable society might be composed of people who had become so law-abiding that an organised police force had been dispensed with. Would that be a society without a "common power"? Of course not. Police power is not the only sort of power. If people generally were *prepared* to take effective action—become *ad hoc* police —in the rare event of unlawful action, so as to punish it and prevent repetition, then the threat of the exercise of such power would—in such a society—be a compelling force, and it would amount to the existence of a "common power". There is nothing in the least farfetched in such a notion: many informal associations—of children, for example—operate peaceably and effectively on such a basis.

Then what conditions would a society have to meet in order that it should be describable as having *no* "common power"? It would have to be the case that it would be predictable that people would not take effective penal or preventive action if breaches of the law occurred or seemed likely to occur. A society of pacifists might seem to fill the bill, but in fact even general pacifism would fall short of the requirement. For a pacifist is one who refuses to engage in overt violence, but overt violence is not the only way of exercising power over others. (My own small daughter is stoical about wounds and bruises, but she will sometimes restrain herself from a misdemeanour from fear of being berated by her school-teacher. The teacher, apparently, uses a telling-off as a (humane) form of punishment. Whether or not the teacher intends it that way, that is how it works: it is, to the child, a disagreeable experience to which she is liable to be subjected as a consequence of committing an offence, and it is a deterrent to committing the offence.) Pacifists have at their disposal a legitimate armoury of weapons which includes the expression of withering disapproval, not to mention lying down in public places. It is probable that in most societies a pacifist system of coercion would not be adequate to enforce the law. But that is a contingent matter, and in any case the point is that *if* it were effective it would be an exercise of power. For even the most highly-organised police forces do not aspire to be on the scene of every projected crime, forcibly restraining the criminal. They are merely the means by which in some, but by no means all, cases the criminal is discovered and subjected to penalties. It is the threat of penalties which compels; and anything may be a penalty if it is an evil, dispensable at the will of those who have it at their disposal, and sufficient to weigh, in the deliberations of a possible offender, against the good to be achieved by the offence. Most parents, skilled in the art of psychological warfare against children, know that violence does not always require strong muscles.

In order that a society should be describable as having no "common power" it would have to be positively committed to abstaining from *any* sort of action which could bring any substantial evil on the heads of offenders. In such a society anyone who was tempted to offend would be able to weigh good against evil without having to take into account any evil which would come on him as a consequence of his action's *being an offence*. If people were extraordinarily and uniformly law-abiding this would not necessarily and immediately lead to any substantial number of breaches of law. Each individual would be able to rely on the orderly behaviour of others, and would have no grounds for despair. But this is a matter of *degree*. Beyond a certain point, to the extent to which the behaviour of people became as predictable as that, to that extent the society would more closely resemble an ant-heap. And, beyond a certain point, to the extent to which the behaviour of people was not predictably lawful the deliberations of individuals would become uncertain. For what the "common power" does is to ensure that a motive exists to keep the law, for anyone who otherwise might lack a sufficient motive. And in so doing (i) it removes from the individual any reasonable temptation to consider anticipatory violence: one might put it briefly by saying that the "common power" *is* anticipatory violence institutionalised. This is an important function, for what makes for maximum uncertainty is a situation where each individual has to do his own anticipating—because even if I am initially prepared to abstain from anticipatory violence against others I must realise that they can foresee the *possibility* of *my* anticipatory violence and cannot *rely* on my abstaining, so that they have good reason to act themselves in anticipation, and I therefore have reason for not abstaining after all. And (ii) the existence of a "common power" is a guarantee that (on the whole) the law will not be broken with impunity—that is what a "common power" *is*. And that can be important even in a society where there is likely to be small inclination to break the law anyway. You might have a very stable society of very law-abiding people. You might think that they were *so* law-abiding that any measures of enforcement, or preparedness to adopt such measures, were unnecessary. But you must be careful here. If *some* breaches were liable to happen, then in the absence of a "common power" they would happen with impunity. That would be a new factor in the situation, not only tempting those who might not otherwise have been tempted, so as to increase the incidence of breaches of the law, but also depriving others of the protection afforded by the existence of the "common power". A law-abiding person does not necessarily have the same reason for keeping the law once offenders have been guaranteed immunity from penalties.

It seems clear that the only viable alternatives are (*a*) a society with a "common power", and (*b*) a society with no "common power" but with members whose behaviour is so predictably lawful that there is virtually no chance of the law ever being broken. Hobbes—to return explicitly to him—does not ignore the second alternative. He discusses the question why it is that when creatures like bees and ants can live peaceably and sociably without a "common power" men cannot do the same. Hobbes gives a number of reasons why not. One of these is that ants and bees do not possess reason, but men do, and this leads them to think that they can reform society, each according to his own ideas, which can lead to "distraction and civil war" (XIV 111). A society which was thoroughly law-abiding, yet with no "common power" would have to be a *very* homogeneous society, with no fundamental disagreements about values. There are two extremes here. One extreme is a completely heterogeneous society with no agreement about values. Hobbes would not expect any "common power" to be able to hold such a society together, since on his view the "common power" derives its power from the consent of the governed. The other extreme is a society so homogeneous that no "common power" is necessary. Hobbes's discussion of the ants and bees amounts to saying that such a society would not be a recognisably *human* society. I think that he is right about that. Now if that is true it is not a psychological proposition, open to the possibility of confirmation or falsification. It does not assert that a human society *could* not develop so that it was able eventually to dispense with a "common power". All that the proposition does is to draw attention to some features of the change that would then have taken place, and to claim that life in the evolved society would be so different from the sort of life that we are accustomed to regard as human that it would be in a sense paradoxical to describe it as a human society at all.

I believe that Hobbes is right about that. At all events it is a proposition which is arguable and which appropriately belongs within a Hobbesian system because it is not a contingent truth about human beings but an unfolding of what is involved in the concept of a human being. If we agree with Hobbes on this point, then, we can regard this part of his system as something which is necessarily true of all human societies, and which therefore properly belongs within a Hobbesian *science* of politics. If we do not agree with Hobbes that a "common power" is necessary for the existence of society and the avoidance of a state of war, then his system, so far as it depends on that proposition, will be true only of those human societies to which the existence of a "common power" is necessary. Then we should have special reason to distinguish very carefully and explicitly between pure political science and applied political science. The pure science would be a system of hypothetical propositions which could be applied and used only in the cases where the condition was met, that society could exist only under a "common power". It would be a matter for empirical investigation to discover (as in my opinion it would be discovered) that all actual or probable human situations are situations in which society cannot be maintained or created without the maintenance or creation of a "common power". If that were established it would have been shown (empirically—not demonstrated) that the pure science applied to all actual or possible human situations. Or it might be shown to apply to many but not all situations. That would not be to refute the pure science but merely to reduce its importance. If it were shown that it applied to none, then the pure science would have become a mere pointless exercise in logic.

Because, as I have argued, I believe that Hobbes's proposition about a "common power" does apply to all recognisably *human* situations I believe both that as it stands it is a formal proposition, belonging within the demonstrative system, and not dependent on any empirical facts, and also that it provides a basis for a precept of reason requiring all men, so far as they are rational and human, to seek peace. I believe that Hobbes has succeeded in showing that it is un-reasonable for any man not to seek peace, whatever his values, so long as he has *some* values, because only in a situation of peace, guaranteed by a "common power", can a man have good reason not to despair.

A conveniently brief way of expressing this would be in terms of a distinction between *necessary* and *contingent values*. A necessary value is some X which necessarily will be desired by any reasonable being, so far as he is reasonable, who also desires Y and Z, whatever Y and Z may be. A contingent value is a value which is not a necessary value. Power, in the sense of the term defined in *Leviathan*, is a necessary value, because if there is anything which a person values he must desire the means of promoting it. A man's own survival is not a necessary value because merely from the fact that a man has some desires it does not necessarily follow that he desires his own survival. Hobbes, however, thinks that a man's own survival *is* a necessary value. But he recognises that there are many contingent values—different men desire different things, as does even the same man at different times. Thus although Hobbes never uses the terms "neces-sary value" and "contingent value", the distinction corresponds to a distinction which he recognises and uses. Thus what I have been saying about Hobbes's argument may be summed up thus: he is mis-taken in supposing that a man's own survival is a necessary value; but he is correct in supposing that necessary values are an important element of the deliberations of one person who is in relation to other people; and he is correct in arguing that peace is a necessary value.

## 2 THE RENUNCIATION OF RIGHTS

Having established the fundamental law Hobbes goes on to derive a number of particular laws—another eighteen of them. The funda-mental law commands us to seek peace, and the other laws point the way to that end.

The second law of nature is "derived", Hobbes says, from the fundamental law, and it is "that a man be willing, when others are so too, as far-forth, as for peace, and defence of himself he shall think it necessary, to lay down his right to all things; and be contented with so much liberty against other men, as he would allow other men against himself" (XIV 85). In order that that should be a necessarily true proposition the reference to self-defence would have to be deleted, since it is the reappearance of the material concept of self-preservation, and the formal concept of the promotion of one's values (or the avoidance of the total frustration of one's desires) substituted. Peace, of course, is to be sought because it is the condition of the effective promotion of values, and the latter has to be kept in mind. For if Hobbes were offered general peace, but at the price of his own life, Hobbes would hold that Hobbes could not reasonably be expected to seize the opportunity. And if someone valued a sense of duty above all else Hobbes would be committed to holding that he could not necessarily be reasonably expected to buy peace at the cost, say, of the total moral corruption of the world. Hence this second law of nature incorporates a double reservation. In the first place, a man should be willing to abandon the natural right to all things only when others are willing to do the same. There is nothing necessarily selfish about that: it is merely that to abandon one's own right unilaterally would be to render oneself impotent to pursue one's values, without gaining in return any expectation that they would be realised in any other way. The second reservation is that even if others *are* willing to make peace, if the consequence of making peace is going to be the existence of the very evils which one was seeking for peace in order to avert, then the abandoning of the right of nature would be contrary to one's values. That is not to say that one would be released from the obligation to *seek* peace, but that one would reasonably prefer to wait, in the hope of better terms.

Hobbes emphasises this second reservation by arguing that some rights are not alienable. When a man transfers or renounces rights it is a voluntary act "and of the voluntary acts of every man, the object is some *good to himself*". Therefore a man cannot be understood to have abandoned the right of resisting attempts on his life or person, "because he cannot be understood to aim thereby, at any good to himself" (XIV 86–87). This applies even to a criminal resisting arrest. If the law threatens a man's life he has the right to resist: his crime consists in the original offence with which he is accused and not in resisting (even a lawful) threat to his life (XXI 142–3). What Hobbes is saying is not so startling as it may sound. This right to resist the law is no sort of *protection* to a man, for there is no obligation on anyone else to respect it. Putting the argument in the formal mode, it is that peace is a means for the promotion of good and the avoidance of evil. The only obligation there is on a man to accept the conditions of peace is the prospect of promoting good and avoiding evil. If this condition is not met then a man is at war with others. When the law threatens a criminal's life then *if* a man's death is, for him, the greatest possible evil he is at war with all the other law-abiding members of society. If a man's own death is not, for him, the greatest possible evil then he does not have an inalienable right to protect his life, but whatever he regards as the complete frustration of all his desires will be that which, if it should threaten, he will be entitled to resist, even if such resistance puts him at war with others, including lawful authority. The significant feature of this right is not so much the fact that it is inalienable but that its exercise is a reversion to the state of war.

Hobbes gives a simple and clear account of what it is to lay down a right. Since in the state of nature every man has a right to everything, one man's renunciation does not give another any right which he did not have before: it is merely that he "standeth out of his way, that he may enjoy his own original right, without hindrance from him" (XIV 85–86). (This is just one of many arguments in *Leviathan* which makes it obvious that by "right" Hobbes means not the absence of external impediments to doing what one wills but the absence of that special kind of impediment called "obligation". For my renunciation of some of my rights could not remove impediments to the exercise of your rights if the existence of a right consisted simply in the absence of external impediments.) This gives an effective twist to the argument. Hobbes has said that laws bind, whereas the essence of right is liberty, and the second law of nature directs us to renounce the right to everything which we have in the state of nature; yet when everyone has a right to everything no one has an effective right to anything, and what the second law of nature directs is that we should renounce some of our ineffective rights in order to make the remainder effective.

## 3 COVENANTS

The next step of Hobbes's argument is an account of *contract* and *covenant*. "The mutual transferring of right, is that which men call CONTRACT" (XIV 87). That seems clear enough. Hobbes goes on to explain that if *one* of the contractors performs his part, leaving the other to perform at some later time, "then the contract on his part, is called PACT, or COVENANT". That also seems clear: a covenant is a contract in which one of the contractors is trusted to perform later. But a few paragraphs later Hobbes says, "If a covenant be made, wherein neither of the parties perform presently, but trust one another . . ." (XIV 89). Hence a covenant is to be taken as a contract in which one *or both* parties trust the other to perform later. What is important for Hobbes's argument, as we shall see, is the *trust* which is involved, on at least one side, in a covenant.

The second law of nature obliges us "to transfer to another, such rights, as being retained, hinder the peace of mankind" (XV 93). Such transference is covenant, for there is no single act or series of acts in which any of the contractors can completely fulfil his part of the contract: what is involved is a reciprocal undertaking to respect the rights of others both now and indefinitely in the future. From this, then, there obviously follows a third law of nature, "*that men perform their covenants made*: without which, covenants are in vain, and but empty words; and the right of all men to all things remaining, we are still in the condition of war" (XV 93). And this, Hobbes claims, is the foundation of the notions of *justice* and *injustice*, for *injustice* is nothing else than failing to perform one's covenant, and the *just* is whatever is not unjust. This argument of Hobbes's applies specially, of course, to that covenant by which men renounce the right of nature. But it is stated generally, so as to apply to all covenants; and the same argument which establishes the obligation to keep the covenant renouncing the right of nature ought to be relevant also to the obligation to keep other covenants. For the important difference between the state of nature and ordered society is the *uncertainty* of the former, which generates anticipation and despair. If a covenant has been made it has been made as something giving each party to it a ground for relying on some action or course of action by the other. So far as such grounds are removed—for example, by breach of covenant—so far one step at least has been taken towards a state of war.

That, of course, is a familiar enough line of argument, and it has its limitations. Firstly, it contains by no means all of the elements which many would consider to be important parts of the concepts of justice and integrity. Secondly, it only provides, at best, a justification for holding that in general covenants ought not to be broken. It does not provide every man on every possible occasion with a rationally compelling reason for keeping every single covenant which he has made. It is no more than a general rule, to which there must be possible exceptions.

These limitations are, however, allowed for within a Hobbesian account. For I have suggested (at the end of Section 1 of this chapter) that Hobbes distinguishes what I (though not Hobbes) call *necessary* and *contingent* values. Thus he establishes that peace is a necessary value. But it is such only under a limitation: it is always reasonable to *seek* peace, but not necessarily to accept it on *any* terms. Peace is not to be promoted at the cost of all the values which it is intended to serve (see Section 2). How this cost is to be calculated will depend on the particular values of each particular person. Hobbes thinks that all men will necessarily agree to regard their own death as too high a cost. But he is wrong about that, and one's own survival is only a contingent value, although it is probably true—and this can be ascertained empirically, and only empirically—that for most men it is a *very* important value. Peace itself might be a contingent value for some, as well as a necessary value—they might, for example, just *dislike* open conflict. Some again might value integrity as a contingent value: that is, they would still value it even if they did not consider it to be a means to the promotion of other values. If Hobbes's argument establishing the third law of nature is valid, then, it shows that a certain conception of justice (not failing to perform one's covenants) is a necessary element of any reasonable person's scheme of values. But the contingent values that a person has may well augment this limited conception of justice, and in such a case justice—in this augmented sense—would be valued partly as a necessary and partly as a contingent value. Thus someone who valued integrity would think that the Hobbesian analysis of justice as a means to the promotion of other values was an *inadequate* account of justice. And he would be right, because Hobbes's account is, and ought to be, an inadequate representation of any actual scheme of values, since it is concerned only with the necessary values which must be incorporated within any scheme of values but which presuppose some (but not any specific) other and contingent values.

Now suppose that a person's contingent values comprised compassion, peace and integrity. Then a world in which these were realised to the greatest possible extent would be, in his view, the best possible world. He would have a very good reason for regarding himself as having an obligation to keep covenants, not only because justice (in the Hobbesian sense) was a necessary value but also because, for him, integrity was a contingent value. Yet if there were an occasion on which the keeping of a covenant were incompatible—as it might be—with acting compassionately or peacefully he would have to consider whether to keep or break the covenant. Keeping the covenant would have to involve a very great threat to his values as a whole in order to outweigh the fact that breaking it would be incompatible not only with the particular contingent value of integrity but also with the necessary value of justice (in the Hobbesian sense), and therefore a threat to all possible values. Nevertheless, such a contingency could conceivably arise, and, if it did, the person involved could not reasonably regard himself as having an obligation on that particular occasion to keep that particular covenant: the obligation in that situation would be superseded by a more stringent and contrary obligation. Whatever scheme of values a person has, unless the only contingent value within it is identical with the necessary value of justice, it will be *possible* for situations to arise in which there are grounds for making exceptions to the general obligation to keep covenants. That is to say that Hobbes's account of covenants is a formal account which of itself provides a ground of a *general* obligation to keep covenants, and at the same time is capable of accommodating both any scheme of values which gives grounds for occasional exceptions and also the rare case of an inflexible scheme of values which permits of no such exceptions.

A special class of exceptions to the general obligation to keep covenants is where there is some feature of the situation that renders the covenant void or invalid. Thus if I have already promised something to Smith and later promise it to Jones, the latter is void, because in promising it to Smith I passed away my right to it, "and therefore the later promise passeth no right, but is null" (XIV 91). Again, a covenant made in the state of nature, in which both parties trust each other to perform later, is void if there is "any reasonable suspicion" that the other party will not perform (XIV 89). Hobbes's argument here is that in the state of nature the contractor who performs first and trusts the other has no assurance that the other will perform his part, so that in performing his own he "does but betray himself to his enemy" (XIV 90). What that argument seems to show, of course, is that in the state of nature no covenants ought to be made, and if made they are void. Yet the laws of nature, including the second law which prescribes the reciprocal renunciation of rights, require us to make covenants, in order to achieve peace, and to keep them in order to maintain it. Hobbes seems to have shown both that it is necessary and also that it is impossible to escape from the state of nature. In fact he manages to solve this problem in the later stages of his argument, when he introduces the notion of a covenant which ends the state of nature by establishing a "common power". The merits of that part of Hobbes's argument will be examined later, when Hobbes's account of the institution of the commonwealth is discussed. For the moment it must be left simply as an unsolved problem.

When he is discussing the validity and invalidity of covenants Hobbes insists that a covenant entered into because of fear is not thereby rendered invalid. I have argued already (Chapter Seven, Section 3) that Hobbes is correct in his assertion that if a person does something incurring an obligation the fact that he did it out of fear does not of itself remove the obligation. He concludes that if a man covenants in the state of nature to pay ransom for his life, then the covenant is not invalid, even although made only out of fear. For that matter, Hobbes adds, even in an organised society, if I save myself from a robber by promising him money I am obliged to pay him unless the civil law releases me from the obligation (XIV 91). Now Hobbes here is pushing the argument too far. From the proposition that a covenant made because of fear is not thereby rendered invalid it does not follow that all covenants entered into because of fear are valid. There may be (and I think that there are) reasons for holding that there are certain special features of some situations in which a covenant is made out of fear which render it invalid. All that Hobbes *needs* to argue is that it is these special features, and not the fear alone, which render it invalid. It is, in fact, possible to argue that Hobbes's account is correct as it stands. If I covenant to pay a robber a large sum of money, under threat of death, I do have an obligation to pay, which the law may *remove*. Against the view that any covenant extorted by threats is wholly void it may be argued that (i) it is reasonable to preserve the possibility of escaping from threat-situations by promising ransom, (ii) that this possibility depends on the robber's assurance that the promise is to be relied on, and (iii) that such reliance depends on a general commitment to keep such promises—i.e. to regard them as creating obligations, so that (iv) the decision to regard such covenants as void would be a decision to deprive oneself of the opportunity of escaping from a certain dangerous kind of situation if ever it were to arise. That argument, if valid, shows that covenants are not necessarily invalid, even if extorted by threat, so that extortion by threat is not one of those special features which necessarily invalidate a covenant. Hobbes, however, does not need to assert that all covenants extorted by threat are valid, nor even that extortion by threat is never a sufficient ground of invalidation of a covenant, because the only sort of extortion which is important to his argument is the case of the conqueror who overthrows a commonwealth (by invasion, for example) and sets himself up as ruler, sparing the lives of those whom he has subdued only on the understanding that they will become his obedient subjects. Hobbes calls that "a commonwealth by acquisition", and he argues later (in chapter XX of *Leviathan*) that the fact that a sovereign has become such by "acquisition" does not in any way diminish his rights or authority. But in order to justify that assertion it is not necessary to hold that all covenants extorted by threat are valid but merely that *certain* covenants are *not* invalidated because extorted by threat (although others may be). The conclusions which Hobbes has already reached about the state of nature provide him with arguments supporting the conclusion that covenants extorted by a conqueror are not invalid although extorted. For if anyone is a conqueror it is only because he has destroyed a previously existing "common power". In such a situation there is a state of nature, unless the conqueror replaces the previous "common power"; and, as conqueror, he is able to destroy those whom he has subdued. The latter, then, are in the same situation as they would be in if a state of nature had come about in any other way, for they have the same need for an ordered society. They have, indeed, an immediate opportunity of achieving that, because they are faced by a ready-made "common power" in the person of the conqueror. The fact that the conqueror is an enemy is not relevant in such a situation: what is relevant is the consideration that when the previous "common power" has been overthrown it is still possible for the conquered to achieve an ordered society by committing themselves to obedience to a new "common power", and this is the only way in which it can be achieved. The conquered have to submit to the conqueror because he is a successful enemy, but his claim to their *continued* allegiance is that his success makes him the embodiment of that "common power" which is a necessary condition of the validity of covenants.

## 4 OBLIGATION, COMPULSION AND NECESSITATION

In his discussion of the reciprocal renunciation of the right of nature Hobbes says that when a man has renounced some of his rights, so as to make effective some of the rights of others, "then he is said to be OBLIGED, or BOUND, not to hinder those, to whom such right is granted, or abandoned, from the benefit of it: and that he *ought*, and it is his DUTY, not to make void that voluntary act of his own: and that such hindrance is INJUSTICE, and INJURY, as being *sine jure*" (XIV 86). Hobbes is offering here a very succinct account of "obliged", "bound", "duty" and "ought". His account is rather *too* succinct, because he simply makes these terms all equivalent to each other. The inadequacies of what he says might be excused, on the grounds that what he is engaged in is not the writing of a comprehensive treatise on moral philosophy but the construction of a political theory, with just as much moral philosophy as is necessary for the purpose in hand. Nevertheless this passage does raise a problem of interpretation. What Hobbes says is that when a man has renounced rights "then he is *said to be* OBLIGED . . .". If what Hobbes is doing here is to offer a definition of "obliged", "ought" etc., then there seems to be an inconsistency between this definition and actual usage elsewhere. For the *first* law of nature is "that every man ought to endeavour peace. . . ." The "ought" which occurs in the formulation of the first law of nature cannot be the "ought" which is defined in the discussion which follows the second law of nature, because we already "ought" to seek peace before we can engage in the renunciation of rights which generates the other "ought". There is a similar difficulty about "oblige" and "obligation". When he concludes his discussion of the laws of nature Hobbes says that they oblige only *in foro interno* and not always *in foro externo* (that is, they oblige merely to the desire that they should take place, but not necessarily to the act (xv 103)). The point is that they do "oblige", even if only *in foro interno*, and the obligation to be prepared to renounce rights (reciprocally, in the pursuit of peace) cannot be an obligation in the same sense of "obligation" as the obligation which by definition arises out of the renunciation of rights.

Yet although Hobbes is involved here in a certain amount of confusion, and although what he says falls far short of being a satisfactory philosophical analysis of obligation, nevertheless his account is of some philosophical interest. Taking ordinary English usage as a guide, there seems to be a clear distinction to be made between *being obliged* and *having an obligation*. I am obliged to leave the house now because it is on fire. I have an obligation to leave the house now because I promised to stay no later. I am obliged to listen to my students' ideas, because I do not know how to stop them talking. I have an obligation to listen to my students' ideas because that is part of my job. Now there are some important similarities between the two types of case.

1. Being obliged and having an obligation both imply a certain degree of constraint. I might prefer to stay in the house, if it were not for the fire, or the promise: fires on the premises and promises to leave are both things that may compel me to leave when otherwise I might have chosen to stay.

2. Nevertheless, although compelled, I still have a choice. I *could* stay and burn to death, as captains used sometimes to choose to go down with their ships, and I *could* stay and break my promise. Sometimes we express the fact that we are obliged to do something by saying that we "have no choice". That, however, does not mean "no choice at all", but "no *reasonable* choice". The shop assistant *could* choose to die rather than hand over his employer's money to the gunman, but he could not be reasonably expected to, and we should readily agree that he had "no choice". Indeed, it is not merely that having no (reasonable) choice *is* compatible with having a choice, but it *has* to be compatible. For the only sort of case in which I can be said

absolutely to have no choice is a case where I *cannot* resist doing what I do, as when I hit you because a very strong man is holding my arm and pushing it into contact with your body. In such a case I have no choice at all; but then it is not that I have actually done something, being obliged to do it, having no choice, but rather that *I* have not done anything, but have had my arm used as a club by someone else who *did* do something. Thus if doing something, having no choice, is really to be a case of *doing* something, the "no choice" must be read as "no reasonable choice", and therefore "being obliged to do something" and "having an obligation to do something" are both compatible with, and both imply, the existence of at least some degree of choice.

3. Both being obliged and having an obligation are related to blame, or the possibility of blame. If prima facie you are disposed to blame me for something, then my showing that I did it, being obliged to, or having an obligation to, has a tendency to lessen or remove the blame. It may, of course, only *transfer* the blame, and not necessarily on to other shoulders—the fire obliged you to leave the house, but you ought to have checked the fire-extinguishers; or you ought never to have promised to leave early. Nevertheless, if any question of blame should arise, being obliged to and having an obligation to are both considerations that must be taken into account.

But there are also some differences.

*a.* If I did something, being obliged to, then to that extent I cannot be blamed: I simply could not help doing it, and merit neither praise nor blame. But to do something, having an obligation to do it, is not at all to be unable to help doing it; and meeting one's obligations deserves praise, if anything, especially when carried out in circumstances of unusual or unforeseen difficulty.

*b.* What obliges one, in cases simply of being obliged, is some particular feature of the actual situation in which one does whatever it is that one is obliged to do—the fire, the talkativeness of the students, or whatever it may be—and the occurrence of such features may be more or less foreseeable, so that one may in some cases, although not in others, be able to predict, with more or less confidence, that one is going to be obliged to do this or that. But if I promise now to start work tomorrow I am not now in a position to *predict* (with more or less confidence) that tomorrow I *shall* have an obligation. The obligation exists *now*, and I carry it around with me until it is discharged. One might be tempted to say that it does not become *operative* until tomorrow, but that would be a mistake, because in some respects it clearly is operative from the moment it is assumed—it commits me now, for example, to a further obligation not to take any steps that will make it impossible for me to discharge the primary obligation tomorrow.

In order to keep the distinction clear, and to have a conveniently brief way of referring to it, it would be useful, and not contrary to ordinary usage, to adopt the term "compulsion" for cases of being obliged, and to reserve the term "obligation" for cases of having an obligation. Now when Hobbes defines "obliged" in terms of renunciation of rights he is giving (the beginnings of) an analysis of what I have called "obligation", and is restricting it by definition to obligations incurred by an act of one's own (such as promising). That is a restriction which is certainly defensible, but also debatable: it would lead one to say, for example, that parents, just *qua* parents, have obligations towards their children, but that children, just *qua* children, do not have obligations towards their parents. That issue, however, is not of primary importance to Hobbes's argument. What is important is that in the first place he uses the terms "oblige" and "obligation" also in ways which are not subject to that restriction, because there is no act by which we *assume* the obligation to seek peace; and that in the second place his account of obligation in the unrestricted sense lies behind his account of obligation in the restricted sense. Thus it is important to determine what precisely the relation is between his two different concepts of obligation.

On one possible interpretation of Hobbes, unrestricted obligation is simply compulsion, and the distinction between restricted and unrestricted obligation is just the distinction between obligation and compulsion. Thus in De Cive the law of nature is "the dictate of right reason, conversant about those things which are either to be done or omitted for the constant preservation of life and members, as much as in us lies", and Hobbes explains that by "reason" he does not mean some infallible faculty but the actual "act of reasoning" (*De Cive*, II 1). He points out also that reason is itself a part of human nature, and he has already claimed that every man avoids evil, and especially his own death, "by a certain impulsion of nature, no less than that whereby a stone moves downward" (I 7). That comes very near to assimilating the law of nature to physical laws, which describe how things do actually happen, and distinguishing it from prescriptive laws, which prescribe what ought to be done, without implying that things do in fact happen that way. Just as a stone moves downwards, so we seek to preserve ourselves, and use our reason to point the way to our preservation. On this account, then, it is not so much that the law of nature itself obliges, as that it describes an inner compulsion, like the inner compulsion which drives the kleptomaniac to steal.

Such a conception of the law of nature, although suggested by some passages from *De Cive*, is not appropriate to the argument of *Leviathan*. I have argued in the earlier parts of this book that in *Leviathan* Hobbes attempts to construct a formal science which leaves no place for descriptions of psychological tendencies, and that the fear of death is, in *Leviathan*, merely the content which Hobbes—mistakenly, but without prejudice to the main course of his argument—insists on giving to the formal concept of fear of frustration of all one's desires. And I have suggested, in Section 1 of this chapter, that Hobbes's account of a law of nature, formalised so as to permit it to belong within the formal system of *Leviathan*, is that a law of nature is a rational precept forbidding a man to do that which would lead to the frustration of all his desires or values, or would prevent him from realising these, and to omit that which would lead to their realisation. The laws of nature do, indeed, "oblige" us, but they oblige because they are "rational precepts". They apply to any man, whatever his values, just so long as he *has* some values, and so far as he is prepared to be reasonable. The proposition that a man's deliberations will not be contrary to the law of nature so far as he deliberates reasonably is a necessary proposition, and a value, such as peace, to which the law of nature directs us is a necessary value. There is no compulsion about it, because men will often enough, and easily, fail to be reasonable. Yet the laws of nature have a claim on us, and a necessary claim, so far as we *are* prepared to be reasonable. The obligation which the laws of nature impose on us, then, is certainly not any kind of compulsion, but it might not be inappropriate to call it "necessitation", because they indicate paths which any rational deliberation necessarily follows.

In considering Hobbes's accounts of obligation, then, three notions have to be distinguished.

1. There is *compulsion*. This is the sort of notion which is sometimes expressed by the term "being obliged to".

2. There is *necessitation*, which is the claim that rational

considerations have upon us (though of course we may not be prepared to be rational).

3. There is *obligation*, which is the existence of a *commitment* to act in some specific way. Some of the elements of Hobbes's arguments in *De Cive* seem to derive obligations from compulsion. But in *Leviathan* the fundamental concept is necessitation, and the pattern of the argument is to show that for any rational being, who has any contingent values, and who is in relation to other such beings, there are certain necessary values, such as peace, which necessitate the taking on and fulfilling of obligations.

## 5  THE PRECEPTS OF REASON

So far I have discussed the fundamental law of nature and the second and third laws. Hobbes goes on to derive a great many more, not all of which either are of great importance to his argument or present any interesting difficulties of interpretation. Examples are the seventh law, of "revenges", which requires that "*in revenges, that is, retribution of evil for evil, men look not at the greatness of the evil past, but the greatness of the good to follow*" (xv 100), and the sixteenth law, "of submission to arbitrement", which requires "*that they that are at controversy, submit their right to the judgment of an arbitrator*" (xv 102). The argument for the sixteenth law is that refusal to submit to arbitration is simply a reversion to war, and since the fundamental law is to seek peace, the sixteenth follows. The seventh law is given a similar derivation. The fundamental law is indeed treated by Hobbes as literally fundamental, because if it collapses the remainder are left without foundation. The question of the validity of the laws of nature in general reduces to the question of the validity of the fundamental law, to seek peace.

In Section 1 of this chapter I have argued that Hobbes succeeds in establishing peace as a necessary value. It is something, that is to say, which rational beings who have contingent values and who are in relation with other such beings will necessarily seek so far as they are prepared to be rational. The proposition that if a man, who is in company with other men, deliberates or acts rationally then he deliberates or acts in accordance with the law of nature is (if Hobbes's arguments are valid as I have presented them) a necessarily true proposition, because the law of nature simply spells out what it is for such a man to deliberate or act rationally. That proposition, however, is a proposition *about* the law of nature, but the law of nature itself is a set of "precepts", requiring us to seek peace, be prepared to enter upon a reciprocal renunciation of rights, and so forth. One may hesitate to apply the terms "true" and "false" to such precepts, because they are of the nature of commands rather than of propositions. Nevertheless, a perfectly good sense, which does not raise any logical problems, can be attached to calling them "necessarily true": to say that a precept, $P$, is necessarily true is to say that the proposition "If a man deliberates or acts rationally he deliberates or acts in accordance with $P$" is necessarily true. In order to show that this is a necessarily true proposition when the laws of nature are taken as values of "$P$", "rational being with some contingent values" has to be taken as involved in the definition of "man", because the form of the argument is to show that peace is a necessary value for any rational being who has contingent values. But of course more than that is required, because peace is only shown to be a necessary value for rational beings with contingent values who are in relation to other such beings. The existence of these relations is presupposed by the argument. There are two different ways in which it is possible to introduce them into the argument. One would be to say that the laws of nature apply only to men who happen to be involved with other men, but do not apply to solitary men. That would leave it as an empirical question, whether the laws applied to any particular man or not. The other, and logically simpler, way would be to incorporate the relations with other men as part of the definition of "man". "Man", then, would be defined as "rational being, with some contingent values, and in relation with other such beings", and Hobbes would then be able to argue that peace was a necessary value for any man. This method of reconstructing the argument is to be preferred, I think.

1. For the only sort of men Hobbes is interested in are men who do have relations with other men, for what he is attempting to construct is a science of *politics*—a set of propositions which are necessarily true within a political context, and not an ethical system valid also for some lonely individual who ekes out a totally solitary existence somewhere, say, in outer space.

2. If we did come across someone who had never had any relations with other people he might be biologically, but not humanly, recognisable as a man.

3. Hobbes himself suggests this by implication, because the discussion of the state of nature and of natural law in *Leviathan* falls in "The First Part—of Man". The definition of "man" as "rational being, with some contingent values, and in relation with other such beings" is certainly not Hobbes's definition, but it is not contrary to his method, and it is true to his argument.

When he comes to the conclusion of his account of the law of nature Hobbes remarks that they "oblige *in foro interno*; that is to say, they bind to a desire they should take place: but *in foro externo*; that is, to the putting them in act, not always" (xv 103). For someone who performed all his promises in a situation where no one else did, would merely "make himself a prey to others, and procure his own certain ruin, contrary to the ground of all laws of nature". This remark has given a certain amount of what seems to me to be quite unnecessary trouble to commentators. Thus in *The Political Philosophy of Hobbes* Professor Warrender suggests that by obligation *in foro interno* Hobbes means obligation not *merely* to desire to observe the law, but obligation to be prepared to observe it when it is safe to do so, and to try to create the conditions in which it can safely be observed. Mr. Plamenatz thinks that Warrender's rendering is "a generous interpretation of Hobbes's actual words", but does not propose to quarrel with generosity (*Man and Society*, I, p. 130).

Warrender's interpretation, however, is not, I think, "generous", but merely natural and straightforward. For, in the first place, Hobbes repeats the point a few paragraphs later, and says:

The same laws, because they oblige only to a desire, and endeavour, I mean an unfeigned and constant endeavour, are easy to be observed. For in that they require nothing but endeavour, he that endeavoureth their performance, fulfilleth them . . . (xv 104).

The use of the word "endeavour" here is suggestive. Hobbes defines it in chapter vi of *Leviathan* as the "small beginnings of motion, within the body of man" (vi 31. See above, Chapter Five, Section 5). As defined there, "endeavour" is a technical term—the most general of the "desire"-family of terms—which means something less than *effortful striving* but a great deal more than mere *inactive wish*. An endeavour is the beginning of an overt action, so that unless it is checked it will continue into an overt action. Unless someone had a tendency to *act* in accordance with the law of nature he could not be said, in the Hobbesian sense of "desire", which is a species of "endeavour", to *desire* its fulfilment at all. There is some indication, indeed, that in this passage Hobbes is not merely using "endeavour" in his own restricted and technical sense, but also relying on some connotation of effortful striving. For (i) he says that the laws of nature oblige "to a desire, and *endeavour*". In his narrowly definde sense of these terms "desire" is merely a special case of "endeavour", and if the words "and endeavour" are to add anything "endeavour" must be taken in a more extended sense. (ii) The insistence on "an unfeigned and constant endeavour" is an emphasis on the *active* element of "endeavour" in this context. (iii) There are other occasions on which Hobbes uses the word in this slightly extended sense. Thus "emulation" is defined as "*Grief*, for the success of a competitor . . . if it be joined with endeavour to enforce our own abilities to equal or exceed him . . ." (VI 37).

In the second place, the assertion that the laws of nature oblige only *in foro interno*, interpreted as Warrender interprets it, merely sums up some points that have already been made clear along the way. The fundamental law of nature itself is a general directive to *seek* peace. The second law of nature does not direct us to renounce any portion of our natural right, but to do so if and only if others are willing to do so. It is not merely, however, that *if* others will renounce their rights we ought to also, but—since the fundamental law directs us to seek peace, and the reciprocal renunciation of rights is a necessary means to peace—that we should seek to bring about a situation in which this condition is fulfilled. The third law tells us to keep our covenants, but only under the condition that keeping them is compatible with the pursuit of those ends which the law of nature directs us towards.

On the other hand part of Warrender's account involves the notion of a "validating condition". The obligation to obey the law is "operative" only if certain conditions are fulfilled (for example, one is obliged actually to keep one's covenants only if one has reasonable assurance that the other party will perform also), otherwise it is "suspended". Two validating conditions, that have to be met, are that there should be "security", or assurance that others will perform also, and that there should be a sufficient *motive* for observing the law. The existence of a sovereign (the common power) ensures both of these validating conditions through effective enforcement of the law (*The Political*

*Philosophy of Hobbes*, p. 144). As Watkins has pointed out, however, the validating conditions of a law can perfectly well be incorporated within the law itself: "Hobbes might equally have said that it is a *universally operative* law of nature 'that men perform their covenants made provided he that performeth first has assurance the other will perform after'. *This* law would not be suspended where he who is to perform first lacks such assurance (a law that parked cars must have lights on at night in unlit streets is not *suspended* where there is all-night street-lighting)" (*Hobbes's System of Ideas*, pp. 88–89).

1. Now I think that in Hobbes's argument the validating conditions *are* incorporated in the law. Thus the full formulation of the fundamental law is "that every man, ought to endeavour peace, as far as he has hope of obtaining it . . ."; and of the second law is "that a man be willing, when others are so too, as far-forth, as for peace, and defence of himself he shall think it necessary . . ." (*Leviathan*, XIV 85). The only reason why they are not incorporated in the formula of the third law is that they require lengthy exposition.

2. Although Watkins suggests that "it makes only a verbal difference whether a law's validating conditions are listed separately, or incorporated into the law itself", I think that in the context of *Warrender's* conception of validating conditions it does make a more than merely verbal difference. There is something wrong with the analogy of the law about parking lights. Under that law a motorist is free to choose whether to park his car, lit, in an unlit street or unlit in a lit street. But under the law of nature a man is not free to choose whether to make covenants, without assurance, and then break them, or to make covenants, with assurance, and then keep them: he is to *seek out* situations in which certain covenants can be made and kept. But Warrender's notion of *suspended* obligation is just as misleading, and for the same sort of reason. In this country the law obliges us to pay a high tax on tobacco, even if we grow it ourselves in our own gardens. There was a period of dollar shortage when the authorities decided to turn a blind eye to the domestic production of tobacco which was, after all, saving dollar imports. The law, and the obligations deriving from it, were, in effect, *suspended* (although *only* suspended, because the law was not repealed and was never officially inoperative). Thus there was a period when *in effect* there was no obligation to pay tax on one's tobacco. But there was no legal obligation, either theoretically or in effect, on tobacco-growers to try

to bring about a situation in which the law could become operative again! The whole point of the law of nature, however, is to direct us to bring about a situation in which we can be obliged actually to keep our covenants.

3. The introduction of the notion of *motive*, as a necessary validating condition, to be distinguished from the law itself, is, I think, foreign to Hobbes's argument. I have suggested that the laws of nature "necessitate"—that is, they are a set of rational precepts valid for every man who is prepared to be reasonable. Because they are necessary values, the contingent values that a man has provide the motive for promoting them, so long as the man is reasonable. What the existence of a common power does is not to strengthen an otherwise inadequate motive for seeking a certain end (although it *may* do that) but to provide the conditions without which the end cannot be effectively promoted, however strong the motive.

Now one commentator has compared the laws of nature with Kant's assertoric imperatives. Kant divided imperatives into categorical which unconditionally prescribe moral actions and hypothetical, which prescribe actions as means to an end; and he further divided hypothetical imperatives into problematic, prescribing means to a *possible* end, and assertoric, prescribing means to an actual end. Watkins suggests that Hobbes's natural laws are to be regarded as assertoric hypothetical imperatives (*Hobbes's System of Ideas*, pp. 82–83). He has already suggested that they are rather like doctor's orders: they are prescriptive, but they are based on facts. The only important difference is that a doctor cannot know that his patient's overriding desire is to preserve his health (pp. 76–77). If my interpretation of Hobbes's is acceptable, however, the laws of nature are to be regarded as in one respect stronger, and in another weaker, than assertoric hypothetical imperatives. They do not direct us merely to the means to actual (contingent) values but establish certain necessary values. These necessary values, however, will be accepted as such only by someone who is prepared to be reasonable.

## 6 "THE TRUE AND ONLY MORAL PHILOSOPHY"

In discussing the state of nature Hobbes says that in it there is no law, no justice and injustice (XIII 83), and later, in his exposition of the third law of nature, he says that "before the names of just, and unjust can have place, there must be some coercive power . . ." (xv 94). Part at least of what Hobbes is saying here is obvious and acceptable. There are some sorts of "justice" and "injustice" which are very obviously dependent on *conventions*. The only reason why it is wrong, in some countries, to drive on the right-hand side of the road is that there is a law requiring one to drive on the left. But the law could, and in some countries does, *prohibit* driving on the left. Again, "stealing" can only be *defined* in relation to property rules and there is a wide range of possible property rules which may be—and are—adopted in different societies. The questions "Was he driving on the wrong side of the road?" and "Was he stealing?" can only be answered when some society has been specified.

But Hobbes describes the science of the laws of nature as "the true and only moral philosophy" (xv 104). Moral philosophy is "the science of what is *good*, and *evil*, in the conversation, and society of mankind". In the state of nature, however, "private appetite is the measure of good, and evil". Therefore all men agree that peace is good, and therefore the means to peace, such as justice, equity, and the other laws of nature. Thus the laws of nature are the only things that are good, independently of the measure of "private appetite", and the science of them is the true moral philosophy. Now I do not think that by saying that all men agree that peace is good Hobbes means that every man as a matter of fact always seeks peace, because he thinks that people by no means always do. He uses a *logical* word here—"and *consequently* all men agree . . ."—and this follows from the reflection that in the state of nature which is a state of war, private appetite is the measure of good and evil. ("For the laws of nature . . . are contrary to our natural passions, that carry us to partiality, pride, revenge, and the like" *Leviathan*, XVII 109.) This is a case where those who are kindly disposed to Hobbes do have to give what may be a "generous" interpretation of his words, and take him to be saying that all men, if they reflect *reasonably* about the state of nature, *must* agree with the conclusion that peace is good, and also the means to peace. Justice, then, is good also, and it is good not merely as a means to an end which all men *do* agree in valuing (there is no such agreement), but as a means to an end which all men *must* value so far as they are reasonable.

But although the doctrine of the law of nature shows that justice is necessarily good, and good therefore in all circumstances, whether in an ordered society or in a state of nature, it does not follow that any distinction between just and unjust *actions* can be made in a state of nature. "A just man therefore, is he that taketh all the care he can, that his actions may be all just: and an unjust man, is he that neglecteth it" (*Leviathan*, XV 97). A just man is thus one who does his best to conform with the requirements of the law, and in the state of nature the only law is the law of nature, which obliges only *in foro interno*. In a state of nature, then, justice consists not in doing this or that determinate class of actions, required by specific laws, but in seeking to bring about a situation in which such laws will be possible. In a state of nature private appetite is the measure, and every man is governed by his own reason. It is not merely that one cannot talk about driving on the wrong side of the road except with reference to some actual Highway Code, but that in a state of nature one cannot even regard oneself as under an obligation of a general sort, to drive with consideration for others. In a state of nature each situation must be "played by ear"; if it can be known that the other drivers are not enemies lying in wait, or lunatics whose driving is dangerous and unpredictable, then one is justified in being prepared to defer to them. But whereas in an ordered society one is justified in adopting a general practice of courtesy and consideration, and, indeed, to be blamed if one refuses to adopt it, in a state of nature the adoption of any general practices, policies or rules is absurd, because a situation is just as likely as not to be such as to make the observance of any rule destructive of whatever values one may have been pursuing in adopting the rule. Therefore there can be no general rules of right and wrong, no possibility of objective moral standards, except for the laws of nature, which do not establish specific obligations, but merely direct us how to bring about a situation in which specific obligations will arise.

That brings Hobbes to the part of his argument which is concerned with the commonwealth, but he has one last, brief word to say about natural laws. They are not "properly" to be called laws, he says, but only "conclusions, or theorems"; for "law, properly, is the word of him, that by right hath command over others". But if these theorems are regarded as commanded by God, then they can be called laws (XV 104–5). It is not to be concluded from this that Hobbes is giving God a supremely important place in his doctrine of natural law. On the contrary, he is dismissing God from it. It is not of the least importance to Hobbes or to his argument to regard God as the author of the laws of nature, or, for that matter, to regard them as "properly" laws. He discusses in great detail the ways in which natural law obliges (or "necessitates"), and it is some of that detail which we have been discussing in the last two chapters. Nothing in these arguments hangs on the issue whether or not these "precepts" or "theorems" are commanded by God; and if Hobbes had decided merely to call them "precepts", and to deny the existence of God into the bargain, the force of his arguments would not have been in the smallest degree diminished—though resistance to their force, in the minds of his contemporaries, would have been greatly augmented!

# CHAPTER NINE

## *Political Science*

HOBBES'S account of man, the state of nature and natural law is the foundation of all his political conclusions. He uses it as the basis on which to construct a detailed discussion of specific political matters, including the institution of a commonwealth, the authority of a conqueror, the nature of sovereignty, the civil law, and so forth. The greater part of *Leviathan* is concerned with these issues, and it is they which constitute his science of politics. My concern has been not so much with whether the political conclusions which Hobbes ultimately comes to are acceptable or not, but rather with the nature of his conception of political science. I have argued that he conceives it—and that, consistently with his doctrine of method, he ought to conceive it—as a formal system of necessarily true propositions; and that the foundations which he constructs for it conform on the whole, though not entirely, with such a formal pattern. Where Hobbes has failed to keep consistently to that pattern I have taken the liberty of reconstructing his argument for him, although what I have done in my reconstruction is not to make additions and revisions but merely to bring out and emphasise certain actual elements of his own arguments. Although I am primarily concerned with the foundations, rather than with the actual system built upon them, some obvious questions about the adequacy of the foundations can best be answered by looking at some features of the developed system. In this chapter I conclude my discussion of Hobbes by first examining his accounts of authorisation, the institution of the commonwealth, and sovereignty, and then discussing what *use* a Hobbesian science of politics can be given, and what sort of confirmation or justification such a formal system can have.

## 1 AUTHORISATION

The state of nature is ended only by the establishment of a "common power". This is done, and a commonwealth instituted, when a multitude of men covenant, each with every other, to give up the right of governing themselves individually to some person who is thereby *authorised* to exercise the right of governing, to the end of securing peace and the common defence. This covenant is at the heart of the whole of Hobbes's political theory, and it employs the notion of authorisation, which Hobbes discusses in some detail before he turns to the covenant.

To have authority, Hobbes explains, is to have the right of doing an action, and an *author* is someone who "owns" the words or actions of another, who is the *actor*, and who acts by authority of the author. Thus $X$ authorises $Y$ if $X$ grants to $Y$ a right such that $X$ will acknowledge $Y$'s acts as his own. An example of this is "power of attorney". If $Y$ has power of attorney for $X$, then obligations which $Y$ enters into on behalf of $X$ are $X$'s obligations. Now a *multitude* can be made one person when they are represented by one person, so long as the representer represents with the consent of every member of the multitude, who then authorises every act of the representative. The representative is a *person*, but not necessarily a single man. A person may be a number of men so long as the decision of the majority is taken as the decision of them all (*Leviathan*, XVI 105–8).

What is important, of course, is the use which is made of the notion of authorisation in the account of the covenant by which a commonwealth is instituted. But there are a few preliminary points that call for comment. In the first place there is Hobbes's assertion that when a person is composed of a number of men—in other words, a committee—its decisions must be what is decided by the majority. He does produce an argument in support of this assertion, but it is rather crude and unconvincing. The argument is that if there are a greater number of negatives than affirmatives then there are more than enough negatives to "destroy" the affirmatives, and the remainder of negatives are therefore left alone as expressing the decision of the committee. That is not so much an argument in favour of majority decision as merely a metaphorical expression of what a majority decision is. Nevertheless it can, I think, be shown in support of Hobbes that a majority procedure must be regarded as the standard procedure for reaching corporate decisions. For there are a great many imaginable procedures apart from the majority procedure, but each, I think, is defective in one or more of a limited number of respects.

1. There might be a positive unanimity rule, but that would mean that on some issues no decision at all could be reached.

2. There might be a negative unanimity rule—a rule that any decision is adopted if and only if members unanimously vote against it. That would in operation be equivalent to a positive unanimity rule, because members who favoured a decision would know that they must vote against it in order to have it adopted.

3. The decision might go by the vote simply of one specific member or of certain specific members. But then the others would be redundant and would not be effective members of the committee, but at most advisers.

4. There might be a negative majority rule: a rule that a decision is adopted if more members vote against than for the decision. That in operation would be equivalent to a positive majority rule.

5. There might be some rather bizarre and specific rule, such as that a decision is adopted if more vote against than for, provided that some vote for. The defect of such a lunatic procedure is that it would make it impossible for members to vote rationally at all. Someone who favoured a decision would not know whether to vote against it, so as to contribute to the necessary negative majority, or for it, so as to contribute to the equally necessary affirmative minority.

Majority vote, then, is standard procedure. Nevertheless there may be deviations from it of certain sorts. Some members of a committee may properly be able each to cast more than one vote. Voting rights may be proportionate to individual power, or interest, or some other relevant factor. Two members of a gang of five hooligans might be much stronger than the others, so that these two together could outfight the other three, although one of the stronger alone would be outfought by the three weaker together. Then in effect each of the stronger would exercise two votes, and each of the others one vote. It would be reasonable for them to reach decisions on that basis, since the decision, as thus voted, would be the same as would be reached if, for lack of an agreed decision-procedure, the issue were fought out. Or four partners might have a different stake in an enterprise—in the proportion, say, of sixty to twenty to fifteen to five. They might reasonably agree to vote proportionately, for one with a lesser share has more to lose by opposing one with a greater than vice versa, since the partnership could more easily survive the withdrawal of a lesser than of a greater share of its capital. Yet even although one member had more votes than the others combined, that would not be the same as simply specifying him as the decision-maker, for he could choose on occasion to exercise no vote, leaving the decision to be made by a majority of the other votes.

Nevertheless, however many may be the possible deviations from a simple majority rule, they must all be regarded as deviations from a standard, and justified by special considerations. There are no reasons for supposing that there are any such special considerations which Hobbes should have taken into account, or that he could not allow for them if they were produced. All that his argument requires is that if a representative person is a committee it must have some workable decision-procedures, and the one which he insists on has the merit of being the standard such procedure.

That, then, is how a representative is constituted. But how does he *become* a representative? Hobbes's answer is, by being authorised, and the sources of his authority are those whom he represents. As a representative he has powers which he does not have as a private individual (or individuals), and it is the act of authorisation which confers these powers upon him. But how can it be that you should acquire real powers merely through my performance of a verbal act, such as my saying "I authorise you . . ."? Or if *that* is not the act of authorising, what is, and how do the represented use it to transfer power to the representative?

Watkins has provided an ingenious answer to these questions. "Hobbes", Watkins says, "often appears to be saying that they transfer something occult and intangible to him—their powers, or their wills, or their persons, or their rights." But of course one man cannot literally transfer his power to another, and what Hobbes really means can be understood well enough if one remembers his thoroughgoing nominalism. What the represented give to the representative is "tokens of their persons, viz. their *names*"—each authorises the representative to *act in his name*. This nominalism of Hobbes's explains both his account of representation and also his assertion that standards of goodness and justice are determined by the sovereign:

Hobbes's nominalist theory of the state might be summarised thus: a multitude of men becomes a body politic when each of them gives to one (or a number) of them the free use of his name, so that the sovereign thereby created may, in the name of them all, allocate such names as *just* and *unjust*, *good* and *evil* . . . (*Hobbes's System of Ideas*, pp. 157–62).

Now that is a suggestion which may well be a major contribution to political theory, but I do not think that it succeeds in making contact with Hobbes.

1. Hobbes's nominalism, in *Leviathan* and elsewhere, is not so uncompromising as Watkins makes it out to be. He refers to Hobbes's "nominalist ontology, uncompromised by 'accidents' " (p. 158). But we have seen (above, Chapter Three, Section 4) that Hobbes's nominalism *is* "compromised" by accidents, and that in *Leviathan* Hobbes actually says, "One universal name is imposed on many things, for their similitude in some quality, or other accident" (IV 19).

2. In his discussion of authorisation in *Leviathan* Hobbes talks of the representative acting "in the name of" the represented. But he does not use this expression very often nor give any indication that he attaches any special importance to it. He uses it merely as an idiomatic way of expressing the fact—already fully analysed without reference to names—that the represented acknowledge the acts of the representer as their own.

3. There is nothing puzzling about the transfer of power. Hobbes has already explained that "reputation of power is power" (x 56). If *A*, *B* and *C* publicly announce that they acknowledge *X*'s acts as their own then *X* acquires some real powers, because if he acts so as to commit *C* to something not only he but also *A* and *B* will hold *C* to it. Each, then, has contributed to create a situation in which many others have grounds for holding him to obligations entered into on his behalf by the representative. *X* thus comes to have some of *C*'s power because in the eyes of *A* and *B* he has the reputation of such power. There is nothing "occult" in the transfer of power, and the notion that it involves some traffic in *names* is not good logic but bad magic. Of course names (in the sense of *words*) have to be used, because something has to be publicly made known, but what is transferred is not names or tokens of names.

4. The reason why Hobbes thinks that the sovereign has the right or power to "allocate" the names "just", "good", etc., is nothing to do with nominalism, which is a theory about names in general, but with his account of these names in particular. The whole of his argument, from his definitions of "desire" etc., through his analysis of deliberation, to his account of the state of nature and natural law, provides a detailed and extended analysis of the use of value terms. There is no magic clue to understanding what he has to say about that: all that can be done is to examine what he actually does say, which means examining in detail the progress of his argument from stage to stage.

I think, then, that there is nothing very mysterious about the notion of authorisation. What matters is the use which he makes of it in his account of the institution of a commonwealth.

## 2 THE INSTITUTION OF A COMMONWEALTH

A commonwealth is instituted when a "multitude" of men (that is, not necessarily a huge number of men, but a mere disorganised *plurality*) come together and unite themselves into an ordered society under a sovereign who represents them. The existence of a sovereign (a "common power") is both a necessary and a sufficient condition of the existence of an ordered society. It has been argued already (above, Chapter Eight, Section 1) that the existence of a sovereign is a necessary condition of the existence of an ordered society, but it is also a sufficient condition, because he cannot exist *as* a sovereign except as an effective "common power", and if a group were not an ordered society then it would follow that there was no effective exercise of "common power". Thus the creating, establishing or instituting of a sovereign is *ipso facto* the creating of a commonwealth.

How, then, can a multitude unite themselves under a sovereign? Hobbes's answer is that this is done by means of a covenant. It is not, however, a covenant between on the one hand a person, thereafter to be held sovereign, and on the other hand the society which he is to govern, because until the sovereign has been instituted no society exists that could be a party to any covenant. It is a covenant between all those individuals whom the covenant is going to make subjects of the sovereign. Each individual gives up his right of governing himself and authorises some person to exercise the right of governing, and that person is thereby made sovereign, with right and power to govern.

In *Leviathan* Hobbes unfortunately gives two different accounts of the precise terms of this covenant. In the first version every man is imagined to be saying to every other "I authorise and give up my right of governing myself, to this man, or to this assembly of men, on this condition, that thou give up thy right to him, and authorise all his actions in like manner" (XVII 112). That might be rendered more briefly as "I authorise this person as sovereign, on condition that you all do too". In this formula some specific person is named and authorised on the condition that everyone else authorises him also. It can be called the *unanimity* formula. At the beginning of the next chapter, however, Hobbes describes, although he does not explicitly state, a different formulation of the covenant of authorisation.

A *commonwealth* is said to be *instituted*, when a multitude of men do agree, and *covenant*, *every one*, with *every one*, that to whatsoever *man*, or *assembly of men*, shall be given by the major part, the *right* to *present* the person of them all, that is to say, to be their *representative*; every one, as well he that *voted for it*, as well as he that *voted against it*, shall *authorise* all the actions and judgments, of that man, or assembly of men, in the same manner, as if they were his own, to the end, to live peaceably amongst themselves, and be protected against other men (XVIII 113).

This introduces the notions of voting and majority decision, but it does not name any specific person: it merely authorises whomever the majority vote for, and it could be rendered briefly as "I authorise as sovereign any person whom the majority name and authorise, on condition that everyone else authorises as sovereign whomever the majority name and authorise". This can be called the *majority* formula.

Neither of these formulae is satisfactory by itself. The unanimity formula requires unanimity not merely in agreeing to covenant but also in naming the sovereign, and the latter especially is a very stiff requirement. The majority formula has one very obvious defect: it is not a procedure for adopting a sovereign but merely an undertaking to adopt a procedure. That defect can easily be remedied by adding to the formula the words "and I name . . .", the gap to be filled in each case by the name of the person preferred as sovereign by the utterer. Then the general adoption of the formula would actually produce a sovereign. Yet the formula is still defective, because it requires unanimity in the adoption of the formula, even although not in the choice of sovereign. If there were some refusals to agree in advance to accept majority decision, which is part of what is agreed to in the formula, the reciprocity condition in the formula would not be met and the whole covenant would be void.

What Hobbes has done, then, is to produce two different formulae, neither of which are very satisfactory. Professor M. M. Goldsmith has discussed sovereignty by institution, distinguishing the two formulae and making some illuminating comments on them. The majority formula, he suggests, is a survival from an earlier account of the institution of the sovereign, in *The Elements of Law*. The unanimity formula really replaces it in *Leviathan*, and the recurrence of the majority formula is probably due merely to an oversight by Hobbes. Goldsmith prefers the unanimity formula. In his view it does not raise any real problems, because dissenters merely do not become members of the society. And it has three advantages. Firstly, it creates an obligation towards a determinate person; secondly, it is general, so that it can create any form of government, democratic, aristocratic or whatever; and thirdly, it provides unanimity (M. M. Goldsmith, *Hobbes's Science of Politics*, pp. 155–61).

Certainly Goldsmith is right in connecting the majority formula with earlier accounts such as that in *The Elements*. But his suggestion that the unanimity formula is to be preferred is debatable. On one possible interpretation of the majority formula, he argues, the covenant *unnecessarily* creates a political obligation in spite of the contrary vote of the minority. I presume that what Goldsmith means here is that the minority have pledged themselves to submit to the choice of the majority, and that this is "unnecessary" because on the unanimity formula they would simply remain outside the society and therefore incur no unwelcome obligation.

There are two chief reasons why I think that the unanimity formula is unsatisfactory. The first is that the notion that dissenters merely do not become members of the society so that no problems arise is an over-simplification. One is required to imagine, perhaps, that the multitudinous inhabitants of the British Isles, weary of the state of nature, journey to a meeting in Salisbury Plain. Most of them agree on Alfred, and so there comes to be a commonwealth of England and a sovereign Alfred. A quarrelsome and dissentient minority do not have any obligation to Alfred, however, and make an orderly withdrawal to resume the state of nature in the mountains of the north and west. I am inclined to think, however, that societies can seldom originate just like that. How societies *do* originate is a question that cannot be answered within the context of a demonstrative "science", and I must make it clear that I am not attempting to engage in armchair historical speculation. The withdrawal of dissenters is something that can and does (on occasion, such as the Pilgrim Fathers) happen. What I am concerned with here is not the question whether it can or does happen (although I suspect that it can and does happen only in rather special circumstances), but the question what attitude a society can reasonably be expected to adopt towards dissidents. To defend the unanimity formula is to deny to society the right to coerce a certain class of dissenters, for if a commonwealth is based on covenant, those who have dissented at the original covenant are not bound by it, and the sovereign cannot enforce an obligation which they have not in fact assumed. But on Hobbes's principles it would be intolerable to place a sovereign under such a restriction. At the moment of becoming merely a dissident minority outside the commonwealth which is instituted by the unanimous covenant the dissenters are still in the state of nature. It is possible that they may agree among themselves, and institute a new commonwealth. But in the first place there is no guarantee that that will happen, and being in a state of nature they are still enemies of every man, including the subjects of the new commonwealth. And in the second place, a new commonwealth may itself be an enemy. It may or may not be impracticable or undesirable to coerce the dissenters, but the sovereign ought not to be deprived of the *right* to do so if, as is possible, there are good reasons for coercing.

Hobbes distinguishes, of course, between sovereignty by institution and sovereignty by acquisition. Sovereignty by acquisition is the rights and powers exercised by a sovereign over those who have been *subdued* by him: they consent to his rule merely because they will die if they refuse, but this is still genuine consent, since fear does not invalidate a covenant. If the unanimity formula leaves a certain gap in the rights and powers of the sovereign, acquisition seems to fill it very adequately. But if one of the chief merits of the unanimity formula was precisely that it should leave that gap, the notion of acquisition seems to leave that a rather empty recommendation.

The second reason why I think that the unanimity formula is unsatisfactory is that it is, presumably, intended to *explain* something. It is not, I think, offered, and certainly should not be taken, as part of an explanation of how societies do in fact originate. It cannot provide an explanation of the sort which is provided by a scientific hypothesis, because it is not offered *as* an hypothesis. What it provides, if anything, is a sort of *moral* explanation: it tells us something about the nature of the obligations which people have in developed societies. Hobbes does not think that obligations are *inherited*, nor does he think that many of us are likely to be faced with the task of constructing a society in a state of nature. If his theorisings are to be of any interest to *us* it must be because it is possible to argue that *our* political obligations are *as if* we had entered into the original covenant. The unanimity formula is so simple a tool that I think that its explanatory powers are insufficient. That can best be shown by showing how much better a job the majority formula can do.

## 3 AN UNCONDITIONAL MAJORITY FORMULA

The terms of the majority formula were: "I authorise as sovereign any person whom the majority name and authorise, on condition that everyone else authorises whomever the majority name and authorise". As it stands that formula has two defects.

1. The uttering of it by a multitude would constitute agreement about a procedure for instituting a sovereign but would not of itself actually institute a sovereign. As I have suggested above, it would be necessary to add the words "and I name . . .". This is a simple enough addition.

2. The condition that everyone else should accept the principle of majority rule is unnecessary and indefensible. If each member of the majority should refuse to bind himself to accept whomever the greater part of the others agreed in selecting, but did in fact make the same selection, then there would be a majority in favour of some specific person as sovereign, though not a majority in favour of the

majority principle. Such a measure of agreement, however, would be sufficient for the instituting of a sovereign.

What conditions must a formula for the covenant meet in order to be regarded as adequate? It must be such that (i) there is a reason why everyone should be prepared to adopt it, and (ii) its general adoption should lead to the instituting of a sovereign. These two considerations are not independent of each other, of course, for if a formula were such that its adoption could not conceivably secure the institution of a sovereign there could be no reason for anyone to adopt it. The unanimity formula is not very well adapted to serve as a means of creating a sovereign, partly for the reasons which I have discussed above and partly because in any case there is no guarantee that there would be sufficient agreement to permit of even a small commonwealth, excluding a vast number of dissenting outsiders. The condition that everyone else should accept the formula is prima facie a defect of the majority formula, because the addition of any stringent condition necessarily lessens the chances of agreement. Some special and compelling reason would have to be found for insisting on it. But in fact its inclusion produces a paradox. For suppose that I accede to the formula, with the condition as stipulated, and that my own choice agrees with the choice of the majority, who have not, however, agreed to the majority principle. Then I have no obligation towards the sovereign, because although he is the sovereign of my choice, and chosen by the majority-procedure which I have endorsed, the fact that no member of the majority *would* have authorised any other person, *if* the other members of the majority had chosen differently, renders my covenant void.

A more readily defensible formula would be simply "I authorise as sovereign any person whom the majority name and authorise, and I name . . .". This can be called the *unconditional* majority formula, because it omits the condition included in the previous formula, which may now be called the *conditional* majority formula. It meets the conditions for an adequate formula. For the law of nature requires that we should seek peace, which requires the institution of a sovereign. Some formula must be found for an agreement instituting the sovereign. There is no reason for supposing that all of those whose agreement is necessary (that is, who cannot simply be left out of the society) will agree in their choice of sovereign, so the formula must incorporate a procedure for reaching a corporate decision. It has been

shown (in Section 1 of this chapter) that majority vote must be regarded as the standard procedure for reaching corporate decisions. It
is merely a *standard* procedure, and it allows of complications and
deviations, if there is some special reason for them, but in a state of
nature, where everything is uncertain, there can be no such reasons,
and a simple and uncomplicated majority-procedure is the only procedure with any reasonable claim to general acceptance. Thus each
individual has reason to regard himself as entitled to cast a vote and
obliged (or "necessitated") to enter into an obligation to accept the
majority decision. But no individual is obliged or entitled to make it a
condition of his acceptance of the majority formula that others should
accept it also, for the reason why he is necessitated to accept it is that
he is thereby maximising the chances of a sovereign being acceptably
and effectively instituted: and it is not a necessary condition of the
institution of a sovereign that the majority should accept the majority
formula, but merely that they should agree on a sovereign, so that to
insist on the *conditional* majority formula would be to lessen the
chances of a decision.

Thus no reciprocity condition need be attached to the acceptance
of the majority principle. Nevertheless a different reciprocity condition *is* incorporated in the formula. It is our old friend, introduced to
us by the second law of nature, which required us to lay down our
natural right to all things, being content with as much liberty against
others as we were prepared to allow them against us, provided that
they reciprocally renounced their rights to the same degree. In the
state of nature, however, there is no security in covenants, and, as
Hobbes has pointed out, in the state of nature natural law obliges
only *in foro interno*. What has to be found is some procedure for the
renunciation of rights which will at the same time create a sovereign,
and therefore an ordered society, so that the renunciation of rights
does not make one merely a prey to one's enemies. That is what the
covenant instituting a sovereign achieves, and since it involves giving
up the right of governing oneself it requires that there should be an
assurance that this renunciation will not be in vain and that a
sovereign will be effectively instituted. It is therefore conditional on
others also having a will to renounce their rights in favour of a
sovereign, since without that the state of nature must continue.

There is, however, one apparent difficulty, whatever formula is
adopted. Hobbes does not merely assert, but places at the heart of his

argument the assertion, that covenants are void unless there is some assurance that the parties will perform, and that a necessary condition of general assurance is the existence of a sovereign exercising coercive power and enforcing covenants. That seems to make a difficulty in respect of the covenant establishing the sovereign. Unless there is a valid covenant authorising him there is no sovereign, but until there is a sovereign there can be no valid covenants. The solution of this problem is expounded by Mr Plamenatz with his usual clarity.

The covenant makes the sovereign powerful, not at all because it involves an immediate keeping of promises, but because it creates a situation in which it becomes everyone's interest that some definite person (the sovereign) should get the better of anyone else he seeks to coerce. I want the sovereign to be able to coerce everyone except me, and everyone else has a desire similar to mine. This is enough to ensure that the covenant makes the sovereign powerful enough to be able to punish anyone who breaks the covenant (*Man and Society*, I, p. 136).

Now at the end of the last section I claimed that the unanimity formula was deficient in explanatory power compared with the majority formula. In order to justify the amount of attention which I have given to these formulae, and to the unconditional majority formula in particular, I must now try to show that the latter does have some explanatory power, and more than the unanimity formula.

The notion of an original covenant has to be regarded as a fiction. That is not to say that there has never been any reality corresponding to it. Some of the elements of it do have instances. For example, as Hobbes himself points out, the relations between sovereign independent states have sometimes been very like the relations between individuals in a state of nature (*Leviathan*, XIII 83); and some societies, in dissolution, may well have reached a condition of anarchy not far removed from the state of nature. Again, some societies may have been instituted, or re-instituted, as ordered societies by means of some covenant. But there is no reason, so far as I know, for supposing that *all* societies must at some time have originated in such an episode. Yet what Hobbes says is something which is meant to be taken as true of *all* societies. It is therefore to be taken as a fiction which purports to embody some important truth.

Now what is a sovereign? A sovereign is a person who governs.

Since the actual business of governing may be carried on through agents, it would be better to say, a sovereign is a person who is supreme in governing. But "person", as Hobbes explains, does not in this context mean "individual". A sovereign may be an individual or may be an assembly of individuals, and the latter is a person so long as it has a procedure for arriving at corporate decisions. A commonwealth can—usually does—become large and complex, so that the business of governing it becomes complex also. Hence various aspects of sovereignty come to be distinguished from each other, and some of these become crystallised in more or less separate institutions. Legislative, judicial and executive functions are different important aspects of sovereignty which have commonly been distinguished. In a simple society ruled by an absolute monarch they are all combined in one individual. In a complex society such as contemporary Great Britain, however, many distinctions have to be made. The one which concerns me here is between sovereign and government. As at present constituted, the sovereign in Britain today is said to be "The Queen in Parliament". That makes good sense, because no acts of the parliament have any legal force until assented to by the Queen, while the Queen herself is limited in her powers, and royal assent is virtually automatic. The government is not the sovereign, but it is the executive agent of the sovereign. Although in practice a government has great power to manipulate Parliament, there is still a real sense in which it derives its power *from* Parliament. For if it chooses (and it *can* choose) Parliament can control the government; and even if it seldom does choose to do so, the fact is that in its broad aspects a government necessarily reflects, and does not determine, the composition of Parliament. Further, the sovereign has a permanency which a government does not have. The composition of Parliament changes from time to time, as do its aims, intentions and decisions. But the sovereign continues through these changes, because it is the sovereign who determines the succession.

There is no perfect form of government, where the disposing of the succession is not in the present sovereign. For if it be in any other particular man, or private assembly, it is in a person subject, and may be assumed by the sovereign at his pleasure; and consequently the right is in himself. And if it be in no particular man, but left to a new choice; then is the commonwealth dissolved; and the right is in him that can get it; contrary to the intention of them that did institute the commonwealth, for their perpetual, and not temporary security (*Leviathan*, XIX 127).

Evidently Britain has a "perfect form of government", because it is the British sovereign who determines his own successor. Parliament, of course, does not decide who specifically are to be members of a new parliament, but it does decide how they are to be selected (whether by universal franchise, or *nearly* universal franchise, and whether by simple majorities or proportional representation, and so forth), and when they are to be selected; and it can indeed prolong its own life as long as it pleases (as it did in 1939). A government, however, does not determine its successor. It cannot choose to prolong its own life any longer than Parliament permits it to, and whereas the sovereign can, and sometimes does, dismiss a government, a government cannot dismiss a sovereign. It cannot even compel the renewal of the sovereign, but merely persuade the sovereign to renew itself. The difference between government and sovereign comes out very clearly if we think of possible crises. Parliament can, and occasionally does, lose confidence in a government, and the government be threatened with collapse. Then there is a crisis of sorts, which may become worse if the government loses the support of Parliament and a new government which can command support is not easily found. Such crises are bad enough, but they are nothing like so serious as the crisis that would develop if the collapse of the sovereign threatened. Suppose that Parliament were dissolved and that before new elections could be completed the government postponed them *sine die*, taking executive action to prevent any further electoral activities. That would be a major constitutional crisis, because the agency which controlled the day-by-day exercise of sovereign power, and which normally is *merely* an agency because required to exercise it under the ultimate direction of the sovereign, which is what makes its acts lawful, would be defying the source of its own power and authority. That would be not merely a critical but a revolutionary situation, and although revolutions sometimes cannot be avoided, no society can afford to make a habit of them.

Some of the implications of the possibility of such constitutional crises will need discussing further in the next section. Here I am merely concerned to distinguish clearly, so far as that can be done, between sovereign and government. Hobbes's covenant is intended to tell us something about the nature and power of a sovereign, and in discussing the power of a sovereign it is necessary to distinguish the power of a sovereign from the power of a government—not merely because the power of a government is derivative, but because the power of a sovereign and the power of a government may vary independently. Although it is a commonplace these days to lament the diminished power of Parliament compared with the augmented power of the prime minister, that is only a half-truth. What has diminished, perhaps, is the power of *members* of Parliament *as individuals*. But, in the first place, the composition of Parliament still determines the nature and general aims of a government. And, in the second place, it is arguable that in this country we have had, on the whole, a strong sovereign but a succession of rather weak governments. Governments have been weak in the sense that they have not often been prepared or able to dominate and control the nation's life and business, preferring instead to follow behind what they imagine popular opinion to be. (That is not necessarily a bad thing, for it is not very easy to combine strong government with democracy.) But the sovereign has been strong, because no attempt to change it—in favour, for example, of a move towards the dictatorship of the proletariat—has been able to present anything more than a derisory challenge. Nevertheless, power of sovereign and power of government are not *wholly* independent of each other, for a succession of governments which were intolerably weak would be liable to bring the sovereign into disrepute and precipitate a revolutionary situation.

Now the sovereign is the person who is supreme in governing, and the point of having a sovereign is to ensure the existence of a stable, ordered society. The sovereign power has to be exercised effectively to that end, and these are two dimensions in which effective sovereign power has to be measured.

1. There is short-term *control*. Executive and judicial decisions have to be made and enforced, and although in this country it is not the job of the executive to make the judicial decisions, it still has the job of ensuring that they are made and enforced. This short-term control is the responsibility of the government, and if government were more than usually weak over a period, the vital interests of a society would suffer.

2. There is long-term *stability*. The institutions through which

public power is exercised must remain fairly stable, and the risk of a
serious challenge to the sovereign must be small, for where there is a
constant danger of revolution no one has a firm basis on which to
deliberate rationally for the promotion of his values. Thus by means
of organised terror a government may succeed in exercising great
power in short-term control. But that is not the same necessarily as
the existence of a strong sovereign. For terror either destroys altogether in its victims the will to resist, and to that extent has made
them less than human, so that a terrorised society may be stable, but
not human; or, so far as it does not destroy the will to resist, necessarily augments the grounds which its actual and potential victims
have for resisting. Beyond a certain point, then, stronger government
makes for a weaker sovereign because it creates reasons for hoping for
revolution.

Thus sovereign power rests necessarily on consent. For even if a
sovereign successfully suppressed the opposition of a majority—say,
through a well-organised minority having a monopoly of sophisticated weapons—its continued existence is necessarily precarious.
That is not to say that it may not survive for a long time, but that it
has no reasonable grounds for *expecting* to survive. For a police
truncheon is effective not because it is a policeman *with a truncheon*
but because it is a truncheon *with a policeman*. The force of a coercive
force is not the sum of the physical powers of the individuals who
compose it. An effective coercive organisation must (*a*) be well
organised, (*b*) have good *morale*, without which organisation is ineffective, and (*c*) have power sufficient to overwhelm any probable
opposition. The organisation and *morale* of a force depend on its incorporating *within* it some necessary values of justice and respect for
the interests of its members, without which the members have no
reason for trying to play their part effectively. A coercive force
employed in coercing and exploiting a dissident majority is engaged in
a task which involves the denial of values on whose acceptance its own
maximum power depends. (That is not *mere* armchair theorising,
because many exploiting minorities have in fact been themselves torn
by internal factions. Nevertheless it is, and is intended to be primarily
armchair work. At this stage of the discussion I am concerned to take
the *a priori* theory as far as it can go. Later in the chapter I discuss the
limitations of such an approach.) Further, an apparently weak police
force may in fact be very powerful because it operates with the

consent and support of the majority. That has the double effect of making opposition less frequent and also uniting auxiliary forces against such opposition as occurs. Consent has the character of being the most reliable source of power, because it both diminishes the opposition and also brings other power with it.

Thus if a situation arises—as, say, in pre-Revolutionary Russia—where people generally do not have an interest in supporting the sovereign, the sovereign is threatened and insecure, and a big step has been taken towards the state of nature. Without consent the sovereign does not have reliable and stable power. The consent that gives power, however, is not merely a momentary consent to this or that act of the sovereign, because that would be to consent to the act and not to the sovereign. The sovereign can act as sovereign only to the extent that he can rely on his decisions being accepted not just because of the sort of decisions they are but because they are *his* decisions. If the sovereign's decisions are not such as on the whole to commend themselves to those who have to accept them, then his subjects will be liable to reconsider whether they have grounds for continuing to consent. Nevertheless, so long as they *do* consent in such a way as to endow the sovereign with effective power, their consent consists *not* in their setting themselves up as judges, to pass a verdict on the acts of the sovereign and to treat him accordingly, but in their regarding themselves as committed to accept his decisions because they are his. They are regarding themselves as having the same obligation to obey that they would have had *if* they had covenanted. And they *do* have this obligation, because to deny it is to destroy the sovereign. In certain situations, of course, the obligation disappears. If supporting the sovereign involves a greater threat to one's values than opposing, then one has no longer any reason for regarding oneself as under an obligation. In the language of covenants, the covenant has then become void. But the previous arguments about the state of nature have shown that such a situation must be a rare and desperate one.

Therefore if one exists in a stable society one exists in a society in which most people have in effect covenanted to obey the sovereign, because they have good reason for regarding themselves as under an obligation to obey. That does not imply that minorities are of no importance, and that if the sovereign should persecute and oppress a minority group there can be no legitimate objection. In the first place, the contingent values of the majority may be inconsistent with suppression of minorities. To some extent it is likely that this will be so in a stable society, for the conditioning which produces a certain degree of respect for the needs and wishes of others, without which one of the foundations of a stable society is lacking, involves some degree of deference to minorities, so far as that is compatible with the preservation of other majority values. And in the second place, everyone is at least potentially a member of *some* minority, and has reason to support at least some degree of tolerance of minorities.

Nevertheless, majority consent, although not necessarily of exclusive importance, is still the feature of primary importance, since it is the condition of the existence of a stable sovereign. The unconditional majority formula thus expresses very well an important aspect of the situation of an individual in a stable society: that he should regard himself as under an obligation to obey a sovereign who has the consent of the majority (and if there is no such sovereign, to make such contribution as he can to the creation of such a sovereign).

## 4 THE ABSOLUTE SOVEREIGN

When people authorise or submit to a sovereign, they "confer all their power and strength" upon him. Hobbes insists that there can be no limits to the degree of authorisation and that what is "conferred" must be *all* of one's power. The sovereign is virtually absolute.

### 1. *Sovereignty is* permanent

Subjects cannot decide to change their allegiance without the permission of the sovereign. Nor can they excuse disobedience by pleading breach of covenant by the sovereign. For what makes the sovereign is the covenant of his subjects with each other, and not with him, for there is no need for any covenant by the sovereign, and therefore none for him to break. And in any case, even if it *were* claimed that the sovereign had broken some covenant, there could be no judge to decide the dispute between sovereign and subjects, and to pursue the dispute would be to revert to the state of nature. That is why the power and authority of the sovereign cannot depend on any covenant entered into by the sovereign. The sovereign is permanent, then, in the sense that only the sovereign himself can decide to renounce his power, and only he has the right to determine his successor. Nevertheless Hobbes insists on two qualifications. Firstly, since the right to defend one's life cannot be transferred or abandoned, a man always has liberty to defend his life, even against the command of the sovereign (*Leviathan*, XXI 142). Secondly, "the obligation of subjects to the sovereign, is understood to last as long, and no longer, than the power lasteth, by which he is able to protect them. For the right men have by nature to protect themselves, when none else can protect them, can by no covenant be relinquished" (XXI 144). Those two qualifications, of course, would have to be restated in the formal mode, as reservations to the effect that a man has no obligation to the sovereign if the sovereign either threatens his values to a greater extent than he protects them, or is unable to provide him with security in the pursuit of them. The second reservation simply amounts to the assertion that the authority of the sovereign depends on his power—that an ineffective sovereign is not a sovereign at all—but the first is more interesting. A person's values might be such that he preferred to live in a situation of maximum danger and uncertainty, rejoicing in the prospect of the frustration of his own and everyone else's values. Such a person then could have no obligation to any effective sovereign, because the function of the sovereign is to reduce danger and uncertainty to the minimum. But the fact that I have the right to resist the sovereign in certain situations does not mean that the sovereign is deprived of his right to overcome my resistance. For we have reverted, in our relations with each other, to a state of nature in which each of us has unlimited right against the other. Therefore the man who totally disvalues security is not to be blamed for resisting the sovereign, but the sovereign must for his part overwhelm him. That is the conclusion of Hobbes's argument, and it is a very acceptable one, because it amounts to saying that dangerous lunatics are to be restrained, but are not to be blamed for their violence and folly.

## 2. *Sovereignty is* unlimited

The sovereign is the legislator, and he is free to make and unmake laws as he thinks fit. No man can claim to be the victim of injustice at the hands of the sovereign, because he has authorised everything the sovereign does, so that the "victim" is the author of the "injustice" which is done to him. Similarly, no subject can ever lawfully punish the sovereign, since he would then be punishing the sovereign for an act which he had himself authorised (*Leviathan*, XVIII 115–16, and XXVI 173). Hobbes is not making so extreme a claim here as might appear, nor is his appeal to the notion of authorisation a mere logical trick. The sovereign's authority is subject to the two qualifications discussed in the preceding paragraph. If the sovereign is meeting the conditions laid down in them then I have, according to the previous argument, reason to regard myself as having an obligation similar to that which I would have if I had, by covenanting, authorised the sovereign; and within these limits I have reason to regard the sovereign's acts as my own. But that does not mean that I may not dispute with the sovereign.

If a subject have a controversy with his sovereign, of debt, or of right of possession of lands or goods, or concerning any service required at his hands, or concerning any penalty, corporal or pecuniary, grounded on a precedent law; he hath the same liberty to sue for his right, as if it were against a subject; and before such judges, as are appointed by the sovereign. For seeing the sovereign demandeth by force of a former law, and not by virtue of his power; he declareth thereby, that he requireth no more, than shall appear to be due by that law. The suit therefore is not contrary to the will of the sovereign . . . (XXI 143–4).

Thus the subject can claim rights against the sovereign: but only by virtue of such law as is made by the sovereign. Hobbes's claim here amounts to no more than that in disputes the last word must remain with the sovereign.

Where that claim has least apparent plausibility, perhaps, is in connexion with constitutional law. Hobbes is denying, among other things, that there can be any constitutional law which stands above the sovereign and which the sovereign cannot alter at will. And there seem to be some obvious counter-examples—the constitution of the U.S.A. for example. Therefore Hobbes is producing as a necessarily true proposition something which is simply contradicted by actual facts. But is that so? Hobbes is describing a "real" sovereign—what a sovereign has to be if he is to fulfil his function properly. The general form of his argument is that the requirements he lays down are such that if they are not met the sovereign will not have the powers which he needs: and to deny the sovereign these powers is to revert to the state of nature. We do not have to suppose, however, that the choice is always starkly between a *perfect* sovereign and a complete state of nature. If the sovereign falls short of the requirements then there is a weakness, but not necessarily an immediate and fatal weakness. All that Hobbes's argument need claim is that a constitution which is set up above a sovereign is a *bad* constitution, and that claim certainly is arguable. For suppose that a constitutional limitation gets in the way of the will of the sovereign. Then the sovereign may either heed it or disregard it. If he disregards it *and* if his subjects on the whole oppose the breach of it, then his position is in danger, because his power rests on consent. In such circumstances he ought not to break it, not, however, because it is a law above him, but because in this particular case it is an act which is destructive of his own power. For suppose that the breach of it is something which his subjects' interests on the whole demand, then he is in a dilemma in which he must either break a law which, supposedly, he has no power to alter, or he must act contrary to his function as a sovereign. That is by no means merely a theoretical possibility. The judges of the Supreme Court of the U.S.A. have the job intermittently of in effect rewriting the American Constitution so as to keep it in line with contemporary political pressures (as in the case of civil rights).

The notion of a constitution which stands above the sovereign and which is therefore unalterable except by revolution is in any case just a sort of moral confidence trick. It is the notion of some moral standard of such importance that no breach of it must ever under any circumstances be permitted. Only if it is as important as that can it justify the position of unchallengeable political supremacy. There is, of course, no objection to the notion that there are some values which are of such importance that they are never to be denied. But a constitutional limitation has to be formulated, *sometime*, *by someone*, and the sort which is under consideration here is a limitation by which its formulators bind not only themselves but all succeeding generations. It involves the assumption not merely that there are some values of supreme importance, but that someone, sometime, can know what they are, and know better than his successors, so that he can deny them the right to change or revise.

### 3. *Sovereignty is* indivisible

Hobbes not merely insists on a long list of rights of sovereignty, but argues that they all belong together—they are "incommunicable and inseparable" (*Leviathan*, XVIII 118). The sovereign must have in his hands all the different reins of power and authority—legislative, judicial and executive. Once again Hobbes's theory seems to be faced by facts which are contrary to it, because there are states in which sovereign power is divided, such as the U.S.A., in which President, Congress and Supreme Court each has certain powers which the others cannot interfere with, and there is no "person" standing above them all—they each occupy different positions at the summit. This, I think, is the position where Hobbes's argument is at its weakest, not because it is at all obvious that his conclusion is false, but because it is not very clear exactly what his conclusion is. The sovereign is one "person", but that is not to say that he is a single individual: he may be any number of individuals so long as these have a procedure for arriving at decisions which can be taken as decisions of the sovereign. If the sovereign were composed of three constituents $A$, $B$ and $C$ who make the ultimate decisions, respectively, on matters of kind $X$, $Y$ and $Z$, then the sovereign would not be divided so long as there was always a standard procedure for determining whether some doubtful issue, $P$, was to be regarded as an $X$, a $Y$ or a $Z$, and therefore to be decided by $A$, $B$, or $C$. If there could arise issues like $P$, without any procedure for determining whether $P$ was an $X$, a $Y$ or a $Z$, then it could not be known what the decision of the sovereign was, because it could not be known whether the decision of $A$ or of $B$ or of $C$ had sovereign authority. Clearly a sovereign so divided would be a weak sovereign, and Hobbes is entitled to that conclusion. But he is not entitled to the conclusion that any particular *form* of sovereignty is preferable. He does in fact conclude that monarchy is preferable, and produces a number of arguments in support of that conclusion. One such argument—the fourth—is "that a monarch cannot disagree with himself, out of envy, or interest; but an assembly may; and that to such a height, as may produce a civil war" (XIX 123). Against that, however, it might be argued that an assembly may be more responsive to popular opinion, and therefore less likely to produce a civil war. Considerations such as these are important: discussion of them, however, cannot usefully be carried on *a priori*, for except in the light of experience of the actual working of different systems there can be no knowing how much weight to attach to them. They cannot fall within a Hobbesian political science, and Hobbes's opinions here are *merely* his opinions.

There are three points of special importance which Hobbes, I think, does establish about sovereignty.

### I. *Power and authority*

It seems obvious that these should be distinguished, because power is a matter of capacity whereas authority is a matter of right—a gun-man has power to make his victims hand over their money, but he does not have the right. What Hobbes has shown is that in some political contexts no such sharp distinction can be drawn. An analogy may be drawn between the relation of parent to children and that of sovereign to subjects: the analogy is illuminating as much for the difference as for the similarity. A parent has the right (and indeed the duty—but it is the right which I am concerned with here) to exercise a sort of sovereign control over his children, and normally he has (a fair degree of) power too. A parent, however, can lose the power—he can find himself unable to exercise effective control over his children. If that happens, so that his children, uncontrolled, are a danger to other people and themselves, we regard ourselves as obliged to re-move them from their parents and to put them under the care of someone who can exercise effective control. Thus the loss of power entails the loss of right. It is not that *any* diminution of power entails a proportionate diminution of right, but that a *sufficient* loss of power entails a *total* loss of right. But it does not work the other way round. If the children come under the influence of someone else, that does not give this other person the parental right, for he may be a rogue or a pervert, who controls the children in such a way as to damage them or make them unacceptable to the society to which they belong. Even if he is not a rogue, and is an ideal foster parent, that of itself does not give him the right, because there are reasons for holding that the parental right should be transferable only by public decision, and only to someone publicly appointed—otherwise children could readily become involved in tug-of-war between parents and aspiring foster-parents. In the case of the sovereign, a sufficient loss of power entails a total loss of right, although a smaller loss of power does not entail *any* loss of right—for if it did, the existence of the sovereign would be too often in dispute. There the analogy with the parent holds. But with the sovereign, a sufficient degree of power does entail right, unlike the case of the parent. The reason for the difference is that it cannot be supposed that a sufficiently powerful sovereign can be damaging his subjects. For since *political* power, if stable, depends on consent, the existence of a sufficient degree of power is a guarantee that the sovereign has been authorised by his subjects. But then, is being authorised the same as having authority—that is, right? The answer is that in this context no distinction can be drawn. If one abstracts from the context of a stable society one may construct whatever scheme of values one pleases, but one cannot claim for them any greater status than merely a set of subjective preferences. One may say that one prefers a state of nature to a society organised in a certain way, and one is entitled to have that preference and to act upon it. One must accept the consequence, however, that then one becomes an enemy of the society in question and at war with it. But it is only within a stable society that the conditions exist for making any objective claim about values—any claim which can demand acknowledgement by others. Within a society the contingent values that one has may not coincide with the values embodied by the society. Then either, because peace is a necessary value, one must, regretfully, subordinate one's own contingent values and seize such lawful opportunities as there may be of changing society in accordance with one's own values, or one must reject peace and accept all the consequences. And the sovereign should view the matter in a similar way. Thus he may decide that conscientious objectors, for example, may be treated with special consideration and not as common criminals. But that is a decision for the sovereign, it is not a right which can be claimed by or on behalf of the conscientious objector. In a very stable society those who commit "political" crimes may be given some degree of special tolerance, but that is only because a very stable society is one in which there is no risk of a high incidence of such crimes. Where the risk is higher such tolerance is inexcusable.

## II. *Qualifications*

These have been discussed already, at the beginning of this section, and again, in effect, in the last paragraph. No man can regard himself as obliged to the sovereign if the sovereign does not offer him the prospect of protecting him in the pursuit of his values. Since peace is a necessary value, any effective sovereign to some extent can claim the support of any reasonable man, but not necessarily to an extent sufficient to outweigh the frustration of his contingent values. Then the sovereign cannot reasonably *expect* his allegiance, but can still reasonably proceed against him as a dangerous enemy, and ought to tolerate him only in those special situations where he is not a *dangerous* enemy. Thus it would be foolish to *blame* communists in a capitalist society for engaging in a criminal conspiracy to overthrow the State. That is what their system of values explicitly requires them to do. We can even admire them for the devotion with which they pursue their selfless cause. But the only good reason for not also putting them in jail is that they might be more dangerous persecuted than merely ignored. (In recent years, of course, there have been signs that some capitalists and some communists have been absorbing a lot of each others' values anyway, so that it is not now clear that they are any longer at war.)

### III. *Priority of political ends*

These considerations can all be summed up in terms of the relation between political and other ends. It is too easy to think of political ends disparagingly, and to imagine that particular social systems can always be judged in the light of some moral standards which are above all basely political considerations. No doubt there are many people who are not tempted by such foolishness. Yet it is not *mere* folly, or at all events it is no worse than the opposite folly, which might be called political positivism—the notion that actual political systems cannot be morally criticised at all. Hobbes's analysis opens up two lines along which political systems can be criticised; and what is distinctive about his account is that both lines of criticism accommodate moral values, yet neither involves the attempt to take up a standpoint outside or above political systems. Firstly, political systems can be criticised in terms of necessary values. Hobbes's political "science" cannot conduct such criticism, because the question whether a given system, or kind of system, is well constructed to promote these values is partly an empirical question. The Hobbesian theory can do no more than provide the theoretical basis of such criticism. Yet even if it provided no more than an assurance that the criticism of political systems was not necessarily completely subjective, that would be something of interest. The status of the necessary values is itself a matter of importance. In a sense they are *supreme* values, because they are the conditions of any other values being obtainable. Yet they are also *derivative* values, because they are only means to the promotion of contingent values. What Hobbes has done is to start with a *Boo-Hurrah* theory of contingent values and derive from it a demonstration of necessary values. Now these necessary values are not to be identified with moral values. I do not know whether it is possible to say what moral values are. There is disagreement not only about what things are morally to be valued, but even about what criteria can be used to distinguish those values that a man has, which may properly be called moral, from those other values which he has and which are non-moral. But even if we do not know what moral values are we are still entitled to say that criticism of a political system in terms of necessary values is at least an important part of any moral criticism that can be made, because necessary values are those values which are conditions of all values, and therefore of moral values.

Secondly, political systems can be criticised in terms of contingent values. On Hobbes's account every individual has to decide whether a given political system threatens his own contingent values to a degree sufficient to outweigh the consideration that it promotes necessary values. And further, even if his dissent falls short of justifying war on the sovereign, he has still to decide whether to seek to make such changes in the political system as it is lawful for him to pursue. Whatever of his values may be regarded, by him or by anyone else, as moral values are, for him, a ground for possible criticism, because the system is good, in his eyes, so far as it promotes both necessary and contingent values to the greatest extent possible. But in order to be justified in appealing to some contingent value as ground of criticism of a political system it is not enough that it should be a value, however deeply held, but it must also be shown to be capable of being incorporated within some workable political system. The holiness of cows is a relevant example. There are people (some tens of millions of them) who regard cows as sacred, and are prepared to sacrifice a great deal to them. When it is pointed out that those who hold cows sacred have to pay a very heavy price in terms of other values sacrificed it is sometimes held that people have a right to their own hierarchy of values, and that if you happen to be a certain kind of person a value-system dominated by cows will be the best system for you. Such a defence, however, is inadequate, because in order that a value or scheme of values should be defensible it must be shown to be capable of being incorporated in some possible political system within which it can be successfully promoted.

Now considerations so general as these are very little more than platitudes. They are capable of a development, however, which is not entirely platitudinous, and I shall suggest a possible such line of development. But before doing that I should like to cite a passage from a recent commentator on Hobbes which suggests that even as they stand they are not so indisputable as to be genuine, first-class platitudes. In the course of a part of his discussion of Hobbes which he describes (too modestly) as "pedestrian", Watkins remarks generally:

There can be no proven or well-justified system of moral propositions. We cannot prove a moral proposition, or justify it in some weaker way, because the premises of any "proof" or "justification" will be at least as unjustified as the original proposition. (The most one can do by way of justification is to show that a proposition follows from, or is supported by, propositions which one's audience accepts; but perhaps some of these have been *wrongly* accepted.) (*Hobbes's System of Ideas*, p. 178).

What I have been suggesting is that Hobbes has shown that there are certain moral propositions—or at least value propositions of a completely general kind, which must have *some* moral content—which must be accepted by anyone who proposes to deliberate reasonably within the context of any scheme of values at all.

## 5 GOD'S PROPHET

Hobbes's sovereign has unlimited—although not, as we have seen, unqualified—rights and powers, and these extend to the controlling of men's speech and opinions. "For the actions of men proceed from their opinions, and in the well-governing of opinions, consisteth the well-governing of men's actions, in order to their peace, and concord"

(XVIII 116). Such a view vividly suggests 1984 and Big Brother. Hobbes is careful to make it clear that he is not defending the right of the sovereign to propagate *falsehood* for the sake of promoting peace. True doctrine, he argues, cannot possibly be "repugnant to peace". For although bad government may have resulted in false doctrine being generally received, so that the truth is "generally offensive", if the "rough bustling in of a new truth" causes turbulence there must already have been a state of virtual war—"For those men that are so remissly governed, that they dare take up arms to defend, or introduce an opinion, are still in war; and their condition not peace, but only a cessation of arms for fear of one another; and they live, as it were, in the precincts of battle continually" (XVIII 116–17).

Hobbes's argument here is, I think, at least a little stronger than it looks. The proposition that the truth cannot be "repugnant to peace" is not an empirical proposition, but neither is it a piece of completely useless armchair theorising or merely a pious wish. The emergence of some particular truth may well be a cause of disorder, but it is reasonable to expect that the general tendency of true knowledge will be to promote peace, since ignorance and delusion create frustration and uncertainty. (If we found generally that acting on what we called "true" beliefs led to greater frustration and uncertainty than not acting on them, we would have grounds for changing our criteria of truth.) The sovereign who seriously attempts to discharge his office of promoting peace (and also the welfare of his subjects) must attempt not only to avoid "false doctrine" but also positively to promote true knowledge.

The sovereign, however, on Hobbes's account, must not only promote the truth but also have and exercise the right of deciding what the truth is. That is the point at which believers in freedom generally, and especially freedom of speech and thought, are liable to feel a sense of outrage. Mill, a classic exponent of liberalism, argued that the truth was most likely to emerge where there was uninhibited freedom of speech. It may well be true, indeed, that the search for knowledge has flourished best in environments where people have had the greatest freedom to think and speak as they pleased. Yet, in the first place, that argument goes no further than to establish freedom of speech on a condition—that the exercise of it should be productive of truth—and not as any sort of natural, still less inalienable, right of individuals as such. And, in the second place, although it may be the case that the highest degree of knowledge depends on freedom, it does not follow that freedom will necessarily produce knowledge. For there is nothing gained in bringing the truth to light unless it can be recognised when found. In some political situations— in the early and unstable stages of "emerging"societies, for example— a large degree of freedom of speech may simply lead to factions and disorder. All that a liberal is entitled to insist on is that freedom generally—and especially freedom of opinion and expression—should be extended as far as is possible. But no general rule can be given for fixing the limits. If it is true that the limits should be set as far apart as possible, it is true also that there may have to be limits, and that it must be a public decision whether there should be limits and what these should be.

Hobbes, then, is justified in reserving this as a right to the sovereign. The justification may seem most obvious when we think of unstable societies on the brink of internal disorder. But it could apply also to stable and sophisticated societies such as our own. If some people or institutions (such as large corporations) found some powerful means (such as television) of propagating dangerous un-truths (such as that car-driving is a sport, or that affluence is impor-tant) among a large number of people, or among an important segment of easily impressionable people, then it would be by no means obvious that the sovereign should leave this unchecked in the sacred cause of freedom of speech. No useful conclusions can be reached about what degree of freedom is permissible except in the light of evidence about the particular society and situation in question, but at least one can try to be clear about what the argument is about. Those whose habits and values are effectively conditioned by the power of advertising are slaves to that power, and *if* there is such a power then the freedom to exercise it is the freedom of one to enslave another. The control, and even prohibition, of the use of such power is a blow against freedom or against slavery depending on whether you think of the freedom of the few who can exercise it or the slavery of the many who can be conditioned by it. What is at issue, then, is not a question of freedom—a conflict between believers in freedom and proponents of control—but a factual question, whether in a given situation advertising is actually as powerful as some people fear (and as its practitioners believe).

The most interesting application of this argument, however, is not to matters such as advertising, but to the relations of Church and State. Since the sovereign has the right of controlling men's opinions generally that must include their religious opinions. The sovereign, therefore, is the "supreme pastor" of his people (*Leviathan*, XLII 355). There is no room in a society for two sovereigns, for then there cannot be peace and order (XXXIX 306). If the sovereign is a Christian then it is a Christian Commonwealth, but if the sovereign is a heathen he is no less sovereign and no less supreme pastor, for he is supreme pastor not by virtue of being Christian but of being sovereign. Hobbes directs a good deal of his argument on this subject to destroying Papal pretensions. Thus he argues that although a sovereign may "commit the authority of ordaining pastors in his dominions to another being, as divers Christian kings allow that power to the Pope", he does not thereby admit a pastor superior to himself: "Christian doctors are our schoolmasters to Christianity; but kings are fathers of families, and may receive schoolmasters for their subjects from the recommendation of a stranger, but not from the command" (XLII 356). The sovereign is not merely pastor, but interpreter of Scripture and, in a word, "God's prophet" (XXXVI 285). For religion is a matter of belief in a supernatural power, but there has always to be decided the question of what the supernatural power requires of us. God does not speak to each and every one of us individually, or if he does then so many of us mishear the message that there is no agreement about what it is. If he speaks through prophets and scriptures, it still has to be decided who are the true prophets and what are the genuine scriptures. If religious beliefs could be as private to the individual as his aesthetic tastes may be, the sovereign would have no occasion to interfere. The sovereign has an interest in interpreting scripture just so far as it is taken as *law* (XXX 254), and therefore he cannot yield his right to authoritative interpretation without yielding his sovereignty.

These arguments of Hobbes's are more than just weapons for using against Popes. They present a serious challenge to any conception of religious ethics, and especially Christian ethics. For one way of regarding the teaching of Jesus is as something which is morally illuminating in a general sort of way without entailing any very specific conclusions about right and wrong in actual situations: something which speaks to the conscience, leaving it still to the individual to decide how to apply the message to actual cases. This is a view which is taken by many, but not all, Christians. Thus although there are some who say that a Christian cannot be a Conservative (or, on the contrary, a Socialist), there are others who believe that Christianity only tells one how to be a *good* Socialist (or Conservative). The other way of regarding the teaching of Jesus is as something which contains a number of specific principles of behaviour, or laws, which can be the basis of a clear decision in actual cases. Thus on the one approach the Christian will say, perhaps, that Christianity does not tell us that we must not fornicate, but only that if we fornicate we must do so with Christian love (which may or may not be a difficult feat to accomplish); while on the other approach he will say that Christianity expressly forbids us to fornicate. Now the second approach presents us with a set of laws requiring our conformity. Then Christians are liable to be faced with problems of double allegiance which can be resolved only by the establishing of a Christian Commonwealth—a sovereign power which embodies Christian ethics in the civil law. Such a sovereign meets Hobbes's requirements, but not necessarily in a way which will satisfy even those Christians who regard Christian ethics as a body of laws. For the sovereign, on Hobbes's view, always has the function of being "supreme pastor" and "God's prophet", and he has it simply by virtue of his temporal sovereign power. Christian would-be theocrats are faced with a dilemma. Either they must suppose that Christians as well as others are bound by the law of nature, so that they must submit to the temporal sovereign in all matters, even of doctrine, and confine themselves to the hope that the sovereign may choose to be Christian; or they must regard Christian ethics as revolutionary doctrine which makes them at least potential rebels, claiming an authority independent of the sovereign. Either way, there must be procedures for arriving at decisions on all matters which may be disputed, and for enforcing these decisions when arrived at, or else Christians are liable to become—as often in history they have become—rival factions, at war with each other, and a source of disorder and confusion. If, in reaction to the problems involved in this legalistic approach to Christian ethics, it is decided that the Christian message is not a body of explicit and specific laws but rather some very general directives about the sort of *attitudes* which people should adopt, and which should inspire them in the things they do and in the laws they make, problems again arise. For either this is just the law of nature (obliging, as it does, *in foro interno*), which stands in no need of Christian endorsement, or it goes beyond the law of nature. But if the latter, then, as has been argued in previous sections of this chapter, no value-system can make good a claim to people's allegiance unless it can be shown to be workable within some specific political context: for a person has to live out his values in a society, or not at all. Thus it is one thing to give no thought for the morrow in a society which makes adequate provision for the welfare of one's children, but quite another to do it in a society in which children are allowed to suffer for the neglectful sins of their parents. Of course a parent who allowed his children to suffer through his failure to make provision for the future would no doubt be told that that was not what was meant by taking no thought for the morrow. The trouble is that when the Christian (or any other) message is taken in this way there is no longer any knowing exactly how to take it, and in cutting it off from any clear political and legal implications it has been pushed a long way towards moral vacuity.

Now I do not believe that in the course of a few pages one can *establish* any conclusions about a matter so complex as the relations between religion, ethics and politics; nor make out even a prima facie case in favour of them. All that can be done is to indicate a few of the kinds of problem that exist. What I have tried to show, however, is that Hobbes may be regarded as having some contribution to make, and that he had more to suggest than merely a crude and cynical subordination of the religious to the political. What he has to offer is an approach based on a systematic analysis of the logic of value-systems generally, and the distinctive nature of the contribution which he makes in that field can be seen, briefly and clearly, in his discussion of *equity*.

## 6 EQUITY

Hobbes describes equity as "that principal law of nature" (XXVI 184). He defines it thus:

Also if *a man be trusted to judge between man and man*, it is a precept of the law of nature, *that he deal equally between them*. For without that, the controversies of men cannot be determined but by war. He therefore that is partial in judgment, doth what in him lies, to deter men from the use of judges, and arbitrators; and consequently, against the fundamental law of nature, is the cause of war (XV 101).

The notion of equity is not limited by Hobbes, as his words here suggest, merely to cases of arbitrating in *disputes*. Equity is the equal distribution of justice in criminal prosecutions, giving no special favour to the rich or powerful (XXX 225), and punishing only the guilty and not the innocent (XXVIII 207). The justification of this as a law of nature, which also must be observed in the provisions and administration of civil law, is that it is clearly a necessary means to peace, since to treat men inequitably is to deprive them of the benefit of law and order and therefore invite them to revert to war.

Now equity—in this sense, which includes forbidding the punishment of the innocent—has often seemed to raise some problems. People may make moral judgments in an incoherent sort of way, appealing to this or that rule of thumb without any clear conception of how the various rules, standards and criteria on which they rely can be related to each other. It seems that they need to be *somehow* related together, because it is possible that a number of different rules to all of which one has assented may lead to conflicting decisions in difficult cases. I may believe that one ought to avoid causing suffering, and also that one ought not to tell lies, for example, and then find myself with a problem when a man whom I know to be dying, and to be afraid of death, asks me to tell him the truth about his condition. The attraction of utilitarian ethics is that it provides a system within which no theoretically insoluble problems can arise. On the theory of what is called act-utilitarianism I simply have to calculate which of a number of actions open to me will bring about the greatest balance of happiness over unhappiness for people generally (or, generally, of good over evil, allowing that happiness *may* not be the only thing which is good). According to rule-utilitarianism I have to act according to rules which are such that general conformity to them will promote the greatest balance of happiness, or good. Thus, given that there are such rules, I do not normally have to ask whether some particular action will promote the greatest possible happiness or good but merely whether it conforms to the rules. In those special cases in which the rules conflict there are a variety of possible moves which I may make. Some rules may take precedence over others, because it may be that general conformity with one rule is a means to greater happiness or good than general conformity to another. Or in the case of conflict of rules I may revert, for that special occasion, to the position of act-utilitarianism. At all events, there are rational and systematic procedures available for resolving the problem, and that is why the system appeals.

On the other hand it is sometimes held that act-utilitarianism gives rise to anomalies. There could be, for example, a situation in which the greatest good could be achieved only by sacrificing an innocent victim. There are some who think that equity is a value of such importance that it would be wrong to do that, even although utilitarian ethics requires it. Rule-utilitarianism, however, may seem to escape this difficulty. For it can be argued that a rule prescribing equitable behaviour must be part of a utilitarian scheme of rules, since general failure to adopt it as a rule would result in general misery and uncertainty. That may seem very like the argument which Hobbes uses—that equity is a means to peace. Yet there is in fact a very big difference. For the utilitarian scheme begins by specifying a certain *end*. For "hedonistic" utilitarians the end is happiness, and for an "agathistic" utilitarian, such as Moore, the end includes not only happiness but such goods as aesthetic experience and personal affection, but however the end is conceived the utilitarian regards moral rules as means to the promotion of some specific end. Now it is a contingent matter whether some particular action, or pattern of conformity to some particular rule, will in fact promote a specific end or not. If equity is conceived as a means to some specific end then it is *conceivable* that this might not be so, and that the world might be of such a nature that conformity with a principle of equity would fail to promote the greatest good. If that were so then on the utilitarian view it would no longer be right to act equitably. Thus utilitarianism is vulnerable to attack by those who believe that it would still be wrong to sacrifice the innocent even if it were not the case that generally equitable behaviour would promote the greatest good. The utilitarian view can establish an obligation to act equitably, but only under a contingent condition, and that is unacceptable to its critics.

What is distinctive about Hobbes's view is that although he presents equity as a means to peace, this does not, in the context of his argument, place it under a contingent condition. For the rule of equity is one of the laws of nature, and the laws of nature embody a scheme of what I have called necessary values (see above, Chapter

Eight, Section 1), and these are values which are means to an end only in the sense of being necessary conditions of the effective pursuit of *any* scheme of ends. To say something is a necessary condition of *any* scheme of ends is not at all the same as to say that it is contingently a means to some particular scheme of ends. A rationally workable scheme of values is one which people generally can adopt with the assurance that they can reasonably hope to promote it. Hobbes's argument is that it is only within the context of an established system of laws that people can make any rational deliberations at all, and that equity is a necessary *element* of any workable system of law, and therefore of any workable system of values, and not contingently a means to its promotion. The position which Hobbes gives to equity is thus different from, and more important than, the position which it can occupy within utilitarian ethics.

## 7 CONCLUSION

My discussion has been limited to only a part of what Hobbes wrote in *Leviathan*. Thus he had a great deal more to say about sovereignty than could be gathered from my brief treatment of it in this chapter. Partly that is because I have limited myself to discussing the foundations of his political theory and have not attempted to follow out his development of it in any detail. This limitation which I have imposed on myself is not, however, merely to keep the book down to a modest size or to spare myself further trouble. It is because what I have been trying to show is that everything distinctive and interesting that Hobbes has to say is contained in the construction of the theoretical foundation. When he comes to discuss in detail such matters as the conduct of government, the merits of monarchy compared with democracy, and so forth, he is no longer constructing a generalised theory but applying it to actual institutions. Some of what he has to say there is penetrating enough, but at that level of discussion conclusions can only be reached in the light of evidence about the actual working of actual political institutions—the sort of considerations which it is the business of political science, in the modern sense of that term, to take account of, but which Hobbes had no great knowledge of, and which, in any case, belonged on his own account within the field of prudence rather than of science.

In Chapter Two I have suggested that the background of Hobbes's thought generally was a revolutionary situation in which many old conceptions of knowledge were being overthrown, with no very settled view of things to replace them; and that a number of diverse influences were bearing upon him. In Chapter Three I have examined his attempts to produce a satisfactory theory of logic, and his failure— not a very surprising one in view of the revolutionary situation in which he was working—to produce a single and consistent account of *truth*. Thus in Chapter Four I have followed out his thoughts on scientific or philosophical method, beginning, as they did, in a state of considerable confusion, out of which emerged two things of special importance: one was an hypothetico-deductive account of physics, which has some merit as a contribution to the philosophy of science, and the other a conviction that a demonstrative, quasi-mathematical structure was the correct model for the sciences generally, except for those which were concerned to provide explanations of particular and actual phenomena. He makes it quite clear in *Leviathan* that his method there is to be the demonstrative, and not the hypothetico-deductive method. By the time he wrote *Leviathan* the distinction between the two methods was fairly clearly drawn, but when he wrote the earlier political works his ideas on method were much more confused. In Chapters Five and Six I have examined in some detail the various accounts of human nature which he gives in his different works. I have argued that the accounts given in *The Elements of Law* and *De Cive* are based on his very pessimistic view of human nature, which he makes a confused and unsuccessful attempt to present in the trappings of a science. In *Leviathan*, however, although this pessimistic view is still in evidence, nevertheless, consistently with his clearer conception of the nature of a science, the pessimistic view is seldom allowed to play an actual part in the argument, which is presented as a formal system of propositions resting on definitions.

What is important for Hobbes at that stage is to construct the notion of a rational deliberation. It is done abstractly, notions such as *desire*, *deliberation*, *good*, and so forth, being formally defined without any assumption about the nature of what actually is desired or regarded as good. In Chapters Seven, Eight, and Nine I have examined the way in which these notions acquire political content. What Hobbes does is to analyse the notion of the deliberation of a rational being with values who is in relation with other such beings, and his political science, so far as it is a body of demonstrated propositions, arises out of the analysis of the structure of any such deliberation. A man, so far as he is deliberating reasonably, must allow not only that there is a possibility that others may threaten his values, but also that others may rationally make allowance for the same possibility. In a situation of maximum uncertainty, where everyone was making reasonable provision for the promotion of his own values, there would be least reason for any hope of actual success, therefore everyone, so far as he deliberates rationally, has reason to aim to avoid such a situation. That is the heart of Hobbes's argument, and although the notion of a universal fear of death is constantly mentioned it does not perform any actual, still less any indispensable, part in the argument, and is a last remnant of Hobbes's earlier and confused attempts to construct a political science resting on his pessimistic view of human nature. When this notion of the fear of death is removed from the argument what is left is a formal system of demonstrated propositions; and the laws of nature, and their consequences, can be presented as necessarily true propositions.

Now it is one thing to construct a formal theory, but it is another to find any use for it. The laws of nature, for example, belong to a system of necessary truths because they are a body of precepts such that if a man deliberates or acts rationally he deliberates or acts according to them; but the proposition that a man who deliberates or acts rationally deliberates or acts according to the laws of nature is a necessarily true proposition only if "man" is defined as "rational being, with some contingent values, and in relation with other such beings" (see above, Chapter Eight, Section 5). The question that cannot be answered within the theory, but which requires an affirmative answer if the theory is to be anything more than an academic logical exercise, is whether the beings who in normal usage are called "men" are "men" according to this definition of "man". For, in the first place, the laws of nature have nothing to say to *you* except so far as you have some contingent values and are prepared to deliberate rationally. In the second place, your obligation to obey the laws of nature *in foro externo* depends on the willingness of others to be reasonable and to obey them also. And, in the third place, and most importantly, while the account of natural law is derived from an analysis of deliberation in the state of nature, the conclusions which Hobbes is arguing towards are conclusions not merely about how we ought to behave in the (unlikely) event of finding ourselves in a state of nature, but also about our obligations in organised society. It is one thing to argue that in a state of nature, where there is maximum uncertainty and no security, a policy of anticipatory violence is reasonable for everyone, so that there is a state of at least incipient war; but it may seem that it is quite another thing to connect that with any feature of political relations in an ordered society. For Hobbes's argument is not merely that the establishing of some public machinery of coercion is necessary to deliver people from the state of nature, but that continued maintenance of the machinery is necessary for the *preservation* of society. It may seem, however, that the facts simply conflict with the theory, since at a political level it is not true that the order and stability of a society varies in proportion to the strength of its government, while at an individual level it is not true that it is only the threat of coercion that drives people to conform with the law. The conflict, however, is not so great as it may appear. For (i) on the theory, as it has been expounded, the stability of a society depends not so much on a strong government as on a strong sovereign (see above, Section 3), and whereas the notion of a strong government involves the *actual* exercise of controlling power, the notion of a strong sovereign involves only the preparedness, capacity and authority to exercise power if occasion should arise—and an important measure of the strength of the sovereign is the infrequency of such occasions. And (ii) the theory does not assert that people only conform to the law for the sake of avoiding its penalties, but that the existence of a coercive agency provides the conditions in which it is reasonable to conform with the law. Nevertheless, the proposition that it is reasonable to conform to the law only when it is backed by coercion depends on the proposition that in the absence of coercion others will rationally deliberate and come to the conclusion that there is no longer any sufficient reason for them to conform, in the absence of the security which coercion affords. But of course other people might not draw that conclusion at all. The very most that Hobbes's *a priori* form of argument can establish is that it would be a *reasonable* deliberation, but it cannot show—nor does it seem that it is entitled to assume—that people will deliberate reasonably. In some situations, perhaps, people will put an unreasonable trust in each other, and the consequences of this unreasonable trust may be peace, while the consequences of reasonable distrust would be war.

Yet I do not think that such a consideration, although it must be conceded, means that Hobbes's theory does not, or does not necessarily, apply to actual situations. For (i) when we imagine situations in which people trust each other we tend to imagine them still within the context of an ordered society. The disposition to trust others is something which it is difficult to imagine developing, except within societies such as we know; and in these the social order is in fact backed by coercion. (ii) The fact that something has a desirable outcome does not of itself mean that it was wisely done: you may be just lucky, in achieving a success which you had no right to expect (see *Leviathan*, XV 95–96).

And (iii) the applicability of the theory does not require that the sort of calculations which it presents as reasonable should in fact always be a dominant element of everyone's deliberations, but only that they should be one important element. People, of course, might become completely irrational. But then there would be no human society because there would be no humans, except in a minimum biological sense of the term. Or they might change so that reliably and predictably their behaviour harmonised peacefully, without the need of any coercive threat. That is a possibility which Hobbes envisages when he compares the societies of ants and bees with human societies (*Leviathan*, XVII 111). What Hobbes says is that humans are just not like that. And some of the differences which he mentions as important—such as the human possession of language and reason—are not merely contingent but are part of the conception of "man". To imagine a society of beings who were capable of living together in peace without any reliance on some coercive order, then, would be to imagine a society of non-humans. On Hobbes's theory, then, *my* obligation to conform to the requirements both of the law of nature and of an actually established legal system, and my obligation to help to maintain such a system so far as I can, are conditional on the existence of others who are prepared to deliberate rationally according to the pattern of deliberation which Hobbes has set forth. The fact that others *sometimes* will not necessarily and wholly conform to that pattern does not affect the validity, nor, within limits, the applicability of the theory. There are many analogies to this. One quite close one is the theory of a game of cards such as whist. In order to decide rationally what card to play at a particular stage of the game a player has to have a grasp of the theory of the game (which tells

him, for example, that two trumps held by each of two partners *can*
produce four tricks through cross-trumping), and he also has to
estimate the chances that this or that card will be held by his partner
or by one or other of his opponents, which estimate depends on the
evidence of the cards already played, assuming the players to have
been playing rationally. But of course the others will have been
playing only *more or less* rationally. Sometimes they may choose to
*ignore* the theory of the game—as some, for example, might have an
eccentric desire not to hold queens longer than possible—and at other
times they may *miscalculate*. A good player will make allowance for
the known eccentricities and limitations of his partner and opponents. But such allowance will be only a special consideration which
may sometimes and in special circumstances affect the good player's
application of the theory of the game, and his success on the whole
will depend on the extent to which his own calculations are rational
calculations which take account of the possible rational calculations
of the others engaged in the game.

The theory of whist, of course, is not an account of how players of
whist actually do calculate when playing, any more than Hobbes's
theory of politics is an account of how people actually deliberate in
political contexts. It is not a substitute for the psychology of whist-
playing any more than Hobbes's political theory is a substitute for
political science (in the modern sense of the term), for the theory of
the game is only one of the elements that enter into the actual play,
and it does so only via the players' knowledge and application of it,
which may be imperfect. Yet this distinction cannot be too sharply
drawn, for (i) it is reasonable to apply the whole theory of the game
only on the assumption that the others are trying to apply it also,
while (ii) it is reasonable to make that assumption, since if it were not
true neither games of whist nor human societies would exist at all
as we know them. Nevertheless Hobbes's political theory is and is
intended to be primarily *prescriptive*, laying down the general rules
which ought to govern the political deliberations of reasonable
people. Moreover, it is limited to such rules as are capable of formal
demonstration, taking no account of special and empirically discover-
able circumstances. It is not surprising, then, that it can have the
appearance of adding up to little more than a collection of platitudes.
Yet I have argued that that appearance is misleading, since propositions which contradict Hobbes's conclusions can seem to be equally

platitudinous—and it is important to get hold of the *right* platitudes and to know that they are firmly based!

The whole of Hobbes's argument can, perhaps, be summed up in a conclusion which has considerable moral significance. It is a distinctive feature of human beings that they have the capacities to reason and to formulate value-systems, each according to his own conception of value. No man could give up these capacities without being less than a man. Yet the exercise of them by people in relation with each other can be wholly destructive of the values which each is striving to pursue. The imposition of coercive law is the only thing which a man can reasonably rely on for the assurance of the realisation of at least some of what he values. Thus even if any given political order does not provide what anyone can regard as the complete good, it is still at the very least better than the only alternative, which is a state of nature. But in fact it is more than that. For in a state of nature each individual would have complete responsibility for the promotion of his values, and would have constantly to decide between either risking the total defeat of all his values or else imposing his power on all whom he could subdue. Thus a "common power" removes from the individual an intolerable burden of responsibility, which he could discharge only if he were God. But it does not reduce him to the status of a bee in a hive, because he still has his own contingent values; and he has to decide both how far these can be pursued within the society to which he belongs, and also whether, given his values, the benefits which a society confers are worth the price which has to be paid— which is a decision either to make war *on* the society or to be prepared to make war *with* it on its enemies. If Hobbes's arguments are valid, then, violence is not a product merely, or even chiefly, of disreputable human passions, so that if human nature could just be improved violence would disappear. It arises, on the contrary, from the relations between rational beings who have values, but not necessarily the same values. Hence there is no question whether violence should be accepted or rejected, but only how best its employment can be regulated.

# Short English Bibliography

"Bibliography" is really too pretentious a title for this list of books and articles by and about Hobbes. It is a selection, and it reflects not only my preferences but also, no doubt, my ignorance. Nevertheless it lists, I think, most recent contributions in English to the study of Hobbes. There are two things which I have aimed at in compiling it. One is to provide some sort of guidance to readers beginning the study of Hobbes. Section A gives an account of what works of Hobbes's are currently available, and in what sort of edition. Section B is a list of books about Hobbes, in chronological order of publication. In most cases I have tried to indicate very briefly whether the book is a comprehensive survey or an examination of some particular aspect of Hobbes's philosophy. Section C may, I hope, help students to follow up recent discussions of some major topics—the dispute about the "Taylor–Warrender thesis", for example. My second aim has been to indicate very briefly some debts which I owe and some disagreements which I persist in. The books to which I am most grateful are those by Peters, Warrender and Plamenatz. I did not read Hood, Watkins or Goldsmith until I had already completed a first draft of this book. In each of them there is much with which I agree, but although I have borrowed—sometimes consciously and sometimes unconsciously— bits and pieces from all of them, and from many other commentators as well, none of them has seemed to me to contain *all* the right pieces or to put them together in quite the right sort of way to make a true picture of *Leviathan*. Thus S. M. Brown, in "Hobbes: The Taylor Thesis" (see 43 below), reconstructs some parts of the argument of *Leviathan* as a formal system. But I think that at best he goes only half-way, for he still leaves some of the foundations as empirical postulates. The critical comments which I have attached to some of the books in the list are not intended as weighty judgments, but should be taken as declarations of prejudice and pointers to the existence of alternative views.

## (A) WORKS BY HOBBES

### FIRST EDITIONS OF HOBBES'S MAJOR PHILOSOPHICAL WORKS

1  *A Short Tract on First Principles.* An early work, first printed in Tönnies edition of *The Elements of Law* (see 12 below).

2  *The Elements of Law.* Circulating in manuscript in 1640, this was first printed in two parts separately—*Human Nature* and *De Corpore Politico*—in 1650. Reprinted in Molesworth E W (see 10 below), Tönnies (see 12 below), and Peters (see 19 below).

3  *De Cive.* 1st edition 1642. 2nd edition, with a new Preface, 1647. Reprinted in Molesworth L W (see 11 below). English version entitled *Philosophical Rudiments concerning Government and Society* published 1651. Reprinted in Molesworth E W (see 10 below) and Lamprecht (see 18 below).

4  *Leviathan.* 1st edition 1651. Many modern editions (see 14–17 below). Latin version published 1668. Reprinted in Molesworth L W (see 11 below).

5  *The Questions concerning Liberty, Necessity and Chance.* 1st edition 1654. Reprinted in Molesworth E W (see 10 below), and a part of it in Peters (see 19 below).

6  *De Corpore.* 1st edition 1655. Reprinted in Molesworth L W (see 11 below). English version entitled *Elements of Philosophy, The First Section, concerning Body*, published 1656. Reprinted in Molesworth E W (see 10 below), and a part of it in Peters (see 19 below).

7  *De Homine.* 1st edition 1658. Reprinted in Molesworth L W (see 11 below).

8  *Dialogue between a Philosopher and a Student of the Common Law.* 1st edition 1681. Reprinted in Molesworth E W (see 10 below).

9  *Behemoth.* 1st edition 1682. Reprinted in Molesworth E W (see 10 below) and in Tönnies (see 13 below).

### MODERN EDITIONS OF WORKS BY HOBBES

10  Molesworth, Sir W. (ed.), *The English Works of Thomas Hobbes*, 11 volumes, London, 1839–45. An unscholarly edition, but it is in fact the most recent printing of a great part of Hobbes's English works.

11  Molesworth, Sir W. (ed.), *Opera Latina*, 5 volumes, London, 1839–45. (Referred to as Molesworth L W.)

12  Tönnies, F. (ed.), *The Elements of Law*, London, 1889. A scholarly edition.

13  Tönnies, F. (ed.), *Behemoth*, London, 1889. A scholarly edition.

14  Waller, A. R. (ed.), *Leviathan*, Cambridge, 1904. A scholarly edition.

15  Pogson Smith, W. G. (ed.), *Leviathan*, Oxford, 1909.

16  Oakeshott, M. (ed.), *Leviathan*, Oxford, 1946. A complete edition of *Leviathan* with modernised spelling and a long introductory essay.

17  Plamenatz, J. (ed.), *Leviathan*, 1962. An abridged edition, with modernised spelling and an introductory essay. Part IV and some of part III of the text are omitted. This is unfortunate, since these parts contain some of Hobbes's finest writing as well as some points of philosophical importance.

18  Lamprecht, S. P. (ed.), *De Cive or The Citizen*, New York, 1949. The 1651 version, with modernised spelling, and with certain chapters (those relating to theology and scripture) omitted.

19  Peters, R. (ed.), *Body, Man, and Citizen*, New York, 1962. Both parts of *The Elements of Law*, some parts of the English version of *De Corpore*, and a small part of *The Questions concerning Liberty, Necessity and Chance*.

## (B) BOOKS ABOUT HOBBES

20  Robertson, G. C., *Hobbes*, Edinburgh, 1886. An introduction to Hobbes's life and philosophy. Old, but still going strong.

21  Stephen, Sir Leslie, *Hobbes*, London, 1904.

22  Taylor, A. E., *Hobbes*, London, 1908. A brief introduction.

23  Catlin, G., *Thomas Hobbes as Philosopher, Publicist and Man of Letters*, London, 1922.

24  Brandt, F., *Thomas Hobbes's Mechanical Conception of Nature*, Copenhagen, 1928. An immensely detailed and scholarly study.

25  Laird, J., *Hobbes*, London, 1934. Laird attempts to give a picture of the whole sweep of Hobbes's philosophy, with an account of his life and times and a review of his influence on the philosophy of his successors. It is a very learned book, and helpful and suggestive at many points. In my opinion, however, it

often presents a completely false picture (especially of Hobbes's psychological theory) through failing to take account of differences between Hobbes's different works.

26   Strauss, L., *The Political Philosophy of Hobbes*, Oxford, 1936. This interprets Hobbes's moral and political views in terms of the concepts of vanity and fear—a thesis which, if true at all, could be true only of Hobbes's earlier works.

27   Gooch, G. P., *Hobbes*, London, 1939.

28   James, D. G., *The Life of Reason*, London, 1949. Concerned not only with Hobbes but with Locke and Bolingbroke also—and, at that, with their views not on ethics and politics but on knowledge, imagination and religious feeling.

29   Bowle, J., *Hobbes and His Critics*, London, 1951. This is a discussion of the criticisms which Hobbes's contemporaries directed against his political theories—Rosse, Bramhall, Clarendon and others. On the whole Bowle agrees with the critics, although, since he is primarily concerned with the critics, he gives only the most perfunctory attention to Hobbes's own views.

30   Peters, R., *Hobbes*, London, 1956. A survey of the whole of Hobbes's philosophy. Remarkably comprehensive, paying careful attention to Hobbes's theories of language and method.

31   Warrender, H., *The Political Philosophy of Hobbes*, Oxford, 1957. Warrender argues the thesis—some of the elements of which had first been advanced by Taylor (see 63 below)—that Hobbes has both a theory of moral obligation and an empirical psychology, which are independent of each other: self-preservation is merely the *motive* for doing what one ought, but the *ground* of an obligation is that it is commanded by God. Although a great many students of Hobbes reject the Taylor–Warrender thesis, so that it has given rise to an extensive and fruitful literature exploring and disputing the points which it raises, it must be regarded as one of the classics of Hobbes-scholarship. No one could fail to learn a great deal from it, but I think that the main thesis of this book is untenable because (i) it does not take sufficient account of the importance of Hobbes's *method*, and (ii) for reasons which I have given in Chapter Two, Section 5, and elsewhere, I do not think that Hobbes gives God any real part to play in his system.

32   Krook, D., *Three Traditions of Moral Thought*, Cambridge, 1959.

This book is concerned only partly with Hobbes. It argues that in contrast with thinkers such as Plato, and even Mill, Hobbes (in company with Aristotle and Hume) takes a "base" view of human nature. In my view this simply confuses Hobbes's private opinions with his philosophical system.

33    Mintz, S. I., *The Hunting of Leviathan*, Cambridge, 1962. An account—complementary to Bowle's (see 29 above)—of the *philosophical* and *metaphysical* criticisms of Hobbes between 1650 and 1700. While this account is of great interest and value, Mintz claims also that it is indispensable to an understanding of *Hobbes*'s philosophy. That seems to me, however, to be very doubtful. What Bowle and Mintz do is to demonstrate how completely Hobbes was misunderstood. That is not surprising, for Hobbes's critics were on the whole a very pedestrian collection. What they did manage to notice was that the general tone of Hobbes's philosophy was secular and subversive of religion.

34    Macpherson, C. B., *The Political Theory of Possessive Individualism*, Oxford, 1962. This includes a study of Hobbes interpreting his theory along Marxist lines. This pays insufficient attention to Hobbes's method, and makes (what I regard as) the mistake of importing Hobbes's views about human nature into his theory of political relations. But it is brilliantly done, and Macpherson–Hobbes is a political theorist hardly less powerful and interesting than Thomas Hobbes.

35    Plamenatz, J., *Man and Society*, London, 1963. Only one chapter of this work is on Hobbes, but it includes an excellent discussion of the covenant.

36    Hood, F. C., *The Divine Politics of Thomas Hobbes*, Oxford, 1964. This is a very thoroughgoing attempt to represent Hobbes as a Christian thinker, and his theory of moral obligation as a religious doctrine. Hood argues that Hobbes's psychology is not egoistic, although still a "descriptive psychology". By contrast I have argued that Hobbes's psychology is not descriptive, but is *sometimes* egoistic.

37    Watkins, J. W. N., *Hobbes's System of Ideas*, London, 1965. This is a fairly brief but original study of the relation between Hobbes's general philosophy and methodology and his political theory. I have discussed it at several points in this book.

38  Brown, K. C. (ed.), *Hobbes Studies*, Oxford, 1965. A valuable collection of papers, two of which are published here for the first time. The papers are listed below (43, 45, 47, 49, 54, 57, 58, 62, 63, 64, 65, 68, 69).

39  Goldsmith, M. M., *Hobbes's Science of Politics*, New York and London, 1966. A study of Hobbes's political theory in the light of his views on method. Goldsmith represents Hobbes's political system as an explanatory theory, and this, I think, confuses the hypothetico-deductive analysis of method described in *De Corpore* with the mathematical method actually practised in the political works. Nevertheless Goldsmith's discussion of the details of Hobbes's political theory is comprehensive and illuminating.

## (C) ARTICLES ABOUT HOBBES

The following abbreviations are used:

| | |
|---|---|
| *Phil. Q .* | *Philosophical Quarterly* |
| *Phil. Rev.* | *Philosophical Review* |
| *Pol. Q .* | *Political Quarterly* |
| *Pol. St.* | *Political Studies* |

40  Brown, J. M., "A Note on Professor Oakeshott's Introduction to the Leviathan", *Pol. St.*, 1953.

41  —— "Hobbes: A Rejoinder", *Pol. St.*, 1954.

42  Brown, K. C., "Hobbes's Grounds for Belief in a Deity", *Philosophy*, 1962.

43  Brown, S. M., "Hobbes: The Taylor Thesis", *Phil. Rev.*, 1959. Reprinted in Brown, *Hobbes Studies*.

44  Berlin, I., "Hobbes, Locke and Professor Macpherson", *Pol. Q.*, 1964.

45  Cattaneo, A., "Hobbes's Theory of Punishment", in Brown, *Hobbes Studies*; reprinted, in translation, from an article in *Jus*, 1960.

46  Engel, S. M., "Analogy and Equivocation in Hobbes", *Philosophy*, 1962.

47  —— "Hobbes's Table of Absurdity", *Phil. Rev.*, 1961. Reprinted in Brown, *Hobbes Studies*.

48  Gert, B., "Hobbes, Mechanism and Egoism", *Phil. Q .*, 1965.

49 Glover, W. B., "God and Thomas Hobbes", *Church History*, 1960. Reprinted in Brown, *Hobbes Studies*.

50 Krook, D., "Mr Brown's Note Annotated", *Pol. St.*, 1953.

51 —— "Thomas Hobbes's Doctrine of Meaning and Truth", *Philosophy*, 1956.

52 Lamprecht, S. P., "Hobbes and Hobbism", *American Political Science Review*, 1940.

53 McNeilly, F. S., "Egoism in Hobbes", *Phil. Q.*, 1966.

54 Macpherson, C. B., "Hobbes Today", *Canadian Journal of Economic and Political Science*, 1945. Reprinted in Brown, *Hobbes Studies*.

55 Nagel, T., "Hobbes's Concept of Obligation", *Phil. Rev.*, 1959.

56 Oakeshott, M. J., "The Moral Life in the Writings of Thomas Hobbes", in Oakeshott, *Rationalism in Politics*.

57 Plamenatz, J., "Mr Warrender's Hobbes", *Pol. St.*, 1957. Reprinted in Brown, *Hobbes Studies*.

58 Pennock, J. R., "Hobbes's Confusing 'Clarity'—The Case of 'Liberty' ", *American Political Science Review*, 1960. Reprinted in Brown, *Hobbes Studies*.

59 Raphael, D. D., "Obligation and Rights in Hobbes", *Philosophy*, 1962.

60 Skinner, Q., "Hobbes on Sovereignty", *Pol. St.*, 1965.

61 Stewart, J. B., "Hobbes among the Critics", *Political Science Quarterly*, 1958.

62 Strauss, L., "On the Spirit of Hobbes's Political Philosophy", from Strauss, *Natural Right and History*, reprinted in Brown, *Hobbes Studies*.

63 Taylor, A. E., "The Ethical Doctrine of Hobbes", *Philosophy*, 1938. Reprinted in Brown, *Hobbes Studies*.

64 Thomas, K., "The Social Origins of Hobbes's Political Thought", in Brown, *Hobbes Studies*.

65 Warrender, H., "A Reply to Mr Plamenatz", *Pol. St.*, 1960. Reprinted in Brown, *Hobbes Studies*.

66 —— "Obligations and Rights in Hobbes", *Philosophy*, 1962.

67 —— "The Place of God in Hobbes's Philosophy", *Pol. St.*, 1960.

68 Watkins, J. W. N., "Philosophy and Politics in Hobbes", *Phil. Q.* 1955. Reprinted, revised, in Brown, *Hobbes Studies*.

69 Wernham, A. G., "Liberty and Obligation in Hobbes", in Brown, *Hobbes Studies*.

# Index

Abstract names, 39–40
Absurdity, 42, 85
Accidents, 34–35, 53, 69
Analytical method, 51–54, 61–62, 71–72
Anticipatory violence, 162, 164–8, 188–9
Apparent good, 125–7
Appearance, 30–31, 102
Appetite, *see* Desire
Atheism, 10, 40
Authority, 236–7
Authorization, 214–24
Aversion, 100–19

Bacon, F., 80
Benevolence, 118–46
Berkeley, Bishop, 18, 40
Berlin, Sir I., 260
Bowle, J., 258, 259
Bramhall, Bishop, 170
Brandt, F., 257
Brown, J. M., 260
Brown, K. C., 260
Brown, S. M., 255–60

Categories, 19, 102
Catlin, G., 257
Cattaneo, A., 260
Cause: 73–74; final causes, 22–23;
    material and efficient causes, 23
Charity, 118, 146
Church, 21–22, 240–5
Circulation of blood, 108, 115
Common power, 186–91
Commonwealth, 186–91, 197–9, 214–31.
    *See also* Sovereignty
Compassion, 118–19
Competition, 143–4; competitive vio-
    lence, 161–2
Composition, 51, 71–72
Comprehension, 47–48, 67
Compulsion, 200–3
Conceptions, 18, 31, 42–46
Conceptual revision, 25–26
Concrete names, 39–40
Consent, 229–31. *See also* Sovereignty
Contentment, 129–36, 139, 145

Contract, 194–9, 214–31
Conventionalist theory of truth, 36–58.
    *See also* Science, conventionalist ac-
    count of *and* Science as a formal
    system
Covenant, 194–9, 214–31
Crombie, A. C., 20–21

Death, fear of, 178–82
Decision, 123–4
Definition, 48, 51–54, 61–63, 111–12;
    and cause, 52–54
Deliberation, 121–9
Delight, *see* Pleasure
Demonstration, 51–53, 60–65, 153–4
Descartes, R., 17, 23–26, 31
Desire, 100–19; object of, 104–6, 116–17,
    130, 160–1
Despair, 180–2
Diffidence, 162
Dissenter, 221, 230, 237–8
Duty, 199–204

Egoism: 11, 12, chs 5 and 6; and
    hedonism, 12, 96–100, 106–14; and
    materialism, 100–6; and pessimism,
    96–97; in *De Corpore*, 106–10; in *The
    Elements*, 110–15; in *Leviathan*, 115–20,
    125–36, 145–55
Empiricism, 78–81
Endeavour, 101, 104–17, 206–7
Engel, S. M., 260
Equality, 160, 163
Equity, 245–8
Essence, 19–20
Euclid, 7–8
Evidence, 41–42, 67–69
Evil, *see* Good
Experiment, 59–60
Explication, 62

Falsification, *see* Verification
Fancy, *see* Imagination
Felicity, 129–36, 139, 145
Final causes, 22–23
Force, 200–3

Freedom, 169–75; of speech, 240–5

Galileo Galilei, 8, 24, 26, 80
Gest, N., 260
Glory: ch. 6; in *The Elements* and *De Cive*, 138–44; in *Leviathan*, 144–7
Glover, W. B., 261
God, 22–24, 211–12
Goldsmith, M. M., 220, 255, 260
Gooch, G. P., 258
Good: 115, 119–21, 125–9; apparent, 125–7; and desire, 119–21, 125; and pleasure, 121
Good will, *see* Charity
Government, 225–9

Harvey, W., 110
Hedonism, 100, 106–10
Hood, F. C., 225, 259
Hume, D., 86
Hypotheses, 71–75, 81, 106–10, 116
Hypothetico-deductive view of physics, 71–75, 86

Ideas, *see* Conceptions
Imagination, 30–31, 101–2
Incompatible objectives, 160–1
Inertia, 26
Injustice, *see* Justice
Introspection, 72, 86, 87, 151–5

James, D. G., 258
Joy, 139–41
Justice, 194, 199–204, 209–11

Kant, I., 209
Kings, *see* Sovereignty
Knowledge: branches of, 29–30; knowledge, original, *see* Prudence
Krook, D., 258–61

Laird, J., 147, 152, 257
Lamprecht, S. P., 257, 261
Language: 18–20, ch. 3; abstract and concrete names, 39–40; absurdity, 42, 85; categories, 19, 102; definition, 48, 51–54; evidence, 41–42, 67–69; marks, 32–33, 41; meaning, 35–43; names and naming, 33–36; arbitrary imposition of names, 36–39; nominalism, 36–39; 216–18; signs and signification, 33–35, 78–79; names of constant and inconstant signification, 37–38; understanding, 35, 41–42, 66–67; universals, 35–47; word-tokens and word types, 34–35
Law of nature: ch. 8; and common power, *see* Power; and covenant, 194–9;

and divine command, 211–12; and equity, 245–8; fundamental law, 184–91; and liberty, 193; and moral philosophy, 209–12; and necessitation, 199–204; and obligation, *see* Obligation; precepts of reason, 184, 204–5, 209; and renunciation of rights, 191–3; and right of nature, 185–6, 192–3; scientific status of, 184, 204–6; and validating conditions, 207–9
Liberty: 169–75; of speech, 240–5

Macpherson, C. B., 259, 261
Majority, 214–16, 219–25
Marks, *see* Language
Materialism, 95, 100–6, 120–1
Mathematics: 60–66, 80–82; and physics, 74–76; pure and applied, 64–65
Meaning, *see* Language
Medieval thought, 16–22
Method: ch. 4; analytical (resolution), 51–54, 61–62, 71–72; and definitions, 51–54, 61–63; *mathematici* and *dogmatici*, 8; in political science, 83–88, 248–54; synthetical (composition), 51, 71–72. *See also* Mathematics and Science
Mintz, S. I., 10, 259
Moderate man, 138–40, 163–4
Molesworth, Sir W., 256, 257
Monarchy, *see* Sovereignty
Motives, 102–6

Nagel, T., 261
Names, *see* Language
Naming, *see* Language
Natural evil, 179–80
Natural law, *see* Law of nature
Natural right, *see* Right of nature
Necessary and contingent: propositions, 49–51; values, *see* Values
Necessitation, 199–204
Nominalism, *see* Language

Oakeshott, M., 257, 261
Object of desire, *see* Appetite
Obligation: 169, 199–204; and compulsion, 200–3; and fear, 174–5, 197–9; *in foro interno* and *in foro externo*, 200, 206–9
Ought, 199–204

Passions, chs 5 and 6
Peace, 184–6, 191
Pennock, J. R., 176, 261
Perception, 30–31, 101–2
Pessimism, 96, 149–51
Peters, R., 12, 13, 14, 146–7, 255, 257, 258

*Philosophia prima*, 60, 61
Physics, 71–75
Pity, 118–19
Plamenatz, J., 12, 147–8, 206, 225, 255, 257, 259, 261
Pleasure, 102, 106–17, 139–43, 178–9; bodily, 139–42; of the mind, 139–43
Pogson-Smith, W. G., 257
Power: ch. 6; and authority, 236–7; common, 186–91; and consent, 229–31; desire of, 144–7, 152, 167–8; relative concept of, 138–9, 167–8
Primary propositions, 52–54, 61–63
Principles, *see* Primary propositions
Prudence, 32–33, 49–51, 66
Psychology, chs 5 and 6

Raphael, D. D. 261
Regulated thought, *see* Thought
Religion: 20–24; and politics, 240–5
Representative, 214–18
Resolution, 51–52
Right of nature: 169–70, 175–8; renunciation of, 191–3
Robertson, G. C., 257

Scargill, D., 10
Science: ch. 4; and causes, 85–86; conventionalist account of, 66–71, 84–85; and experience, 32–33; as a formal system, 66–71, 76–88, 115–19, 150–5, 164–8, 180–2, 184–6, 190–3, 204–6, 248–54; and hypothesis, 71–76; in the Middle Ages, 16; and philosophy, 29–30, 59–60; and prudence, 49–51, 84–85; and religion, 20–24
Self-evidence, 25–26, 54–55, 60–70, 72
Self-preservation, 168–70, 175–82, 192–3
Sense, *see* Perception
Signification, Signs, *see* Language
Singular propositions, 39, 48–49
Skinner, Q., 261
Solicitation, 111–14
Sovereignty: ch. 9; by acquisition, 197–9; and authorization, 214–24; and common power, 186–91, 218; and consent, 229–31; and government, 225–9;

indivisible, 235–6; institution of, 218–31; and monarchy, 235–6; and opinion, 240–5; permanence of, 231–2; and power, 228–30; and religion, 240–5; unlimited, 232, 234
State of nature, ch. 7, 209–12
Stephen, Sir L., 257
Stewart, J. B., 261
Strauss, L., 258, 261
Subjectivism, 119–21
Synthetical method, *see* Method
*Summum bonum*, 129

Taylor, A. E., 257, 261
Thomas, K., 261
Thought: 30–32, 42–43; regulated, 31–32
Tönnies, F., 256, 257
Truth, 36–58

Understanding, *see* Language
Universal propositions, 32, 48–51
Universals, 19, 35–47
Utilitarianism, 246–7

Validating condition, *see* Law of nature
Values: moral and political, 238–45, 254; necessary and contingent, 191, 195–6, 238–40, 247–8
Verification and falsification, 54–57, 75, 80–82, 85–87, 147–55
Violence: 159–69; anticipatory, 162, 164–8, 188–9; competitive, 161–2; self-glorying, 162–3
Vital motion, 103–4, 107–13, 115–16
Voluntary, 101, 103–5, 115–17

Waller, A. R., 257
War, 159, 185–6
Warrender, H., 12–13, 206–8, 255, 258, 261
Watkins, J. W. N., 34–35, 170, 178–80, 208–9, 216–18, 240, 255, 259, 261
Wernham, A. G., 171, 261
Will, 121–4
Woozley, A. D., 36